Praise for *More than a Dream*

"More Than a Dream tells a vivid story of the power of education to change lives. As we as a nation confront the still-growing challenges of ensuring quality educational opportunity in our poorest communities, Cristo Rey provides an important and inspiring model."

—JOHN DEGIOIA, president of Georgetown University

"Cristo Rey schools are one of the most fascinating and innovative programs in American Catholic education. By combining academic excellence, social responsibility and challenging opportunities for youngsters from disadvantaged families, they present all who enroll with a chance for a better life. I hope these schools will continue to multiply throughout our country."

—CARDINAL THEODORE E. MCCARRICK,
   archbishop emeritus of Washington

"*More than a Dream* is a compelling, fascinating read of how Cristo Rey took root and changed the lives of young people in Chicago's Pilsen neighborhood. The students' stories are amazing and deeply moving, the founders' vision profound and faith-filled, the faculty's commitment inspiring and challenging. Read *More than a Dream* to learn how one single program can make a difference."

—THOMAS H. SMOLICH, SJ, president of the Jesuit Conference

"G. R. Kearney brilliantly tells the story of Cristo Rey Jesuit High School, an imaginative, creative solution to the problems of urban education today."

—NEWTON N. MINOW,
   senior counsel at Sidley Austin LLP,
   a proud employer of Cristo Rey students

"Cristo Rey Jesuit High School is one of the most important innovations in Catholic education in recent decades."

—Rev. John I. Jenkins, CSC,
president of University of Notre Dame

"The Cristo Rey model is one of the most successful new educational models of our time. It offers an extremely high quality education combined with great family, faith, and moral values with the best quality of all, hope for the future."

—Paul Purcell,
Chairman, President & Chief Executive Officer of
Robert W. Baird & Co. Incorporated

"The Cristo Rey high school model can be a model for the nation. It has certainly influenced my thinking on high school reform."

—Paul Vallas,
superintendent of the Recovery School District of New Orleans
and former CEO of the Chicago Public Schools

"Kearney describes superbly the people and the concepts behind the immensely successful Cristo Rey Jesuit High School in Chicago and the expansion of the idea through the country. These schools located in impoverished areas have with growing success turned high school–age students with very little chance into winners. It is a must-read about the work of the Lord in today's America."

—William J. McDonough,
vice chairman of Merrill Lynch and
former president of the Federal Reserve Bank of New York

"*More Than a Dream* is a compelling narrative that carries the reader from the moment of creation through the first decade of success of an entirely new kind of school. The Cristo Rey model, designed to help the poor, is now renewing and revolutionizing Catholic secondary education."

—William J. Byron, SJ,
president of St. Joseph's Preparatory School, Philadelphia,
and author of *Jesuit Saturdays*

"Cristo Rey is a wonderful example of 'Jesuit-style ingenuity' for the twenty-first century—a fascinating, innovative way to serve a population that (to our country's disgrace) has not been well enough served by the education system; and G. R. Kearney does a wonderful job in chronicling how this ingenious school system was launched."

—Chris Lowney, author of *Heroic Leadership*

"The story of Cristo Rey is one of the most exciting educational success stories in decades. G. R. Kearney's inspiring and entertaining new memoir offers a behind-the-scenes look at how the Chicago Jesuits and their colleagues revolutionized education for a group of poor Hispanic children in the inner city. Their innovative model, in which students work in real-world jobs during the school year, has spread with astonishing speed across the country. Relive the excitement (and anxiety) of starting a new venture, meet the remarkable students, teachers and administrators who dared to dream a hopeful future, and be reminded how with God all things can be made new."

—James Martin, SJ, author of *My Life with the Saints*

"Anyone who cares about improving education should read this book . . . and prepare to be inspired. The Cristo Rey story is proof that a small group of creative individuals who are committed to a mission and willing to take a risk can indeed change the world."

—Tom Vander Ark, president of the X Prize Foundation

"We hear a lot about what's wrong with our schools. *More than a Dream* is an inspiring story about a school where things are going right."

—Larry Colton, best-selling author of *Counting Coup*

"Cristo Rey schools are remarkable examples of what can happen when dreams meet opportunity. Cristo Rey graduates are tomorrow's leaders in industry, education and public service."

—Richard J. Durbin,
   United States Senator & assistant majority leader

"All children deserve the opportunity to enhance their futures through access to quality education. *More than a Dream* highlights the success of the Cristo Rey school model, an innovative private-partnership tuition payment program that is opening new doors for students in over a dozen schools nationwide."

—CHUCK HAGEL, United States Senator

"All the armies in the world, said Victor Hugo, can't stop an idea whose time has come. Cristo Rey is one of those ideas, and G. R. Kearney tells the story as only a gifted 'insider' could."

—FR. MARK LINK, SJ,
author of the Challenge/Vision 2000 series and
founder of Staygreat.com

More Than a Dream
The Cristo Rey Story

THE CRISTO REY STORY

MORE THAN A DREAM

*How One School's Vision Is
Changing the World*

G. R. Kearney

LOYOLAPRESS.

CHICAGO

LOYOLA PRESS.

3441 N. ASHLAND AVENUE
CHICAGO, ILLINOIS 60657
(800) 621-1008
WWW.LOYOLABOOKS.ORG

Excerpts from the feasibility study, "Ministers of the Word Sent to New Frontiers," [Chapter 5] are reprinted with permission of Rev. James Gartland, SJ, and the Chicago Province of the Society of Jesus.

Excerpts of newspaper article on pages 111–112 are as published in the *Chicago Sun-Times*. Copyright 1995 by *Chicago Sun-Times*, Inc. Reprinted with permission.

Excerpts from Board Meeting Minutes of Cristo Rey Jesuit High School are reprinted with permission of the school's past and current administrations, as represented by Rev. John P. Foley, SJ and Rev. James Gartland, SJ.

Mission Effectiveness Standards excerpts [Chapter 27] reprinted with permission of the Cristo Rey Network™

Cover imagery: Steve Donisch
Author photo: Mary Henebry
Map illustration: Bill Wood
Cover design: Kathryn Seckman Kirsch
Interior design: Tracey Sainz

Library of Congress Cataloging-in-Publication Data
Kearney, G. R.
  More than a dream : the Cristo Rey story : how one school's vision is changing the world / G. R. Kearney.
    p cm.
  ISBN-13: 978-0-8294-2576-5
  ISBN-10: 0-8294-2576-4
  1. Cristo Rey Jesuit High School (Chicago, Ill.) 2. Poor children—Education (Secondary)—Illinois—Chicago. 3. Children of immigrants—Education (Secondary)—Illinois—Chicago. I. Title.
  LD7501.C4K43 2008
  373.733'11—dc22
                                                            2007037847

Printed in the United States of America
07 08 09 10 11 12 M-V 10 9 8 7 6 5 4 3 2 1

To my wonderful wife Tara.

*Thank you for the kick in the pants
that got me to write this book.*

Contents

A Story That Needs to Be Told

WHEN I ARRIVED AT Cristo Rey Jesuit High School in 1999, I had no idea I'd just taken what amounted to a front row seat for one of the most improbable, exciting, and inspiring educational stories in decades. In truth, it was more than that. It was one of the most improbable, exciting, and inspiring *stories*—period.

Five years earlier, a group of Jesuit priests had proposed opening a private college-preparatory high school in Pilsen, a predominantly Mexican immigrant neighborhood on the Lower West Side of Chicago. The cost per student at the school would be at least $5,500 per year, maybe $6,500. The average family income in the neighborhood barely surpassed $20,000 per year, and the average family size was five. There was little doubt the neighborhood would benefit from a new school, but funding it seemed a virtual impossibility. Families would have to part with more than 25 percent of their annual income to send just one student to the school.

To make the school more affordable, its founders adopted a bold new funding model. It was the kind of model that when proposed in most boardroom brainstorming sessions would elicit a chuckle and a few harrumphs. Someone would probably say, "Yeah, wouldn't it be nice if we could." Inevitably, though, it would be dismissed in favor of something more practical, something that had already been done, been tested, and proven successful. The new approach would

> The model proposed for the new school was untested and certainly unconventional. But the Jesuits decided . . . to try it anyway.

fall silently from the table, its potential snuffed out by a refusal—or maybe an inability—to think of what *could* be.

In this case, though, the new model defied the odds and stayed on the table. The Jesuits were determined to start a school for the children of the working poor—and they vowed to make it happen, even though every passing year in Chicago saw a few more small but venerable Catholic schools shuttered in the face of skyrocketing labor costs and falling enrollments.

The model proposed for the new school was untested and certainly unconventional. But the Jesuits decided, after substantial consultation and discernment, to try it anyway. From its genesis to its ultimately overwhelming success, the school they opened has transformed the lives of countless young men and women. It has challenged others to think the unthinkable and to attempt to change what once seemed unchangeable. This one school sparked a revolution in education in urban America.

❋

I STUMBLED INTO THE middle of this story eight years ago when I agreed, along with two of my classmates from Georgetown University, to volunteer for two years at Cristo Rey. Two years of teaching journalism, English, and computer skills, of grading papers, directing retreats, and chaperoning rainy camping trips. Two years of coaching Cristo Rey's basketball, baseball, and volleyball teams to four losing seasons and one canceled season. Two years in which the unfolding lives of the young women and men at Cristo Rey—sometimes desperate and sad, sometimes joyous, often precarious—substantially altered my understanding of the world and my place in it.

During my relatively brief time at Cristo Rey, many moments, such as the class of 2000 graduation, led me to fall deeply in love with the school. That year there were only twenty-two seniors. Just about every teacher in the school had taught them. They were all Latino: eight boys and fourteen girls. Almost all the graduates were either children of immigrants to the United States or immigrants themselves. These students had succeeded despite a host of challenges. Many of their neighborhoods were plagued by gang violence. Some of their home lives were, at best, messy. Most of them had come to high school unprepared by their grammar schools for the rigors of a college prep curriculum. But they'd made it. They were, in most cases, the first in their families to graduate from high school and go to college.

Most of the teachers sat in the back row of the gym at the graduation ceremony. This struck me as odd. For anyone who works in a school, graduation is the payoff. Why not sit up front? Then, just before the graduates began their slow recession from the stage, the teachers stood and filed quietly into a cramped classroom with stained carpet at the back of the gym. I followed. Onstage, the music began to play. Through the open door of the classroom, I strained to catch glimpses of maroon gowns filing down the stairs and turning into the aisle. Only then did I realize they were coming into the classroom. The throng of teachers split apart, creating a large open space near the door. When the first student came in, the room exploded with joyous applause. One by one the others filed in. On each of their faces was a look of surprise, then a knowing smile. Soon the room was full. The applause grew louder. Outside the room, parents, grandparents, brothers and sisters, aunts and uncles continued to clap. Inside, many of the teachers cried. They cried because they understood the stories of their students.

During the two years I spent at Cristo Rey—and the three subsequent years I spent as the girls' basketball coach—I was privileged to witness these stories: the struggles, the heartbreaking failures, and the triumphs. This book is about those stories, and about how a school can sometimes change the trajectory of people's stories and lives.

This book is not about my experience at the school. When I was at Cristo Rey, I had no idea I'd later decide to write this book. Now, looking back, it's clear that the countless moments I spent with the students—coaching, playing basketball, disciplining, riding buses, advising, camping, counseling, teaching, struggling to teach, failing to teach, playing catch, watching pro baseball—made this book possible. Cristo Rey, like the sprawling mosaic on the building's facade, is a collection of stories. The story of the school, and its improbable success, can't be separated from the stories of its students. They are embedded in the larger story, an integral part of the composition, the sum of its meaning. Without them, the larger story is incomplete, incongruous, and meaningless. Without them, the school is little more than an empty building and an interesting idea.

This book reflects that. It tells the story of the school's development. But it also tells the stories of four students: their struggles, hopes, and dreams. What they achieved, and, sometimes, what could have been.

I haven't set out to write a book about my experience at the school, but that experience has informed this story in myriad ways. I've returned to Cristo Rey numerous times, not as a former volunteer and teacher, but as a reporter in search of a story. I've talked to those who originally dreamed up the idea for the school. I've sought out those whose labors launched it. I've spoken with many of the first teachers and students, as well as with current students, parents, and the school's principals, deans, security guards, campus ministers, and volunteers.

The result, I hope, is a factual account of Cristo Rey, its founders, and its students. It's a big story because it's about a school built for people with smaller stories, people who are often forgotten and ignored. It's a big story because the risks taken have reaped enormous rewards. It's a big story because the seemingly impossible idea worked. And because it's still working.

PART 1

The Vision Takes Shape

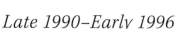

Late 1990–Early 1996

Here's to the crazy ones, the misfits, the rebels, the troublemakers, the round pegs in the square holes, the ones who see things differently. They're not fond of rules, and they have no respect for the status quo. You can quote them, disagree with them, glorify or vilify them. About the only thing you can't do is ignore them, because they change things. They push the human race forward, and while some may see them as the crazy ones, we see genius, because the people who are crazy enough to think they can change the world are the ones who'll do it.

> *Apple Computer advertisement*
> *(often mistakenly attributed to Jack Kerouac)*

Opening the Envelope   1

L ATE IN 1990, AN envelope was mailed from Chicago to Rome. The envelope contained a *terna*, Latin for "threefold." Three names: three Jesuit priests. One of them would be chosen by the Jesuit order's father general to become the next provincial of the Chicago Province of the Society of Jesus. Only nine people, all of them Jesuits, knew whose names were in the envelope. And none of the nine could begin to fathom how the decision would ultimately affect education for the poor in Chicago and around the United States. The envelope, mailed from the Chicago Province's headquarters in Lincoln Park, a posh neighborhood on the city's North Side, was bound for 4 Borgo Santo Spirito, the Jesuit Curia, the worldwide headquarters of the Society of Jesus, a stout fortress-like stone building situated just a few steps from St. Peter's Square and the Vatican.

❇

THE JESUITS HAVE BEEN headquartered in Rome since September 1540. There were only ten Jesuits then. Their leader, Ignatius of Loyola, was a diminutive Spaniard of noble descent who had come to his religious vows late in life, at least for that time. His military career had ended at age thirty, when a cannonball shattered his leg during a battle against the French at Pamplona, Spain. Profoundly bored during his extended recuperation, he requested some popular romance novels to pass the time. None were available, and he ended up reading instead a life of Christ and a book on the lives of the saints. Those stories prompted a conversion in him, a very real change of heart. The once proud soldier known for his bravery and love of women laid down his arms, saying that he wanted to fight not for the kingdom of Spain but for the kingdom of God.

Once healed (as healed as he would ever be—he walked with a limp for the rest of his life), Ignatius set out on a pilgrimage to the Holy Land. En route, on the banks of the Cardoner River in Manresa, Spain, he experienced a profound religious enlightenment, one he eventually recorded and sought to replicate for others in a small booklet. Today, those writings, *The Spiritual Exercises*, serve as a guide for millions of spiritual seekers around the world. They also contain the essence of Ignatian spirituality, which unites the roughly twenty thousand Jesuits serving in 127 nations on six continents.

After spending ten months on the banks of the river, Ignatius made his way to Rome, where he was granted permission by Pope Adrian VI to make a pilgrimage to the Holy Land. Ignatius wanted to spend his life imitating Christ and figured there was no better place to do it than the Holy Land. But almost as soon as he arrived, he was sent back to Rome by a priest with authority over the region because the situation in Jerusalem—where Turkish vigilantes who controlled the Holy Land regularly kidnapped and killed Christians—was far too dangerous.

By the time he'd made his way back to Europe, Ignatius had decided he wanted to become a priest. Unfortunately, he didn't know a word of Latin, a prerequisite for university study and church ministry. So in 1524, in his thirties, he enrolled at a school for boys in Barcelona to study Latin grammar. It was the beginning of an eleven-year period of educational formation, during which he studied at two Spanish universities before enrolling at the University of

Paris. During his years of study, Ignatius encountered his share of difficulties. He was beaten nearly to death in Spain and saw his closest companion killed. His teaching of the catechism drew the ire of the examiners for the Inquisition, who told him he needed a "license" to teach. He was brought to trial on several occasions, censured, and twice imprisoned. Despite this, he soldiered on, eventually earning a master's and a licentiate in theology from the University of Paris.

A small group of students in Paris were heavily influenced by Ignatius, who taught them to pray and directed each of them in early versions of some of the spiritual exercises he'd begun to devise in the wake of his riverside experiences in Manresa. In 1534, Ignatius and six of his companions from the university—Peter Faber, Francis Xavier, James Laynez, Alonso Salmerón, Nicolás Bobadilla, and Simón Rodríguez decided together to take vows of chastity and obedience. They vowed, too, to go to the Holy Land in two years, when their studies were complete. There they would attempt to do what Ignatius had tried to do years earlier by modeling their lives completely on the life of Christ. If they couldn't reach the Holy Land, they would put themselves at the disposal of the pope in Rome.

Repeated efforts to travel to the Holy Land failed, and late in 1537, after all of them had been ordained priests, Ignatius, Faber, and Laynez made their way to Rome to offer themselves to the pope. Ignatius called them La Compañía de Jesus, which translated roughly to the Company of Jesus. Pope Paul III responded positively to the proposal they laid out, in part because they'd opted after much debate to take a vow of obedience to the pope himself. Paul III expressed a desire to send the priests to various parts of the world to work as missionaries, and he invited the rest of the companions to come to Rome to work under his direction. On September 27, 1540, the papal bull formally creating the Society of Jesus was issued. It limited

When he created the society, Ignatius had not intended to include teaching among its ministries. Today it is perhaps the ministry for which they are best known.

the society to sixty members. In April 1541, Ignatius was elected the society's first superior general. He insisted on a revote and was again elected—his vote being the lone dissenting vote. Ignatius would spend the remainder of his life, fifteen years, working in a small office in Rome and directing the society by writing letters to its members, who were dispersed to every corner of the globe.

The society he founded proved very popular with young men of the day. The sixty spaces allowed by the papal document filled up almost immediately. Two years later, when the limit was lifted, men clamored to join the new society, and its membership swelled. Ignatius opened schools in Italy, Portugal, the Netherlands, Spain, Germany, and India to educate the new members. Then, in 1548, he received an odd request from magistrates in the Sicilian town of Messina: they asked him to open a school to educate their sons as well as Jesuits. When he created the society, Ignatius had not intended to include teaching among its ministries. The sole purpose of the schools he had opened was to educate new Jesuits. Despite this, he responded to the need in Messina and dispatched five Jesuits to open a school there. Today, Jesuits operate thousands of primary schools, secondary schools, colleges, and universities throughout the world. It is, perhaps, the ministry for which they are best known.

❈

St. Ignatius College Prep, located on the Near West Side of Chicago, is one of those schools. It was founded in 1869 as St. Ignatius College by Fr. Arnold Damen, SJ, who had come to Chicago roughly a decade earlier at the request of the city's third bishop, Anthony

O'Regan. The plan had been for Damen to serve as pastor of Holy Name Church, the bishop's parish, but he set out instead to open a new church. Catholics were plentiful in the center of the rapidly growing city, so it came as a surprise when, in 1857, Fr. Damen chose for the site of the new church a seemingly uninhabitable section of land in the vast prairie southwest of the city. He opened the church, Holy Family, in a temporary building that same year. By 1860, he'd raised enough money to erect a permanent church, which still stands today. In 1869, he opened St. Ignatius College. It would later be divided into a college and a high school—Loyola University Chicago and St. Ignatius High School, now known as St. Ignatius College Prep. The high school today occupies the original St. Ignatius College building. Over the past 139 years, it has become one of Chicago's preeminent educational institutions, educating generations of civic, business, and church leaders.

In hindsight, Damen's decision to open the church and school southwest of the city was nothing short of brilliant. Chicago continued its rapid growth and before long extended far beyond St. Ignatius in every direction. The once uninhabitable prairie was chewed up by the city's grid and became home to thousands of Chicago residents.

One of the factors spurring growth to the south of St. Ignatius's campus was Mayor John Wentworth's Battle of the Sands. The Sands, a burgeoning red-light district on the Near North Side of the city, had become occupied by a rapidly growing population of Bohemian Czechs. In an effort to strengthen Chicago's moral fiber, Wentworth—a six-foot-six Dartmouth-educated newspaper man turned politician (who, according to legend, drank a pint of whiskey a day)—launched a vicious police campaign on the Sands in 1857. Police are reported to have blitzed the neighborhood, burning houses and beating and sometimes killing residents. The

Bohemian population fled the neighborhood and settled half a mile south of St. Ignatius in a neglected area of the city they named Little Pilsen.

Later it became simply Pilsen, and Bohemian immigrants to Chicago gravitated toward the neighborhood. Eventually the immigration tide shifted to Scandinavians. They, too, flocked to Pilsen. So did Austrian, Russian, Hungarian, and Polish immigrants, making Pilsen the primary port of entry for Chicago's immigrants. The neighborhood, stretching from Halsted Street on the east to Western Avenue and from Sixteenth Street south to Twenty-Sixth Street, was a checkerboard of ethnic enclaves, each centered on a church.

Today, the neighborhood is still dotted with spectacular steeples climbing skyward above the small brick apartment buildings that line vaulted sidewalks and narrow streets. It remains a port of entry for Chicago's immigrants, but the ethnic enclaves are gone. Pilsen is now populated almost entirely by Latino immigrants, many of them from Mexico, who began arriving in the neighborhood en masse in the 1960s, during the fourth major wave of American immigration.

WINTER HAD DESCENDED ON Chicago in January of 1991. The grass was covered with a thin layer of hard, windblown snow that had already turned gray from city grime and exhaust. Sunlight was scarce. Even in midafternoon, the sky was dark when Fr. Bradley M. Schaeffer, SJ, turned off Halsted Street and onto Roosevelt Road on his way to a meeting at St. Ignatius College Prep. Schaeffer had graduated from St. Ignatius in 1967, just as the wave of Latino immigration to Chicago was beginning to peak. Later that year, he entered the Society of Jesus at the Jesuit novitiate in Milford, Ohio.

Looking back on his reasons for becoming a Jesuit, Schaeffer, who was raised in a working-class neighborhood on the northwest side of Chicago by parents whose own parents had immigrated to the United States from Germany, Italy, and Ireland, says, "I thought God was calling me to it. I looked at my father and the Jesuits around me. I thought I could be happy as a husband and father. I thought I could be happy as a Jesuit. And it seemed I could be called to be a Jesuit. Over time, I've become convinced it was my vocation. But it has deepened and become more sophisticated. At the same time, it's simple. It seemed right. It still does. This is where God called me and continues to call me."

Schaeffer made his way down Roosevelt, past the University of Illinois at Chicago and toward St. Ignatius. After his ordination in 1979, he'd served as assistant principal at St. Xavier, a Jesuit high school in Cincinnati, before becoming principal at St. Ignatius, a job he held until 1989, when he was named the provincial assistant for secondary education and pastoral ministry. On this winter day he stopped for a red light at the intersection of Roosevelt and Blue Island Avenue, waiting to turn right into St. Ignatius's campus. He gazed down Blue Island, a diagonal street that cuts southwest from St. Ignatius six blocks to Eighteenth Street, the epicenter of Pilsen.

When he was principal at St. Ignatius, Schaeffer often gazed out the window of his fourth-floor office toward Pilsen and thought to himself that the Jesuits should be there. The first Jesuits had offered their order to the pope so they could go where the need was greatest. Schaeffer knew that in Pilsen and Little Village the need was enormous. More than a hundred thousand people, many of them undocumented immigrants, lived in the two neighborhoods. Tens of thousands were school-aged, but there were just two underperforming high schools serving them.

> The neighborhood was populated almost entirely by immigrants from Mexico and Central America who had come to the United States in search of a better life.

Driving south into these two neighborhoods is almost like crossing the border into Mexico. South of the Sixteenth Street viaduct, there are no Laundromats or barber shops, only *lavanderías* and *peluquerías*. Restaurants, businesses, and churches all advertise in Spanish. Sprawling murals—many of the Virgin of Guadalupe—painted by local artists adorn the sides of brick apartment buildings. Smells from taquerías and tortillerías sneak into the streets, tempting passersby to stop for a handful of tiny taquitos or a plateful of steaming enchiladas.

From its earliest days, Pilsen was a refuge for immigrants. Schaeffer knew that hadn't changed. The neighborhood was populated almost entirely by immigrants from Mexico and Central America who had come to the United States in search of a better life. They found the work so often elusive in Mexico. But work in the U.S.—in factories, on landscaping crews, on temporary labor forces, and in building maintenance—was difficult, and the pay wasn't great.

Like any parents, these new immigrants wished for their children to have even better lives, with more opportunities. But they realized that those opportunties depended on education. They wouldn't get the education, but it was their hope that their children would. With a good education, all their dreams for their children could come true.

Schaeffer knew that existing educational options in the neighborhood weren't giving every child and every family a chance at the better life they sought. The two public high schools serving Pilsen and Little Village were overwhelmed. Dropout rates in the neighborhood were sky-high. Gangs, violence, and drugs pulled far too many students out of school. It happened when a group of students skipped school to roll joints in someone's basement and get high. It happened when kids from the neighborhood were harassed on their way home by gang members. It happened when their friends convinced them that being in a gang was cool because you could earn money and you always had protection. It happened the first day a student made the decision to wear gang colors to school. And every time it happened, parents' dreams for their children began to slowly and painfully dissolve.

The Jesuits should be in Pilsen—Schaeffer knew it. Not only was the need great in the neighborhood, but Latinos had also become, in just a few decades, a significant presence in the Catholic Church in the United States. Studies suggested that, in as little as two decades, they could represent more than 30 percent of the church population. These were people the Jesuits needed to serve.

Schaeffer's hands were tied while he was principal at St. Ignatius. Authority for the direction of the province's various ministries—and the creation of new ones—fell not to young high school principals, but to the provincial. In 1989, he became the provincial's assistant for pastoral ministry and secondary education, a job that charged him with overseeing schools and pastoral ministries. A job that put him on the provincial's staff and afforded him the opportunity to participate in discussions about how the Jesuits could respond to the greatest need. In the winter of 1991, he still sometimes pondered what it would take to get the Jesuits into Pilsen.

A few days later, a document arrived from Rome naming Fr. Schaeffer the thirteenth provincial of the Chicago Province, the youngest in the province's history.

We Wanted to Be with the Poor

2

B RAD SCHAEFFER WAS INSTALLED as provincial of the Chicago Province of the Jesuits in August 1991. In February 1992, six months into his new job, he began acting on his instinctual belief that the Jesuits should be working in and for Chicago's Latino community. He penned a letter to Joseph Cardinal Bernardin, leader of the Chicago Archdiocese, asking permission for the Jesuits to assume pastoral care of a parish in a Latino neighborhood.

It is fairly common practice for a religious order to ask—for any number of reasons—to staff a diocesan parish for a certain period of time. Dioceses and archdioceses welcome the assistance and almost always offer up financially strapped or understaffed parishes. Upon receipt of Schaeffer's letter, Bernardin promptly wrote back, offering two parishes, one in Pilsen and one in Little Village, a Latino neighborhood just west of Pilsen.

THE WEATHERED BASKETBALL DROPPED to the pavement with a thud. It was a few minutes after eight on a February morning. Moments earlier the sun had climbed above the roof of Davis Elementary School, a massive brick building near the intersection of Pershing Road and Kedzie Avenue on the southwest side of Chicago, and now it shone on the school's asphalt basketball court.

Audelio "Leo" Maldonado Jr. blew into his hands and picked up the ball. His breath was visible as he yelled "¿Listo?" to his friends. "Sí. Sí," they said, nodding. Leo tossed the ball to Juan José, who flipped it back to him, officially starting the game. Leo looked to his left, then to his right. He slung a pass to Eduardo. That morning, he, Eduardo, and Pablo were playing against Juan José, Jorge, and Orlando. They were all classmates in the fifth grade's lone bilingual classroom. The six of them came to school an hour early every morning to play basketball; they also ate lunch together and played together after school. They had to. As bilingual students, they were shunned by the mainstream English-speaking Mexican American student body at Davis. Most of Davis's students were second- or third-generation Mexican Americans and fluent English speakers. Leo and his friends were first-generation. Most of their parents had come to the United States from Mexico as undocumented immigrants.

Leo's dad had come to the United States during the early 1970s. Like the other people with whom he crossed the Rio Grande under the cover of darkness, he came in search of a better life, of opportunities that didn't exist for a young man in Mexico. Three years after moving to the States, he returned to Mexico and married Leo's mom, Teresa. They returned to the States, again illegally.

Both were able to find jobs that required them to speak only a little English. Audelio Sr. landed a job in the shipping department at a metal stamping, fabrication, and assembly plant on the northwest side of the city. He spent his days pulling and pushing skids full of metal products off and onto the beds of trucks. Most weeks he worked six days; most days he worked twelve hours, sometimes more. Occasionally, when they weren't busy, he got off a little early. Teresa took a job at a plant that manufactured workplace and storage furniture.

On September 8, 1981, they had a baby boy, Audelio Jr. Growing up, Leo didn't speak English at home. Spanish was the language of family parties, trips to the store, the breakfast table, the TV, and the radio. When he began kindergarten in 1986, Leo was assigned, not surprisingly, to a bilingual classroom. By the time he'd reached fifth grade, he'd rarely been called upon to speak English at school and was still assigned to the bilingual class. But the classes, he recalls, were hardly bilingual. His fifth-grade teacher was a Puerto Rican who himself had very limited English skills.

"Even though it was a bilingual class," Leo says, "they focused on Spanish, not English, so I didn't really learn English well until I got to high school. It's supposed to be a classroom with the teacher teaching in both languages. But that's not how it worked at Davis in those years. I don't know how it works now, but in those years it was basically just all the Mexicans who only knew Spanish in one little spot where the teacher spoke Spanish."

The fact that limited English skills generally inhibit success was lost on Leo, who says the Spanish-heavy education "didn't really bother me. Back then I didn't know. I wasn't really aware."

On the basketball court, Leo flashed across the lane. "Lalo, Lalo, aquí," he said, clapping his hands. Eduardo fed him the ball and he turned to the basket, looking for a shot. Orlando slid over, his arms high in the air. Like everyone else in the class, Orlando was taller than Leo. Leo turned, faked a pass, and then sneaked past Orlando for a layup. He missed, but Pablo, who was under the basket, collected it and scored. Leo's team erupted into loud chatter, in Spanish. They played "make it, take it," so they got the ball back. Leo blew into his hands again. Snow still ringed the pavement, but with a couple more sunny days it would be gone. Leo checked the ball with Juan José to start the game. He passed to Pablo, and the gym shoes

> He wasn't particularly interested in learning; he just wanted to keep from flunking.

once again began to slide across the pavement. The chatter continued as the six boys competed in the sacred dance of playground basketball. When the bell rang at 8:55, Leo and his friends would once again enter a world where they were ostracized for being "retards," or just for being different.

Inside school, Leo didn't distinguish himself as a particularly fastidious student. Early on, he figured out how much he'd have to do to get by, and that's exactly what he did—nothing more. He wasn't particularly interested in learning; he just wanted to keep from flunking. He came to school to see his friends, to play basketball with them in the morning, and to talk about the games at lunch. When the bell rang in the afternoon, they left school together. There were more games to be played, mostly football and basketball in the alleys surrounding Leo's house.

To get from school to those alleys, Leo and his friends walked down Pershing, then up Kedzie to Thirty-eighth. Every day they walked past a handful of gang members, all of whom were easily recognizable by the black and beige clothes they wore, the close-cropped hair, the hooded sweatshirts. The gangbangers lingered around street corners, slouched in doorways, or leaned against light posts. Occasionally they sold some drugs, but really they were watchmen, guarding their turf against rivals. And they were always on the lookout for new members, younger boys who would eventually be able to replace them on the corners so that they could move into the houses. There they would become more involved in the dealing of drugs. They would make more money and have more power.

Leo and his buddies walked past them every day. The gang members knew them; they were the ESL kids—the ones who couldn't speak English. The losers. The gang members, like the kids at school, weren't interested in the outcasts. They wanted nothing to do with Leo and his friends. Being left alone by the gangs was the one advantage to being left out at school. They didn't have to explain why they didn't want to be in the gang. They could play games in the streets and just be kids.

But they couldn't be kids forever. Unfortunately, the free pass from gang life they now enjoyed would eventually expire.

✳

IN THE SPRING OF 1992, Brad Schaeffer made unannounced and unofficial visits to the two parishes in Pilsen/Little Village that Cardinal Bernardin had offered. He attended Sunday Mass at both. The first parish, in Little Village, was made up mostly of first- and second-generation immigrants. Many of them had worked themselves into the middle class, and the parish's relatively healthy balance sheet reflected this. The Pilsen parish was much poorer, many of the parishioners having just arrived in the United States. The Spanish Mass Schaeffer attended was a free-for-all. "The place was jammed," he recalls. "There were kids everywhere, running around, screaming and crying." The parish, which offered mostly Spanish Masses on Saturday evenings and practically every hour on Sunday, received a hefty annual subsidy from the archdiocese.

It may have been wishful thinking on the archdiocese's part to offer the Jesuits the second parish, knowing well that they would do their homework and dissect the financials for both. The first parish seemed the logical choice, but Schaeffer never seriously considered it, settling instead on St. Procopius, the poorer of the two. "There were a variety of reasons," he explains. "St. Procopius had lots of young families, intact families. I saw what appeared to me to be husbands and wives with kids. There were kids running all over the place. On the day I visited, I just had a feel that the Eucharist was really engaging." Ultimately, Schaeffer chose St. Procopius because, he says, "we knew we had to be with the poor in some way. We wanted to be with the poor."

The poorest of the poor are the modern equivalent of biblical lepers—people shunned and easily forgotten. Why then do the Jesuits desire to be with the poor? "It's the gospel, for one," Schaeffer says matter-of-factly. "And our General Congregations, the documents that determine who we are as a religious order, have asked us to be with the poor." He pauses for a moment before adding, "It just makes sense."

But it might not make so much sense to an outsider, who might also wonder why a remarkably talented young man like Schaeffer would choose to forgo married life, family, and a career in corporate America to pursue a vowed life of poverty, chastity, and obedience. In the modern world—as in St. Ignatius's time—the decision to become a Jesuit doesn't make sense to a lot of people. But for a handful of men, a life of prayer and service, a life without sex, without a diversified investment portfolio, without a house in the suburbs, and without children does in fact make perfect sense.

Every Jesuit would answer the question "Why this life?" in his own way. Most would probably say, though, that they feel called. For some it's a leap of faith. For others it's a commitment to faith. For each and every Jesuit, it's a decision to live in a way that is radically countercultural.

More than 450 years ago, St. Ignatius literally gave away all his worldly goods. Today's Jesuits make the same—sometimes subtler—decision. They turn their backs on the values espoused by the predominant culture and aim instead for lives of love and service.

Yet the Jesuits have, since their founding in 1540, been committed to working *in the world*. The Society of Jesus is not a cloistered order—Jesuits don't lock themselves in monasteries. They work with and for other people in the world. A central tenet of Jesuit spirituality is that God is present in all things. In cities. In jobs. In churches. In hospitals and schools. Jesuits try to work in many of these places.

> For a handful of men, a life of prayer and service, a life without sex, without a diversified investment portfolio, without a house in the suburbs, and without children does in fact make perfect sense.

The only way to understand the radical decisions Jesuits make, such as choosing St. Procopius over a wealthier and stronger parish, is to understand that their values are, quite simply, different from the values that dominate our culture. Schaeffer's radical values, though, weren't the only thing influencing his decision to go with the poorer parish. "I wanted a parish with a grade school," he says, and the other parish didn't have one. "A parish without a grade school seems unnatural in a place like Chicago."

But there was more to it than that. The acquisition of a grade school was the first part of a much larger and surprisingly ambitious plan.

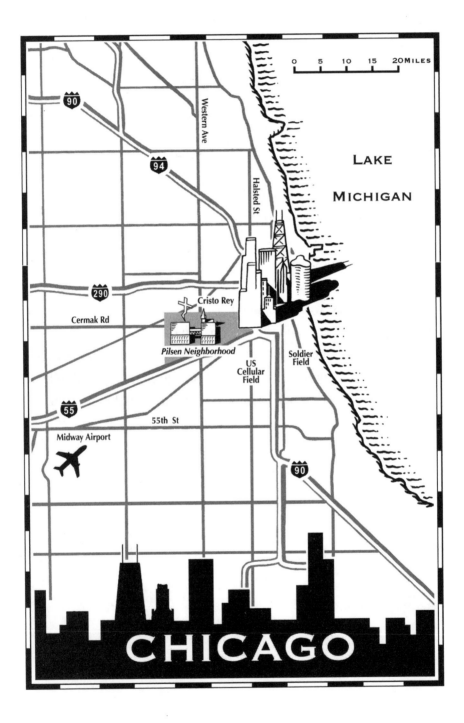

CHICAGO

What the Hell Is a Feasibility Study? 3

L ATE IN THE SPRING of 1992, Brad Schaeffer went to see Dr. Elaine Schuster, Superintendent of Schools for the Archdiocese of Chicago, to tell her about his plan for Jesuit works in Pilsen. He fully expected her to enthusiastically support his plans. By that time, the Jesuits were finalizing the contract through which they would assume pastoral responsibility for St. Procopius. They planned to move into the parish in October. Fr. James W. Schulz, SJ, would be pastor. The Jesuits would name their house in Pilsen in honor of Fr. Miguel Pro, SJ, a Jesuit priest who carried out a clandestine ministry in Mexico during a period of violent anti-Catholicism in the early twentieth century, and who was eventually caught and killed. He refused a blindfold for his firing squad execution. Moments before he was killed, he forgave his executioners and proclaimed, "¡Viva Cristo Rey!" ("Long live Christ the King!").

Brad Schaeffer often equates the province's acquisition of the parish with "establishing a beachhead in the neighborhood." The ultimate goal, he readily admits, "wasn't to run a parish in Pilsen. We wanted to build a comprehensive educational package, something that would benefit the entire community. A high school was always in the back of my mind. But a parish seemed like the best way to get in." So as soon as he'd inked the deal for St. Procopius and made the necessary preparations, he turned his attention to some of the other pieces of the proposed educational package. That's when he went to see Dr. Schuster.

Since January 1991, Dr. Schuster had been serving as superintendent of the nation's largest Catholic school system. As a sophomore in college, in 1963, she entered the convent of the Sisters of Charity of the Blessed Virgin Mary. Seven years later, in the aftermath of the Second Vatican Council, she left the order. She often says, "I left the religious community but never left the ministry." She's devoted her entire career to education. She and Schaeffer first met in the mid-1980s and fast became friends.

Schaeffer knew that Schuster's support would be critical. A Catholic high school couldn't be opened in the archdiocese without the approval of the cardinal, and Schuster was well respected and trusted by archdiocesan officials and the cardinal in particular. Garnering her support, Schaeffer figured, would be a cinch. They were friends, and they shared an abiding love for Catholic education. She'd be excited about a new school—the archdiocese hadn't opened one in decades. During the 1970s, more than seventy-five schools had operated within the archdiocese; by 1992, only fifty remained. The others had either closed or merged with existing schools. Each passing year saw enrollment in the archdiocese's schools drop even more.

Schaeffer made what he thought was a compelling pitch to Schuster. He explained that the Jesuits had a strong sense that they needed to be ministering to the Hispanic community and would take over St. Procopius in October. They would use the parish as a base for a new comprehensive educational initiative, and the next step would be a high school.

A high school. Schuster smiled.

Schaeffer went on to say that he wanted to open the high school less than a year later, in the fall of 1993. Once fully constituted, the school would have an enrollment of one thousand students. Schaeffer said the project was "a no-brainer." Much to his surprise and chagrin, Schuster wasn't convinced. She seemed only lukewarm about the idea. "Brad, I think you've got to prove there's a need there," she told him.

"Prove there's a need? There's clearly a need. There's a neighborhood full of Catholic people and there's no Catholic school. And the public schools serving the kids there are overcrowded. There's a tremendous need."

"I know there's not much space in the public schools. But the families will have a hard time affording private school. And if they can't afford it—"

"We're working on a model that people will be able to afford. We know that's an issue. I don't know how we're going to do it yet, but we're going to make the school affordable."

Looking back on that first conversation, Schuster says, "His vision for this school clearly gave him life and energy. It was like he was saying, 'We're Jesuits. I'm proud of our schools, St. Ignatius and Loyola Academy and Loyola University and the medical center.' But he wanted the Jesuits in this province to meet the needs of the Hispanics in this city. He felt called to do that. There was so much energy—this was his conviction. I think many of his Jesuit brothers were skeptical. I know some of them had to think, *What is he talking about?* This was a point in time when schools were becoming more expensive every year. Catholic schools were struggling to stay open. But he had his own personal and very deep convictions."

Schuster appreciated those convictions, and deep down she agreed with him. But in their first meeting, she didn't show her cards. She still had a job to do.

"Brad," she said, "as superintendent, one of my biggest jobs is to keep the leadership of these schools together and talking. We just

"You've got to confirm the need, and then confirm that the school you are proposing will address the need."

had one messy transition to coeducation, and we're starting another. A big part of my job is making sure we don't kill each other in the process. These decisions—changing the status of a school or opening a new one—affect other schools. Not everyone is going to say, 'Oh, great. There's no school in Pilsen and the Jesuits are going to open one.' Other schools are drawing students from Pilsen. How will this affect them? These are important questions. And you also have to make sure that your school is addressing a need. I'm not denying that there's a need in the neighborhood. Clearly there is. But will families in the neighborhood be able to take advantage of your school? If not, then it won't really address any needs. That's why I think you ought to do a feasibility study."

"A feasibility study?"

"Yes, you've just got to take a closer look. You've got to confirm the need, and then confirm that the school you are proposing will address the need. Basically, you've got to figure out if what you want to do is at all feasible."

By the time Schaeffer left the meeting, he already knew the person he wanted to conduct the feasibility study. The only problem was that the Jesuit he had in mind still had a year of theology studies to complete before he'd be ordained a priest.

❁

MARITZA SANTIBÁÑEZ-LUNA WAS SAD.

For the moment, though, the sadness and uncertainty had been pushed to the back of her mind by the bullfight unfolding in the ring below her. Like her cousins, Maritza sat on the edge of her seat. It was the summer of 1992. She was eight and had just finished the third grade at Sor Juana Inés de la Cruz in the Mexican city of Morelia, in the state of Michoacán. Thin as a rail and quiet compared to her cousins, Maritza watched the fight intently. The matador, Alejandro Silvetti, held his red cape with arms extended. He challenged the bull, luring him closer. The bull began his charge and quickly gathered speed. Silvetti stood his ground, the cape dangling before the bull, now only a few feet away. At the last moment, Silvetti, a thin man clad in an ornate blue and gold costume, danced deftly out of the bull's path. The crowd erupted into frenzied applause, then fell silent as the bull stopped, turned, and set his sights once again on Silvetti.

Maritza and her cousins were in the best seats in Plaza Monumental, the elegant fifteen-thousand-seat bullring in Morelia. With the exception of two months in the United States—while her biological father was working on horse farms in California and Florida—Maritza had spent her entire life in Morelia.

For the last month or so she'd been living with her aunt and uncle, and that's why she was sad. Not because life there was bad—it wasn't. They lived in a nice part of Morelia. Her uncle managed Silvetti, the bullfighter, so they always had good seats at the fights. Their house was beautiful. They had people who worked in the house, cooking and cleaning. Maritza had spent many happy nights there with her cousins, one just a few months younger than she and one who was five years younger.

But living there would take some getting used to. For years she had lived with her grandparents. Her grandfather was a carpenter who owned a successful small business making custom furniture. At the end of the school year, Maritza's grandmother slipped on the patio and broke her ankle. She couldn't walk; plus, she had diabetes and a host of other health problems. She was an older woman, and there was no way she could continue to care for Maritza.

She returned to Mexico six months after she left. Much to her surprise, her bank account was empty—someone in her family had taken all the money. She returned to the States.

Maritza found out after school one day. The driver who took her and her cousins home from school each day took her to her aunt's house. Later, Maritza asked when her grandmother would be there to pick her up. Her aunt told her that her grandmother wasn't coming and that Maritza would be staying with them. Maritza knew there was no use explaining that she loved living with her grandparents, where she was the only child and got "all of their love and affection." Her grandparents' house was spacious and their neighborhood nice. Maritza attended private school. She had everything she could ever want.

That night at dinner, the first night of her new life in her aunt and uncle's house, Maritza kept thinking back to the weeks after her mom, María, left. Maritza was only four at the time. She remembered not knowing where her mom had gone, or why she'd gone. Or if she was ever coming back. Maritza's mom and two friends had gone to the United States, to Chicago. They were looking for adventure. But María also wanted a job, a good job. She was going to work for six months or a year in the States and send all the money back to Mexico. She planned to use the money she saved to open a drugstore in Morelia.

She returned to Mexico six months after she left. Much to her surprise, her bank account was empty—someone in her family had taken all the money. She returned to the States. The next time she came home to Mexico, she had a baby daughter. She'd created a life for herself in Chicago and probably wouldn't be coming back. Maritza, though, stayed in Mexico with her grandmother. Her mom called every Sunday, but, as Maritza would say a few years later, "for a little child, that's not enough."

As she sat silently above the bullring in the warm afternoon sun, Maritza wondered if she would ever be able to move back in with her grandmother. And if her mom would ever come home.

❈

IDEALLY, JESUITS GO WHEREVER the need is greatest. Until 1992, Fr. Jim Gartland, SJ, was one of those ideal Jesuits: he was open to just about any ministry out there.

Then he fell in love with Peru.

It was the summer of 1992. Gartland, who was thirty-four at the time, had asked his Jesuit superiors for permission to teach in Lima, Peru, during his summer break from theology studies. Peru was a long way from Ohio, where the young marathon-running Jesuit had grown up the fifth of eleven children. His dad was a fireman and drove a truck for Roadway on his off days. As a teenager, Gartland had worked at a gas station during the school year and on a landscaping crew in the summers to help pay his tuition at St. Ignatius High School in Cleveland and then Xavier University in Cincinnati, both Jesuit schools. At Xavier he was an accounting major before switching to theology.

Most of his siblings stayed in Cleveland, but Jim headed straight for Chicago after graduation and found a job teaching religion at Loyola Academy, a Jesuit high school in Wilmette, Illinois. He lived in the North Side neighborhood of Rogers Park, not far from Loyola University Chicago, and commuted to the suburbs. He enjoyed his single years. He was surrounded by a group of friends from Xavier, and he had no problem expanding that circle of friends. His social calendar was packed with parties, trips to the bars, and dates.

Then, in 1982, he was invited to lead a Loyola Academy student trip to Peru. "There was part of me that was afraid to go," he recalls. "I was afraid it might screw up my life. I was having a great time. I remember thinking long and hard about the decision to go, because I could stay home and hang out at Butch McGuire's on Division Street all summer, or I could go to the Peruvian Altiplano." Eventually he agreed to go, despite his misgivings "that the trip would probably have a powerful impact on me."

He spent six weeks working in Jarpa, a tiny Peruvian mountain town, with students from Loyola Academy and St. Xavier High School in Cincinnati. Fr. T. Mattingly Garr, SJ, a Jesuit stationed in Peru, coordinated the work for the American students and teachers, most of which consisted of digging a latrine for farmers who came down from the mountains each day to work. The students and teachers slept on the floor in the classrooms of a local school building. The work was hard, the days long, and the nights cold.

Nevertheless, the experience, as Gartland had predicted, had a profound effect on him. Much of it seems to have come directly from Garr. A Louisville, Kentucky, native and a graduate of St. Xavier High School, Garr had entered the Jesuits in 1963 and had been assigned to Peru since 1976. When Gartland visited, Garr was living in the rectory of a small adobe church. "He lived in this little place with no light, no hot water, no electricity, and walls made of adobe bricks," Gartland recalls. He was fascinated by Garr's decisions.

In high school, Gartland had been intimately involved in the school's campus ministry program. Just a few years earlier, in 1973, Fr. Pedro Arrupe, SJ, the father general (a position roughly equivalent to CEO) of the Jesuits, had delivered a speech that called for Jesuits and alumni of Jesuit schools to be men and women for others. Those words were adopted as a slogan by Jesuit schools around the world. Gartland liked the idea of being a "man for others," and it led him to participate in high school service work and a service trip to Haiti when he was a college student. But it wasn't until he visited Peru and saw Matt Garr sleeping on the floor in a mud hut that he realized exactly what it meant to be "a man for others."

> "I wanted to be broken by being forced out of my comfort zone, challenged to learn a new language, and challenged to learn lessons from the poor about trust and humility."

He also realized, at that moment, that he wanted to do the same thing with his life. "I realized then that it's not about comfort. It's not about me. It's about giving. It was so blatant there. I wanted to let go of my life and give it to God." Once he was back in Chicago, it still felt like a "perfect match." He entered the Jesuits in the fall of 1983 and spent the first two years in the Jesuit novitiate, a sort of laid-back spiritual, intellectual, and ministerial training camp. Next came three years of philosophy and theology studies at Loyola University Chicago. After these "first studies," Jesuits begin a two- or three-year period called "regency," during which they work in a Jesuit ministry. Most young American Jesuits do this in one of the Jesuit high schools in the United States.

Jim Gartland was different. He'd taught for three years at Loyola Academy before entering the Jesuits and didn't feel he needed to do it again, so he asked to spend his regency in Peru. "I wanted to be broken," he says of his desire to go to Peru, "by being forced out of my comfort zone, challenged to learn a new language, and challenged to learn lessons from the poor about trust and humility. I thought it would also make me more available as a Jesuit if I spent some time in 'the missions' and picked up a second language." So after a few months of Spanish language study, he was assigned to Cristo Rey

Jesuit High School in Tacna, Peru's southernmost city, where he was a full-time teacher and counselor.

He doesn't mince words when talking about the experience: "The first year there was horrible." One of its low points came on an overnight bus trip with Fr. John P. Foley, SJ, a Jesuit priest who'd been in Peru since the early 1960s. Foley had graduated from Loyola Academy and tried to keep in touch with Gartland during his first year in Peru. Foley knew firsthand how difficult the transition to life in Peru could be. On a semester break, Gartland and Foley were traveling home to Tacna from Lima, where they had gone for the celebration of the feast of St. Ignatius and the ordination of a handful of Peruvian Jesuits. The bus to Tacna was full of people and live pigs, Gartland recalls. Foley asked him how things were going—an innocent question—and it brought Gartland to his knees. Soon he was in tears. "I'm a failure," he said. "I was a good teacher at Loyola. And I get down here and all of a sudden I'm awful at it. My Spanish is awful. I'm teaching senior ethics and philosophy, which is hard enough in English, let alone in Spanish. I have all these concepts in my head that I want to explain, and I can't. I'm afraid I'm failing these kids." Foley listened patiently. It was all he could do. Decades earlier, he'd felt much the same way.

For the first time since his high school athletic career flopped, Gartland was forced to face his limitations and failures. "As Jesuits, we're supposed to pray to be poor like Christ, humble like Christ, humiliated like Christ," he says. "As a novice, I said, 'I don't want that.' Who does? And it kind of bit me in the ass. That first year in Peru humiliated me. In retrospect, it was good for killing my pride, which is my huge sin."

By the end of his second year in Peru, Gartland didn't want to leave. What brought about the change? "What the Peruvians taught me was that it wasn't about me and what I do for them," he says.

"They taught me that what was most important was my desire to be there, with them." His Spanish also improved. He began to connect with students. He once again started to feel that he was teaching, that he was serving others and not just fumbling around in the dark.

At the end of two years in Peru, Gartland reluctantly returned to Berkeley, California, where he began the three years of theology studies required to become a Jesuit priest. But by then, Peru was in his blood. In 1992, during his second year of theology studies, Gartland asked if he could spend the summer teaching in Peru. His provincial, Brad Schaeffer, said yes.

In May of 1992, Gartland took up residence in El Agustino, a four-mile-long former squatter settlement in Lima, Peru, and began teaching at a Fe y Alegría (Spanish for "faith and joy") school affiliated with the parish there. The Fe y Alegría educational movement was started by Fr. José María Velaz, SJ, a Jesuit who wanted to educate children living in the slums of Caracas, Venezuela. Velaz founded his first school in 1955 when a local, Abraham Reyes, donated the home he and his wife had built with their own hands after hearing about Velaz's vision for the school. Velaz quickly converted the home into a small schoolhouse and began offering tuition-free education. News of Velaz's work spread, and by 1966, there were Fe y Alegría schools serving the poor in Ecuador and Bolivia as well. Over the next three decades, the movement continued to grow. By the time Gartland arrived in Peru in 1992, there were well over five hundred Fe y Alegría schools in Latin America.

Gartland considered his summer in Peru a test run. During his previous years there, the Peruvian people had affected him profoundly, and he felt that he'd like to return after ordination. "Many times I asked myself, in the face of such dire poverty, how can these people be so faith-filled and so hope-filled? They challenged my categories, and my control issues. I like to know schedules. I like to plan my life in such a way. They can't plan; they live day to day. Their faith is one of the only constants. They have so little, and yet they have this faith."

Before committing himself to a lifetime of ministry in Peru, Gartland needed to be certain it would be a good fit, that he could be useful and effective there. He spent the summer teaching at a twelve-hundred-student K–12 school. In a corner of the room, he kept a tall stack of paper and a cup of pencils, because most of the forty students who sat in the shabby desks in his classroom each day didn't have their own. They didn't have electricity at home either. During the short days of winter—Peru is in the Southern Hemisphere, so its winter coincides with summer in North America—it was virtually impossible to assign homework, because most students didn't have lights at home. The school, with its cinder-block classrooms, sat on an unpaved road in the heart of El Agustino. Each morning, a layer of dust that had sifted in from the road covered just about everything in the school building.

To many teachers, such conditions would be nightmarish. To Gartland, they were perfect. He knew in his heart that he was supposed to be there, and he'd even begun discussions with the folks at Fe y Alegría's central office about possible job openings. He hoped to begin work there as a teacher. Fe y Alegría's leaders, though, wanted Gartland to consider traveling to different cities and schools in Latin America to offer training and retreats to the primarily lay faculty and staff members.

It was an intriguing proposal, and Gartland brought it up with his provincial during Schaeffer's scheduled visit for the Feast of St. Ignatius, on July 31. Schaeffer nodded as Gartland spelled out the specifics of the proposal.

"How do you feel about it?" Schaeffer asked.

"This is where I'm supposed to be," Gartland said. "I'd really like to come back and continue this work after ordination."

Schaeffer nodded again. "I'd like you to think about something else, too."

"What?"

"Well, I've been in a conversation with Cardinal Bernardin. We don't know where exactly this is going, but the question in my head and his head is, given the huge population explosion among Latinos in Chicago, and given their educational needs, is there some possibility of the Jesuits using our resources to meet these needs? And we're thinking of you—because you're bilingual—moving to Pilsen after ordination to do a feasibility study."

"A feasibility study? What the hell is a feasibility study?"

From Peru to Pilsen   4

IN 1991, SOME FASCINATING computer programming came out of Conseil Européen pour la Recherche Nucléaire (CERN), the famed particle physics research and accelerator laboratory outside Geneva, Switzerland. In an effort to increase collaboration among CERN's physicists, Tim Berners-Lee had developed an interactive method for transferring and sharing information digitally across a computer network.

Berners-Lee believed that the ability to store and update information on a central computer accessible to other users would facilitate CERN's research; scientists would be able not only to access relevant information as they needed it—as opposed to waiting for hard copies, exchanging floppy disks, or relying on face-to-face communication—but also to contribute their findings to the network. To make it possible, Berners-Lee developed Hypertext Markup Language (HTML), a computer language that made digital files interactive by linking them to one another. The user—in this case, a scientist—could use the links to move from file to file or page to page and could go to the exact information he wanted.

Berners-Lee also developed a means for transferring HTML files. It was called Hypertext Transfer Protocol, or HTTP. To facilitate accessing files located on the central computer, Berners-Lee cooked up a rudimentary piece of software that would allow users to receive and interpret data. It was the first Web browser. The new system was first used on a computer network at CERN in May of 1991. Its existence was announced to the public in August of the same year.

In 1992—while Jim Gartland was in Berkeley studying theology and preparing for his life as a Jesuit priest—seven University of Illinois students working at the National Center for Supercomputing Applications (NCSA) came across the work Berners-Lee had done. The students, led by Marc Andreessen, felt the programming was brilliant but far too complex for the layperson with no advanced computing knowledge.* It had, after all, been created for physicists. The students thought it would be fun and worthwhile to develop a more user-friendly and robust Web browser. Early in 1993, they released the NCSA Mosaic browser. By August 1993, the students had built UNIX, Mac, and PC versions, all of which were made available for free download on the Web, provided the browsers weren't used commercially. In the days that followed, thousands of copies were downloaded.

Andreessen and his fellow Mosaic creators were sitting on a gold mine. Remarkably, they had no idea.

❋

JIM GARTLAND AND TWO of his fellow Jesuits lay facedown on a slab of marble before the altar at St. Francis Xavier Church in Cincinnati while the congregation—made up mostly of Jesuits, family, and friends—chanted the Litany of the Saints. By the end of the two-hour ceremony on June 5, 1993, Gartland had received the sacrament of holy orders and had become a Catholic priest. The following day he presided over his first Mass.

A week later he traveled to Mexico, where he enrolled in an intensive Spanish review course. In late August 1993, he returned to Chicago

---

*http://www.pbs.org/opb/nerds2.0.1/wiring_world/mosaic.html

to begin work on the feasibility study for the Jesuits' proposed new school. It hadn't been easy for Brad Schaeffer to convince Gartland to take the job. Gartland had thought Schaeffer was kidding when he first brought it up a year earlier. When he learned Schaeffer was serious, he cried. Then he said, "Seriously, what is a feasibility study?"

Confusing the matter even further, Schaeffer said he wasn't sure what the feasibility study was . . . or what Gartland would find. "I've been talking with the consultors [a group of Jesuits who serve as advisors to the provincial], and we think you can go into the neighborhood, talk to the people, and figure out what the needs are and then formulate some kind of response. I don't really know what the response will look like."

"I was disappointed," Gartland recalls. "Here I was, back in Peru, and I really felt called to be there." He tried to dissuade Schaeffer. But the decision didn't have to be made for a year, since Gartland was still in studies at Berkeley, and Schaeffer told him that all he had to do was think about it.

Think about it he did. He made a list of pros and cons, and, he says, his cons "far outweighed the pros." By the time he saw Schaeffer again, in Berkeley in the fall of 1992, Gartland had prepared what he thought was a bulletproof defense of his life in Peru. Schaeffer stood his ground. They both knew Schaeffer had the upper hand. When Gartland became a Jesuit, he had vowed to obey his superiors. But Schaeffer didn't want to resort to that. He wanted Gartland to choose the job. And after their third meeting, Gartland did.

All he knew for sure when he arrived in Chicago in August was that he'd have an advisory committee. The rest, it seemed, was totally up to him. "The marching orders," he recalls, "weren't really very specific." It quickly became clear, though, that Brad Schaeffer had chosen the right guy for the job.

✳

ON MAY 6, 1993, Maria Hernandez* returned from the hospital to her apartment at Twenty-first and Paulina, in the Pilsen neighborhood. In her arms she cradled Ignacio, her seventh child. Three days earlier, her water had broken just after midnight, and almost immediately she'd begun to experience painful contractions. During six previous pregnancies she'd never felt pain like that. She called for help. Her oldest daughter, Mayra, rushed into the room and, seeing immediately that something was wrong, called an ambulance. Fortunately, the phone was turned on. Often, because of the family's inability to pay the bills, it wasn't.

Ignacio's birth proved difficult, and Maria spent three days and two nights in the hospital. Mayra's birth, seven and a half years earlier, had been much different. Maria was seventeen when she became pregnant with Mayra. She'd married her husband, Rafael, in May of 1985, days after she graduated from Benito Juárez, the lone public high school in Pilsen. The doctors told her the baby would come in early January.

Mayra, though, came three months early. She was born on October 16. Maria remembers her stomach hurting that night. She felt like she had to go to the bathroom. When she did, she felt something inside her give. She looked down and, much to her surprise, saw her new baby's head. It was three o'clock in the morning. She and Rafael didn't have a car. She woke him up, and he pounded on the doors of their neighbors. "A lot of the neighbors," Maria says, "worked nighttime factory jobs. No one was home." Eventually they found a fourteen-year-old willing to take the family car for a drive.

---

* I have attempted to accurately accent all Spanish names that appear in this book. Some of the individuals in this story do not write the accents in their names. In these cases, I have omitted the accents.

Maria crouched in the back of the navy blue Chevy Impala as it raced north from Pilsen on Ashland toward the hospital. She was afraid that sitting down would hurt the baby. She never made it to the delivery room, instead giving birth to Mayra in the lobby as the doctors raced out of the emergency room toward her.

Eleven months later, she gave birth to her first son, Rafael. Fifteen months after that, she had her second son, Juan Enrique, whom they called Henry. Nine months later, Amanda was born, with Stephen coming eleven months after that. Two and a half years later, in January of 1992, Maria Isabel was born. And then, on May 4, 1993, Ignacio came into the world. Joy filled Maria when she first held him, just as it had when she first held the other babies. Raising him, though, wouldn't be easy. The family lived in a cramped three-bedroom basement apartment in the heart of Pilsen. Maria had been living in Pilsen since she was a fourth grader. She'd come to the States a year before that, after crossing the border near Los Angles with a "coyote"—a guide paid to smuggle undocumented immigrants into the United States—and her aunt, her cousin, and seven of her siblings.

Maria had long wanted to come to the States. Her parents had come to Chicago in the early 1970s in search of better jobs and better lives. During that time, Maria and her five brothers and two sisters stayed with their aunt in Mexico. Life there was not good. Their aunt, who had only one child, was young and didn't know how to handle so many kids. She also liked to go to parties. Her solution was to lock the kids in an upstairs bedroom. "Sometimes we'd be in there for a full day without any food," Maria says.

A few years later, in the mid-1970s, Maria and her siblings came to the States and settled with their parents, who were living and working on the northwest side of Chicago. She attended a public school but was

"We learned English the hard way, with lots of embarrassments and insults from teachers and students."

ridiculed for her inability to speak English. "We learned English the hard way," she says, "with lots of embarrassments and insults from teachers and students."

A year later, the family moved south to Pilsen. Maria worked hard at school and after completing junior high was excited to enroll at Benito Juárez. She wanted to become a nurse, and Juárez had a pre-nursing program. She applied as a junior but wasn't accepted, she was told, because she wasn't a senior. She applied again before her senior year. To her dismay, she was again rejected. This time, they told her she wasn't the right age. The program's leaders had decided it would be more effective if they enrolled juniors and put them through a two-year program. During the second semester of her senior year, Maria started dating Rafael. They fell in love and were married days after their graduation.

By the time Maria gave birth to Ignacio, several years later, things between Maria and Rafael had begun to sour. Rafael had proven unable to hold a steady job. He drank a lot and spent more time partying with his friends in the neighborhood than he did taking care of the kids. The family was getting by on public aid and the piñatas that Maria made and sold to some of the neighborhood stores.

Rafael hadn't gone to the hospital with Maria and hadn't been there when Ignacio was born. He hadn't been at home either, leaving Mayra, who was only seven and a half at the time, to watch the other kids while her mom was in the hospital.

❋

Joey Garcia, unlike most of his classmates, couldn't wait to get his hands on his report card. It was the last day of his second-grade year at Pilsen's Irma C. Ruiz Elementary School. As a student in the Chicago public school system, Joey received four report cards a year. In the fall and spring, parents came to school to pick up the cards and have conferences with the teachers. Right before winter break and summer break, the teachers gave the cards to the kids to take home. Today's card would be Joey's twelfth. So far, he had gotten the highest possible mark in every class he'd taken.

Joey was small, by far the smallest in his class, and he already sported a pair of glasses with lenses that looked thick enough for someone ten times his age. He sat at his desk, hands folded, smiling, waiting patiently as the teacher thumbed through the cards and his classmates squirmed in their seats, summer break minutes away. "I was a bright child," he says today, reflecting on his career at Ruiz. "Super bright."

Report card day was a quarterly confirmation of his intelligence. And, more important, it was an opportunity for him to shine in his mother's eyes, to show her how well he was doing and how good he was. Joey's mom had been smart, too. "She told me that she was the smartest girl in the world," he says. "Well, not in the world, but I mean out of the family, because she's one of nine." And she stressed to her only son the importance of education. "My ma always taught me that education was the key to everything." When Ms. Vasquez handed him his report card, Joey pulled it in close to his body, opened it, and scanned it quickly. Perfect. Again. As soon as school let out, he headed for home, half walking, half jogging, anxious to share the good news with his mom, to show her that he knew education was important and was doing something about it.

Looking back on his childhood, Joey describes himself as "a house kid." His life outside school was spent almost entirely in the two-bedroom third-floor apartment he and his mom shared in Pilsen. They lived above Joey's grandma just a few blocks from school.

"I stayed in the house most of the time. I never had many friends outside school. I'd just come home from school and do all my homework and stuff and then watch TV or jump around, you know, like kids do." He didn't want to play with other kids, go to the park, or go get a slice of pizza after school, "because I didn't need anything like that. I don't know, my ma gave me everything I needed, so there was no point hanging out outside with all my friends. I had a whole bunch of friends, but I didn't need to see them, because I had my mom."

Joey took the steps to the apartment two at a time, pushed open the door, and rushed in to hand his mom the report card. She read it. Then she pulled him close and hugged him.

JIM GARTLAND WALKED TOWARD a group of four gangbangers who stood in the shadows next to a brick building, just beyond the yellow light cast by a nearby street lamp. He was scared. Their gang affiliation was clear in the way they wore their clothes, their hair, their shoes. They were out on patrol. It was a hot night in September, and Gartland—dressed in a Roman collar, comfortable chinos, and a pair of Teva sandals—was walking the neighborhood and talking to people. He slowly approached the group, his hands in his pockets, and tried to look self-assured. He knew they were watching him. His white face shone in a sea of Latinos.

This was one of Gartland's first face-to-face interviews, and it's worth noting that as he approached the young gang members, no one had his back. In a literal sense, he walked the streets alone, following the clearest orders he received from his superiors, to "go out and meet people and tell us what, if anything, we should do." In a figurative sense, Gartland was conducting the feasibility study with very little support from his fellow Jesuits. Even as he walked the streets, many of them were voicing their opposition to the idea of a new ministry, particularly a school.

From 1992 to 1993, the number of Jesuits in the province fell by four, from 318 to 314. Since 1970, though, when there were 571 Jesuits in the province, the number had dropped by 257. Over the same twenty-three-year period, enrollment at all the province schools had grown considerably. Many Jesuits in the province felt they should be focusing their energy on maintaining the province's existing ministries rather than devoting resources to studying the possibility of a new one. Many Jesuits felt that there were too many ministries already, too few Jesuits, and far more important tasks to be done.

In the nineteenth and twentieth centuries, Jesuit high schools in the United States were founded to provide education to the children of immigrants, almost all of them white, almost all of them of European descent.

On the flip side, some Jesuits were suggesting that the incredibly strong Jesuit network of schools—at the time, twenty-eight colleges and universities and forty-five high schools in the United States—wasn't really fulfilling the Jesuit mission. The Jesuits had, since their founding, served the *greatest* need. In the nineteenth and twentieth centuries, Jesuit high schools in the United States were founded to provide education to the children of immigrants, almost all of them white, almost all of them of European descent. After graduating, many of them had become successful in the world. When they started families, they wanted to send their children to Jesuit schools, too. Most Jesuit schools are now populated with a number of second-, third-, and even fourth-generation students, the children of bankers, attorneys, lawyers, consultants, and CEOs, and the nature of the schools themselves has changed. So in the 1980s and '90s, some Jesuit educators said the schools were no longer addressing "the greatest need" and that the Jesuits should be turning their attention elsewhere.

In Chicago, Brad Schaeffer had picked Jim Gartland to seek out that greatest need and help the Jesuits determine how best to address it. To do so, Gartland went into Pilsen to talk to—and, more important, listen to—parents, teachers, school principals, students, community leaders, church leaders, and even gangbangers.

As Gartland drew near the gangbangers standing in the shadows, they turned slowly to face him. He was surprised by how young they seemed, with thin mustaches and beards, and tattoos emblazoned on their shoulders and arms. Still, they succeeded at appearing menacing. Gartland could barely manage to say, "Hi, guys."

A Frontier in the City   5

O NE SPANISH WORD FOR a Caucasian is güero. As Jim Gartland strolled toward that first group of gangbangers, trying to look casual, they must have been wondering, *What is this crazy-ass Güero doing?*

When he said hello, they didn't know whether to laugh or to knock him to the ground. So they nodded. And then Gartland started asking them questions. To his surprise, they started talking.

Gartland ended up conducting scores of these casual interviews, and they were, he believes, crucial for the feasibility study. Something hadn't worked for these young men, the gangbangers standing on corners. They were teenagers who should have been in school learning about congruent triangles and the periodic table, but instead they were carrying weapons, selling drugs, and trying to scare the hell out of people.

Pilsen was crawling with gangs: Two-Six Party People, La Raza, Latin Kings, Ambrose, and Morgan Boys. Somewhere along the line, the kids in these gangs had probably made bad decisions, as kids sometimes do. But something larger was at work. Or something larger wasn't working. Gartland needed to know what had gone wrong.

He can't remember the specifics of that first conversation, save the fact that he didn't get his head kicked in. Many more conversations took place, and common threads eventually emerged. "Before I did it, I wondered how you talk to gangbangers. But you'd be surprised how

"I would ask, 'When you're twenty-five, what do you want to be?' And they'd say, 'We don't think that way. We only think about now. We're just trying to survive.'"

easily they'll tell you their story. I'd just ask them, 'How long have you been out of school? Why don't you go? What do your parents think about that? How come you stopped going? What are you hoping for? You're here—what would you like to see in the neighborhood?' Over time, the answers all started to sound the same: Dysfunctional families. Dad is an alcoholic. Dad isn't around. Mom gave up on them. Some were second-generation gangbangers. They all went to school but didn't get a lot out of it. There were a lot of problems at school, mostly fights. So they ended up on the streets and would say, 'Now what do I do? There are no job opportunities. I make a whole lot more selling on the corner than I would at McDonald's. I lost my brother. I lost my friend.' I would ask all of them, 'When you're twenty-five, what do you want to be?' And they'd say, 'We don't think that way. We only think about now. We're just trying to survive.' Then I'd ask them, 'Well, what means the most to you?' Usually, it was 'my homeys, my boys here.' There was no sense of future. That was one thing they all had in common."

Gartland's work on the feasibility study involved much more than talking to kids on the street. During the 1993–94 school year, he tried to meet with ten people every week. He spent countless hours on the phone arranging interviews and meetings. He spent his nights on the streets, talking and listening. He talked to pastors in the neighborhood and to teachers and principals at public and private grade schools. He talked to local business owners and Hispanic business leaders in Chicago. Through parishes and community organizations, he formed focus groups of mothers in the neighborhood. He visited administrators from other Catholic high schools. Every meeting or interview yielded more names, other people he should see.

In an effort to learn more about the educational history and needs of the area, he visited the local high schools, Benito Juárez Community Academy and David G. Farragut Career Academy, and spoke to teachers and administrators there. In those schools he found some deeply committed individuals who seemed limited by bureaucracy and sometimes bitter infighting. Both of the public schools were overcrowded. People in Pilsen/Little Village had already called on Chicago Public School officials to open another school in the area.

Area pastors were, Gartland says, "definitely into the idea of the Jesuits launching a school of some kind." The Resurrection Project—a powerful neighborhood organization that seeks to build healthy communities through education, outreach, development, and affordable housing—also loved the idea of the Jesuits starting a new initiative in Pilsen. Parents were excited about the possibilities. Gartland says that the mothers "were worried about safety in the schools." Many parents expressed a desire for a school of their own, a school they could understand and one that understood them.

But not everyone thought it was such a great plan. Some community leaders were skeptical. Gartland recalls them saying, "It's great that you're here, but we don't need a study. We don't need a plan. We need to know that you're going to stay." Leaders of other Catholic schools in Chicago—both junior high schools and high schools—were almost unanimously opposed to the idea of the Jesuits opening a new school. Early on, Gartland asked Elaine Schuster for permission to make a presentation to the council of Catholic school principals. Schuster thought it was such a good idea that she asked Gartland to give regular progress reports to the council. Gartland wanted to be the first to tell them about the Jesuit study, but he wasn't. By the time he made his presentation, rumors had begun to circulate about the Jesuit plan for Pilsen. With each meeting, the opposition swelled and strengthened.

Gartland doesn't fault any of the school leaders for opposing the new school. He admires the work they were doing then and continue to do today. "The Catholic schools, both the grade schools and the high schools—all their energy is spent surviving," he says. "They're incredible at surviving with so little. But they have little energy left for creative thinking. They have neither the time nor the luxury. And here I come, this Young Turk who doesn't have a job other than hitting the street and thinking ideas."

Gartland recalls one particularly heated exchange. "One of the principals said, 'If I have open seats here at my school, why are you going to open a new school?' I remember asking how many students from Pilsen attended her school. The principal said, 'That's beside the point.' I said, 'No it's not. It's not at all beside the point. In Pilsen, there are lots of kids not in high school. The majority are not in high school.' At first, they didn't buy this. They thought a new school would doom them. And all we were doing was *thinking* about a school, *talking* about a school. We hadn't settled on anything. But the idea of a high school or a junior high school upset them."

Gartland and the Jesuits who were involved with the project in its early stages remain eternally grateful to the one supporter they did have: Br. Michael Quirk, FSC, who helped run the De La Salle Institute, a high school located a couple miles southeast of Pilsen.

Quirk was in attendance at one particularly contentious council meeting when some Catholic school principals were haranguing Gartland and accusing him of plotting to steal their students. In the middle of the meeting, Quirk stood up and said, "Jim, I'd love to tell you not to pursue this study, because De La Salle would like to have more students from Pilsen. But I know there's a need there. I know God wants the children in Pilsen/Little Village to have a better education. So start something in Pilsen. And know that you'll have my support, the support of De La Salle, as you do so."

Gartland also conducted much of the feasibility study on the road. As soon as he began talking to people about a school in Pilsen, people started telling him he should go see such-and-such school that was trying to do something similar. Many of them mentioned Nativity schools, the first of which was started in the early 1970s by Jesuits on the Lower East Side of Manhattan. Today there are more than forty Nativity-model middle schools around the country. By relying on the generosity of private donors, they're able to offer tuition-free education, small class sizes, extended school days, and extended school years to economically disadvantaged young men and women.

So Gartland hit the road and visited Nativity schools in New York, Boston, and Baltimore. He visited Pine Ridge, South Dakota, where Jesuit priests and the Lakota people run the Red Cloud Indian School. He visited Detroit, Michigan, where the Jesuits had just opened Loyola High School, which seeks out underperforming students who seem susceptible to the high dropout rates plaguing inner-city Detroit. He visited Los Angeles, where a Jesuit priest, Fr. Greg Boyle, SJ, had launched a number of initiatives designed to rehabilitate, educate, and empower former gang members.

The road trip underscored the fact that Jesuit ministries can, and do, dramatically impact people's lives. It also helped Gartland understand that, despite centuries of experience in education, there was no template in place in 1993 for starting a Jesuit school to serve the poor. A lot of different things were working. A lot of different things, it seemed, could work.

❋

THOUGH MAYRA HERNANDEZ TURNED eight on October 16, 1993, she had many of the responsibilities of a parent. She had to, because her dad was rarely around—and was usually drunk when he was. Mayra changed the diapers of her little brothers and sisters. She regularly fed Ignacio, the youngest, and knew how to burp him. She cradled her baby brother carefully, as if he were her own. In the mornings, after getting ready for school, she would help her younger siblings get dressed. She helped her mom cook.

But Mayra was still a kid. And like any kid, she loved going to the park.

Her mom didn't have the time or the energy to take the kids to the park. Trips to the store were enough. But Mayra's Uncle Sergio— one of Maria's younger brothers—did have time. He lived nearby in Pilsen, wasn't married, and didn't have any children of his own. Mayra says Sergio was "a sports addict." During high school he had played any sport he could—on school teams and intramural teams. Once he was out of high school and working, he joined some of the men's leagues in Pilsen. When he didn't have games, he'd go to the park looking for pickup basketball games.

Sergio also made time to help his older sister. He'd stop in three or four times a week—almost always with a basketball under his arm—to do whatever he could. Sometimes the greatest service he could offer was taking the kids out of the apartment to let them blow off some steam. He usually took them to a play lot near the intersection of Twenty-first and Ashland. There was a paved basketball court there, and the kids could also get onto the fields at Benito Juárez, the local high school.

The first time Sergio took them to the park, the kids all wanted to shoot baskets with his ball. Most of them were too small for the full-sized basketball, and the hoop was too high. Soon all the kids shifted their attention to something else—everyone but Mayra. She stayed a few steps from the front of the basket and kept trying to heave the ball over the rim and in. After the first one fell through, she was hooked.

※

By the end of 1993, more than one million people around the world had downloaded the Mosaic browser. In December, the *New York Times* published its first story about Mosaic and Web browsing. Marc Andreessen had since left the University of Illinois in Champaign to take a job at a software company in Silicon Valley. He was still largely oblivious to the potential of the browser he and his buddies had created. There was someone in Silicon Valley, though, who wasn't oblivious.

Jim Clark had been a professor at Stanford University for years before helping found a company called Silicon Graphics Inc. (SGI), which had become a major player in the burgeoning personal computer business. Early in 1994, Clark became disillusioned with the company and left. He recruited Andreessen—and many of his colleagues from the University of Illinois—to launch a commercial version of the Mosaic browser. They set up shop in Mountain View, California. At first, they named the company after their product, Mosaic, but they soon changed the name to Netscape. Late in 1994, they put the finishing touches on the beta version of the first product, a Web browser called Netscape Navigator.

The world was about to change.

※

In the spring of 1994, after many months of study, conversation, and prayer, Gartland put pen to paper. On June 22, he submitted his feasibility study—titled "Ministers of the Word Sent to New

Frontiers"—to his provincial, Brad Schaeffer. Gartland framed the purpose of the study by asking, "If the glory of God is the human being fully alive, how are we corporately offering our talents and energies to Jesus' desire to see a world at once more human and more divine?"

The study was composed of three parts. Part 1 described the neighborhood, its people, and their needs. Despite being neither a demographer nor a sociologist, Gartland offered solid research in this section. Below is a sampling of the information he collected and used as the basis of the study.

- According to the 1990 census, Hispanic Americans are the second-largest minority group in the United States and will soon be the largest. About 10 percent of the current population is Hispanic. During the 1980s, the Hispanic population in the United States grew by 53 percent, eight times as fast as the non-Hispanic population.

- The poverty and unemployment rates among Hispanics are growing. One in every four Hispanic households and two in every five Hispanic children are poor. Despite the high poverty rate, Hispanic men have higher labor-force participation rates than non-Hispanic men, 78.2 percent compared to 73.9 percent. Yet in 1990, the median earnings of Hispanics were remarkably lower than those of non-Hispanic men, $14,141 versus $22,207, and the income gap between whites and Hispanics is widening.

- Only 50 percent of Hispanic adults are high school graduates. This drops to 43 percent for Mexican Americans. Less than

10 percent of Hispanic adults have a college degree, and for Mexican Americans, it is only 6.2 percent.

- In 1970, Latino students made up 9.8 percent of the total enrollment in Chicago public schools. In 1992, they made up 29 percent of the enrollment, a jump of 111 percent. Over the same time period, the enrollment for white students dropped 76 percent, and the enrollment for African American students dropped 27 percent.

- According to the 1990 census, the population in Pilsen/ Little Village is 126,809, of which 109,028 are Latino. Forty percent of the Latino population is under the age of eighteen.

- In Pilsen/Little Village, 2,640 youths between the ages of sixteen and nineteen are not enrolled in high school and don't have high school diplomas. Only 27 percent of the Latino adults in this neighborhood are high school graduates, and less than 3 percent have college degrees.

- Benito Juárez High School and Farragut Career Academy are the two high schools in the area of study. In 1992, Juárez had 2,157 Latino students enrolled (98.6 percent of its enrollment), and Farragut had 1,602. The class of 1991 dropout rate was 55 percent at Juárez and 73.1 percent at Farragut. Because these figures do not include those who never reached the high school level, local community leaders in the area often refer to a 75 percent dropout rate.

- Forty-six percent of Chicago Public School teachers send their children to private schools.

- Of the 5.6 million people who reside in the Archdiocese of Chicago, 2.3 million (41 percent) are Catholic. In 1988, 30 percent of the Catholics in the archdiocese were Hispanics.

In the second part of the study, Gartland attempted to connect faces with the statistics. At one point, he recounted his interactions with young Hispanic men incarcerated in Cook County Jail.

> The conversations I have had this past year with Latino adolescents in Cook County Jail haunt my sleep. Once given the opportunity to step out of the machismo of their gang world, these young men return to the childhood they never had. They simply want to work, have families, and live in peace. Unfortunately, they do not know how to attain these goals. Through tears of frustration and fear, they kept questioning me, "What do I do?" and "Where do I go now?" . . .
>
> The faith of some of these prisoners inspires me. One seventeen-year-old told me about his nightly Bible reading. Locked in a room with fifty others, this young man quietly read about the life of Jesus after the lights were turned off each night. He wanted to avoid verbal and physical abuse, so he prayed while the others were sleeping. He, along with several other inmates, made his first communion in Cook County Jail this past year.

In the second part of his study, Gartland also addressed the issue of funding such a new school, noting that many parents in Pilsen/Little Village wanted to send their children to private Catholic schools because of the poor performance, overcrowding, and sometimes dangerous conditions in local public schools. Most parents, though, couldn't afford private school tuition. Making any new educational venture affordable would therefore be critically important.

In part 3 of the study, Gartland made his recommendations. He stated that it would be a great risk to open a new educational center in Chicago while the number of Jesuits in the province continued to shrink. He believed, though, that a ministry with the poor would breathe new life into the province, its Jesuits, and its existing ministries. The need for a new school was indisputable, and he believed the Jesuits were uniquely qualified for the work. In the end, Gartland recommended that the Jesuits begin to seek funding for a new educational center. Because of the difficulties of such a venture, he urged his fellow Jesuits to approach the project realistically.

> Of course dreams and zeal for this project need to be grounded in fiscal reality. Is there money? The next phase must be geared toward raising money. With this alternative model of education designed to meet the needs of families in the Pilsen/Little Village area of Chicago, can we contact foundations, apply for grants, and raise money from the corporate world in Chicago?

Gartland ended the study with a list of eleven presuppositions for the proposed educational center—what he usually called it. By using this label he seemed to suggest that the school would be different from all the other schools out there. In the list of presuppositions—summarized below—he laid out, like a master architect, much of what would, over time, make the school different.

1. The educational center will be Catholic and Jesuit and will have a clearly articulated mission statement.

2. Based on the needs of the students and the parents, the center will strive for academic excellence. The hope is to provide quality education for the people of Pilsen.

3. The goal is not to replace existing parishes and their schools, but rather to work with them.

4. Ongoing collaboration with Catholic high schools will also be important. The goal is simply to provide more families in Pilsen/Little Village with the option of a quality Catholic education.

5. The hope is to educate families. Parental involvement will be necessary for the school's success. Adult education and spiritual development will be an integral part of the center.

6. Community involvement in the planning and functioning of this project will be crucial. This center has the opportunity to model a new way for schools to collaborate with communities.

7. The curriculum and atmosphere of the center will be culturally sensitive to the Mexican American community it serves.

The model and programs of the center will be different from traditional ways of proceeding. The hope is that the administration, staff, and faculty will be culturally sophisticated in order to welcome and accommodate the families they serve. This will include encouraging students and their families to appreciate their culture, heritage, language, and traditions while being integrated into the larger society.

8. This project will be for the people of Pilsen/Little Village. It will be located in the neighborhood and restricted to residents of the neighborhood.

9. The school will begin by accommodating students at the junior high and high school levels. It could start with a group of seventh graders and grow year by year until it has full junior high and high school enrollment.

10. The principles and objectives will be formulated by an advisory committee that will include parents, educators, community leaders, church leaders, business leaders, and Jesuit personnel.

11. The project will have the support of the Chicago Province of the Society of Jesus. Support for the proposed endeavor cannot be provided only by the provincial and a few Jesuits.

No one knew it at the time, but the thirty-five-year-old Jesuit had prepared a blueprint for a school that would change people's lives. Many

Jesuits reacted with skepticism, fearful still that the province simply couldn't sustain another new ministry. Brad Schaeffer welcomed the feasibility study with open arms. Within days of receiving it, he sketched out a plan for the second phase of the study, which would attempt to answer the largest question Gartland had raised: "How are we ever going to pay for this?"

Dollars, Cents... and Sense   6

JUST ABOUT EVERYONE INVOLVED in the early stages of the Jesuits' proposed school in Pilsen points to provincial Brad Schaeffer's leadership as the primary reason for its eventual success.

Brad Schaeffer, on the other hand, points to good luck and suggests that Providence may also have had a role.

The second phase of the feasibility study is proof that they were both right.

❋

THE SECOND PHASE OF the study was shaped primarily by two issues. Jim Gartland had determined definitively in the first phase of the study that there was both a need and a desire for a new educational center in Pilsen. He'd recommended that the province move toward opening one but hadn't said for sure what the school would look like. A determination had to be made about what the school would be: a junior high school, a high school, or both.

And then the Jesuits had to figure out how to pay for it. Financing the school was critically important, and tricky. As Elaine Schuster had pointed out, the school would be useless if people in the neighborhood could not afford it. The tuition model employed at most Jesuit schools around the country would not work.

To figure out the financing, Brad Schaeffer needed someone with a businessperson's ability to analyze and structure financing arrangements. But he also needed someone with a desire to serve, someone who implicitly understood why opening a new school in Pilsen made sense. One Jesuit in the province seemed to fit the bill: Fr. Ted Munz, SJ.

In 1980, just before he began theology studies—the final stage of preparation for the priesthood—Munz earned an MBA at the University of Chicago's Graduate School of Business. He was, he readily admits, an oddity among his classmates.

"I went to business school because my perception was that it would provide me with tools that were extremely flexible in terms of any work in the Society of Jesus, tools that would give me a strong analytical grounding and a way of understanding the structures of how people live." His fellow graduate students had different plans. "I think the hot thing then was investment banking. That's what everyone seemed to want to be doing."

Munz, as a person, was also quite different. He didn't own many nice clothes. When he needed to get dressed up, he put on a nylon pullover. For most of his life as a Jesuit, he has slept on a thin mattress on the floor. As a young priest, he drove a beat-up old car that some of his closest friends and colleagues referred to as a "ghetto sled."

Munz was ordained in 1983. Four years later, he and two fellow Jesuit priests founded the Heartland Center in Hammond, Indiana. Heartland's purpose was to fuse social research and analysis with grassroots social action. Munz, Fr. Philip Chmielewski, SJ, and Fr. Tom Florek, SJ, were driven to open the center by the thirty-second General Congregation, a meeting of Jesuits from every province and region in the world, which called Jesuits to work toward a world that is more just and humane.

Munz and Chmielewski, a sociologist, shared the belief that grassroots social movements often were not grounded in objective statistical reality. Because those seeking to bring about change didn't have all the facts—or, in some cases, hardly any of the facts—their efforts for change were largely unsuccessful. "Way too often, activism and research are separate," Munz says. "You have people who are passionate about a cause. They imagine themselves as the next Martin Luther King or Gandhi. They get excited and say, 'We have to do something.' But very often they don't have the analytical tools to understand politics, sociology, or economics. So their movement fizzles or they burn themselves out. On the other side, there are people who are absolutely brilliant at understanding the structures of injustice. They talk about it and write about it, but they have no insertion point. They're standing on the outside." Munz, Chmielewski, and Florek wanted to change that.

"Way too often, activism and research are separate. You have people who are passionate about a cause. . . But very often they don't have the analytical tools . . . So their movement fizzles or they burn themselves out."

Munz was completing his seventh year at Heartland Center when Schaeffer called in the summer of 1994 and asked him to become part of the provincial staff. As provincial assistant for social ministries, Munz would oversee the various social initiatives—including the Heartland Center—run by the province and would direct the second phase of the feasibility study for the proposed educational center in Pilsen. Munz moved to Chicago in early August.

"The first step was to figure out what kind of school we should open," Munz recalls. "Jim's work had identified the educational needs in the community. The conclusion wasn't surprising to him or anyone else. Educationally, it's a community that has huge needs. There were very limited educational resources. The question was, how should we as Jesuits respond?"

Throughout the fall of 1994, Munz retraced Gartland's steps and conducted countless interviews with pastors, community leaders, and educational leaders. The conversations helped Munz understand that the educational needs in the community stretched from preschool to adult education. In September, he assembled a task force of lay and religious educators and thinkers to brainstorm possibilities for the school. Gartland, who'd become the pastor at St. Procopius, was a member, as were Fr. Larry Reuter, SJ; Fr. John Costello, SJ; Agustín Gómez; and Sr. Judith Murphy, OSB. Reuter had served previously as president of Loyola Academy and was Loyola University's vice president for ministry. Costello was the Chicago Province's chief fund-raiser. Gómez, a Loyola Academy graduate, worked as an architect in Chicago and lived in Pilsen. Murphy had just stepped down as president of St. Scholastica, a highly regarded girls' high school on the North Side of Chicago. They met every couple of weeks to discuss the new educational center. They talked about the right student body for the school—grade school students, high school students, or adults? Males, females, or both?—and about how a school could connect with students and make an effort to respect their culture. They began to think about curriculum, and how different models could address the educational needs of the students in the neighborhood.

"Sometime in early November," Munz recalls, "I began saying to myself, 'We can do whatever we want, and, in a community that has huge needs, it will be valuable. But what is it that we really know how to do? High schools.' There were ten thousand high school–age students in Pilsen/Little Village and no Catholic high schools. My one conclusion was if we can do high school, that would be a huge contribution."

On November 17, Munz submitted a report to the provincial. In it, he recommended that the province open a high school, and he actually put forth a comprehensive educational plan, named "The Pilsen Project: Jesuits Educating," that would address more of the neighborhood's educational needs. In addition to investing in a new high school, he recommended that the province continue to invest in the grade school at St. Procopius and develop an after-school program that would provide classes and activities for both children and adults. Such a program would not only provide new skills and opportunities for the parents, but would also prepare them to take a more active role in the education of their children. Munz suspected the plan would be approved quickly. But the second big question still remained to be answered: how would they pay for it?

❀

LEO MALDONADO SHIFTED HIS weight back and forth while a high school kid he'd never seen before packed marijuana into the bowl of a pipe and then fished a lighter out of his pocket. Leo looked around the basement. He didn't know whose house he was in. The ceiling was low, and the tiles sagged in a few places.

It was the second time he'd seen one of these pipes. The first was at a party a couple of months ago, right at the end of seventh grade. That time, he hadn't been sure what the small ceramic contraption was for. He and his friends from the neighborhood—the ones who were also assigned to his ESL class—had never stolen beer from their parents' fridge. They'd never wanted to smoke cigarettes, and they'd certainly never laid eyes on a dime bag of weed. They were too busy trying to outdo each other with killer crossovers in their alleyway basketball games.

Leo knew, though, from watching the people at that party a few months ago—the way they fidgeted and watched and waited for the "bowl" to be passed to them—that it contained more than just regular tobacco. And he knew he probably shouldn't have any of it, so he backed away from the group, pushed himself into the shadows against the wall, and watched as they passed the pipe, wrapped their mouths around it, lit it, and inhaled.

Now he was at another party in another basement, and there was another bowl. Only this time, there was nowhere for Leo to go. He watched as the kid with the bowl held the flame against the pinch of weed he'd just packed into it. It started to burn. Leo could remember the smell from the last time. It was a hard smell to explain, but he remembered it clearly, its thickness and strength. The kid closed his eyes and inhaled. Then he pulled the bowl away from his mouth, tilted his head back, and exhaled. He passed the bowl. The guy next to Leo had it now. Leo was one of only four people in the room, and he knew he couldn't leave. All of a sudden, the bowl and the lighter were in his hands and he was lighting and inhaling. He passed the bowl and exhaled, coughing a bit as the smoke left his body.

The smoke left something behind. He felt it in his face—a strange but somewhat pleasant feeling. By the time Leo left the party an hour later with Rafael and Juan, his head felt normal again. He'd been hanging out with these two guys more and more. They met halfway through seventh grade, even though Leo wasn't looking for new friends. He had his boys, his friends from the neighborhood and from his class at school. Leo, though, was doing fairly well at school, despite the fact he rarely did his homework. It was clear to his teachers that he was learning to speak English. So, at the beginning of seventh grade, they took Leo and two other students out of the Spanish class for two or three class periods each day and put them into mainstream classrooms.

At first the other students ignored him. Leo was an ESL kid; to them, that meant he was dumb. Over time, though, the students in the mainstream classrooms warmed to him. Soon he had more friends—friends who were connected to gangs, drugs, and girls.

Leo didn't know it at the time, but he'd just taken his first steps onto a well-worn path toward drug abuse, gang life, and sexually transmitted diseases. Thousands of kids in Pilsen/Little Village were already on the path. It was possible to enter it without even knowing it, from neighborhood basements, backyards, even the bathrooms at school. There were so many ways to enter the path that being on it seemed normal. It was where most teenagers seemed to be.

Leo didn't know it at the time, but he'd just taken his first steps onto a well-worn path toward drug abuse, gang life, and sexually transmitted diseases. Thousands of kids in Pilsen/Little Village were already on the path.

❊

IN EARLY JANUARY 1995, Brad Schaeffer accepted Ted Munz's recommendation for the Pilsen Project. The Jesuits would—provided they could pay for it—open the first new Catholic high school in the Archdiocese of Chicago since 1963. But the feasibility of a new high school depended on the Jesuits' ability to make it affordable. Figuring out how to do that was Munz's job, but he didn't have to do it alone. Fr. John Foley, SJ, a smiling, bespectacled Jesuit, had just returned to Chicago from Peru at Schaeffer's request to help with the project.

Foley had spent more than thirty-four years in Peru and could have stayed—the provincial there would have been happy to have him. Not to mention that returning to Chicago was a leap of faith since he didn't know exactly what he was coming back for. Schaeffer himself didn't know what the project would be when he first approached Foley about returning, in 1992. But Foley agreed, because he thought it was what a good Jesuit should do.

It was the same attitude that had landed him in Peru decades before. The son of a successful car dealer in Chicago's North Shore, Foley graduated from Loyola Academy in 1953. After graduation, he almost entered the Jesuits. "It was that mentality that you better do what God wants, or you're going to be in big trouble," Foley recalls. "I felt that I was supposed to be a priest, but I thought I'd drawn the short straw. I didn't like the idea at all. I liked living high off the hog. I enjoyed life too much. I thought it was going to be such a downer to be a priest." His counselor at the school, Fr. Douglas Pearl, SJ, figured all this out and told him, "If that's the way you feel, then you should just go to college."

He enrolled at Georgetown University. After stumbling onto the funeral of a Jesuit priest in the school's chapel, he experienced a profound change of heart and realized he wanted more than anything to become a priest. The summer after his freshman year, he entered the Chicago Province's Jesuit novitiate in Milford, Ohio. After six years of Jesuit formation, he wrote a letter to the provincial offering himself for the missions in India. "I didn't really have any desire to go, and I think I said that in the letter, but I said I was willing if they needed me. I thought it was what a good Jesuit should do."

In 1961, just a year after Pope John XXIII asked every U.S. religious order to send 10 percent of its personnel to Central and South America, Foley learned he would be one of the first Jesuits sent from the Chicago Province to a new mission in Peru. At the time, Jesuit assignments to the missions were for life. Foley said good-bye to his family, expecting never to see them again. In Peru, and briefly in Mexico, he studied for the priesthood. After his ordination in 1967, he served as a teacher, spiritual counselor, principal, and president at Jesuit schools and centers in the Peruvian cities of Arequipa, Piura, Cuzco, and Tacna. He was involved in traditional high school education, adult education, and the administration of a social service center for the working street children of Tacna.

It was Foley's experience with educating the poor, and educating them in Spanish, that had gotten Schaeffer's attention. Schaeffer visited Peru in 1992 and asked Foley if he'd ever think about coming back to the United States to work with Hispanics in Chicago. Though Foley had spent two-thirds of his life in Peru and expected to spend the remainder there, though he loved the people and the work he was doing, he said he would be willing to return. It was what a good Jesuit should do.

✻

As soon as the Chicago Jesuits' attention shifted toward making the new school affordable, Munz asked Fr. John Costello, the province's chief fund-raiser, to join the discussion. Costello, a smooth, silver-haired Jesuit, raised money for the province and its many ministries from the financial and social elite of Chicago and Cincinnati and was a fixture at black-tie galas in Chicago. Just a few years earlier, Costello, working in partnership with the Detroit province, had successfully completed a twenty-five-million-dollar capital campaign for health care for aged Jesuits.

Munz, Costello, and Foley put their heads together to come up with ways to make the school affordable. Most of their early discussions were focused on raising money from private donors and foundations. There was no doubt that the province's donors would play a substantial role in the creation of the school, but could they alone finance the construction or purchase of a new school? More important, could they keep the school open once it was up and running?

The private-donor model had worked for the Nativity middle schools then beginning to spread across the country. Each of the Nativity schools had succeeded in raising enough money to avoid charging tuition—and the cost per student, because of extended school days and extended school years, far exceeded the cost at public or parochial schools. Each year the Nativity schools sought out donors willing to sponsor a student for a year to four years. And each year they found them.

But the Nativity schools are much smaller and have far leaner budgets than those of a high school. Most Nativity schools don't have janitorial staffs but rely instead on students doing "chores" to keep the schools clean. Few Nativity schools educate more than one hundred students. The Jesuits hoped to educate ten or twenty times that number in their new high school. It would be difficult to raise enough money annually—whether through pledges or the creation of an endowment—to cover the tuition for a thousand students.

Not that this hadn't been done before. Regis High School, located on the Upper East Side of Manhattan, has long provided tuition-free college preparatory education of the highest quality to its students. In 1912, a parishioner at St. Ignatius Loyola Parish in New York presented the pastor, Fr. David W. Hearn, SJ, with a generous gift for the construction of a new school. She also promised that she and her family would support the school through the future to ensure tuition-free education. From 1914—the year the school was founded—to the late 1960s, it was the private charity of the foundress and her family. Late in the 1960s, the family somewhat reluctantly agreed to let Regis alumni contribute financially to the school. By that time, it had educated generations of young men—most from modest backgrounds. Many of them went on to great success in the world and desired to share that success with their alma mater. Today Regis—thanks to a remarkable endowment and substantial annual giving from its alumni—continues to offer tuition-free education.

Couldn't the Jesuits do the same thing in Chicago?

For a number of reasons, Costello, Munz, and Foley knew the answer was a resounding no. Opening a school was a dramatically different undertaking in the 1990s than it was in 1914. First of all, the cost of real estate had increased exponentially. And while there were certainly plenty of people with considerable wealth in Chicago, and maybe even some capable of making a gift large enough to build or buy a school, building the school was only half the job. They also had to keep the school open.

> It would take ten to fifteen Jesuits to start a tuition-free school and even more to sustain it once it reached full enrollment. This new school would be lucky to get three Jesuits.

The new school would have to rely on paid labor, the cost of which had skyrocketed. When Regis was founded, it cost very little to run because it was staffed almost entirely by Jesuit priests, brothers, and scholastics (Jesuits preparing to become priests or brothers) who did not take salaries in exchange for their labor. In the 1970s, though, after the Second Vatican Council and in the midst of the sexual revolution, many Jesuits left the order. Jesuit high schools and universities were expanding, but the number of Jesuits available to staff them was shrinking. The pattern continued through the 1970s and '80s and into the early '90s, when there was widespread concern in Jesuit communities, in the Chicago Province and around the country, that soon there wouldn't be enough Jesuits left to staff *existing* schools.

It would take ten to fifteen Jesuits to start a tuition-free school and even more to sustain it once it reached full enrollment. This new school would be lucky to get three Jesuits. That meant it would have to rely on lay teachers, and employing lay teachers—even those who were content to work for less than their peers in suburban public schools—was an expensive proposition. In 1995, the average cost per student at Loyola Academy and St. Ignatius College Prep, the two Jesuit high schools in greater Chicago, was well over six thousand dollars per year. Raising that kind of money for the new school would be difficult, maybe even impossible.

Munz, Foley, Costello, and Schaeffer all knew that families in the neighborhood couldn't begin to pay for a new school. Jim Gartland's study showed that the average family size in Pilsen/Little Village was five and that the average family income hovered around twenty-thousand dollars. Even if the Jesuits could cut the cost per student at their new school to four thousand dollars, there was simply no way they could ask families with three or four children to part with 20 percent of their annual income to educate just one of their kids.

Brad Schaeffer suggested inviting different religious orders around the country to assign one or two people to the school. These priests, brothers, and sisters would basically work for free, just as the Jesuits had at Regis early in the twentieth century. Funding the school through private donations would then become more feasible. But there were loads of logistical issues. There was the question of cooperation. Who would want to participate? There was some concern that religious superiors would send those members of their order who hadn't worked out in their own schools. But the real issue was diminishment of numbers of religious. It wasn't just the Jesuits who saw their numbers falling; this was happening in every religious order. What would happen when there weren't enough religious left to staff the school? The school would be back at square one. The idea was tabled for fear that it wouldn't work over the long haul.

What, though, would work? The Jesuits knew there was an answer out there, but by mid-February they were stumped.

Backyard Brainstorm   7

IN EARLY FEBRUARY 1995, Rick Murray's phone rang. It was John Foley, a Jesuit priest he'd met a couple of years earlier. "Rick, your name has come up as someone who might be able to help us with a new project," Foley said. "Is there any way you could meet me and a couple of other Jesuits late this week or early next week for a meeting and lunch?" They agreed to meet at St. Procopius.

It was only when he hung up the phone that Murray, a real estate attorney and developer, started to wonder what they wanted to talk to him about. Murray had an undergraduate degree from the University of Michigan in environmental design and a law degree from Loyola University Chicago, and had once worked on a debt-conversion strategy that Jesuits in third-world countries might use to benefit their ministries.

A few years earlier, Murray, who volunteers with a variety of civic and charitable organizations, was working with the Nature Conservancy on a bioreserve plan for the Great Lakes Basin and learned about a debt-conversion strategy the conservancy had used to acquire sizable pieces of land in Africa, South America, and certain third-world countries. The process fascinated Murray, and he started thinking about other groups who might be able to use variations of it for applications other than conservation.

As a student at Loyola Law, Murray had met a Jesuit, Fr. Keith Esenther, SJ, who'd spent time in Africa. Murray tracked him down and told him about the idea. Esenther didn't know quite what to make of Murray's scheme and referred him to Fr. Daniel L. Flaherty, SJ, the province's treasurer. Flaherty, in his mid-sixties at the time, was a no-nonsense, old-school Jesuit. He had entered the society after graduating from St. Ignatius High School in 1947 and had gone on to serve as director of Loyola Press (the province's publishing house), provincial of the Chicago Province, and executive editor of *America*, the prominent weekly Jesuit magazine published in New York. He was tapped eventually to become the province's treasurer because of his managerial and financial experience, his desire to serve, and his pragmatic approach to just about everything. Over the phone, Murray's idea sounded far-fetched to Flaherty, but he agreed to meet with him.

At their lunch meeting, Murray explained to Flaherty how the Nature Conservancy—or the Jesuits—could buy the bad debt of a foreign government from a bank who'd already written the debt off as a loss. Instead of trading the debt for a piece of land, like the Nature Conservancy had done, Murray proposed converting it to local currency at an advantageous rate. Flaherty, the financier of the province's multitude of ministries, understood the consequences. There was an opportunity to multiply the U.S. dollars that were helping fund Jesuit ministries in foreign countries. It didn't take a treasurer to recognize that this was a good idea.

Flaherty suggested that Murray connect with Jesuits on the ground in India, Nepal, and Peru, the province's three mission territories. "Call John Foley," Flaherty told Murray. "He's a Jesuit from Peru, but he's back here raising money." Murray and Foley went to lunch and discussed the idea. Foley didn't completely understand how he could make it work but agreed to investigate it further when he was back in Peru. What Foley did understand, though, was that Rick Murray was uncommonly bright and seemed to want to help the Jesuits. And as far as Foley knew, Murray wasn't asking for anything in return. So when the Jesuit team working on the new school couldn't come up with a way to make it affordable, Foley called Murray. "He's clever with numbers," Foley had said to Ted Munz and John Costello. "Maybe he can come up with something."

※

JOEY AND HIS MOM walked on the cracked sidewalk that ran along Cermak Road on their way to Jewel, the large grocery store where they did most of their shopping. It was the middle of the afternoon late in the winter of 1995. The snow had finally melted away, and there was a hint of spring in the air. Joey pushed a small four-wheel grocery cart past the windows of a dollar store, which displayed rows of tall glass candles decorated with images of the Virgin of Guadalupe.

This was their first trip to Jewel in several weeks. It had been a hard winter, with an ice storm followed by a snowstorm in January. All the schools were closed for a couple of days. The snow didn't melt right away, and the sidewalks were treacherously icy, making the small grocery cart almost impossible to push. So instead of walking to Jewel, eight blocks away, they had walked the three blocks to Walgreens. Their money didn't go as far at Walgreens, but the trip to Jewel was just too much for Joey's mom.

The hard winter was part of it, but Joey's mom was also sick. Exhaustion was a symptom, but she never mentioned it to Joey. Exhaustion, nausea, and weakness had put her in the hospital back in 1992, when Joey was seven. In addition to those symptoms, she'd suffered a searing pain in her stomach. Joey remembered her being gone at the hospital for three weeks or a month. For most of that time, he lived with his grandma.

And then one day his mom came home. As far as Joey could see, she was fine; she hadn't changed. What she knew, though, was that scar tissue was overtaking her fifty-year-old liver. The condition was called cirrhosis. The scar tissue, which the doctors said usually resulted from hepatitis or chronic alcohol abuse, would grow and grow, taking over a little more of her liver each day. It wasn't curable and would eventually take her life.

She wanted to know when. They told her three years.

When she returned from the hospital in 1992, she didn't tell Joey any of this. By the winter of 1995, she figured she was close to the end of her life. A lot of parents pushed their children to get out of the house and make friends, play in the neighborhood, and join team sports. But Dolores Garcia didn't push her son to do any of those things.

She was forty-three when she had Joey. She hadn't planned on having a child and thought of his arrival as a miracle. "God broke the mold when he made you," she often told him. Joey was her angel; he'd changed her life. As soon as she'd become pregnant, she'd stopped the drinking and partying that had been habitual since her teenage years. She realized now that she hadn't stopped soon enough. She knew, too, that she'd eventually have to say good-bye to her son and that every moment spent with him—including a walk to the grocery store—was precious.

At the grocery store, they loaded their cart mostly with bread, rice, cereal, tortillas, and potatoes. They bought very little meat and few fruits and vegetables. Their grocery money came out of the welfare check. Joey says his mom "could stretch a dollar with the best of them." The welfare checks were not calculated to include her nephew Nick, who didn't get along with his mother and had been living with Joey and his mom for months. Joey's mom would figure out a way to feed Nick as long he needed to stay there. "She didn't want to see him fail," Joey explains.

By the time they got home with the groceries, it was dark. As soon as they stepped into the apartment, Joey's mom told him to get started on his homework, and he did.

✺

As Rick Murray climbed the concrete steps to the old brick rectory just north of St. Procopius, he was still wondering about the nature of the meeting he was about to attend. Whatever it was, the Jesuits had offered to buy him lunch, and the aroma of tortillas and grilling steak drifting up Allport Street past the small houses and beat-up cars already had him looking forward to the meal. Murray rang the bell and was ushered through the windowless door and up three long creaky staircases to a dusty fourth-floor office. Munz, Foley, and Costello were waiting for him there. Murray, who wore a suit for the meeting, was taken aback by Munz's casual attire—blue jeans and an untucked shirt. *What exactly are they working on?* he wondered.

The three Jesuits began a long-winded explanation of the work they were doing in the grade school and after-school program at St. Procopius. They introduced Munz's Pilsen Project to Murray, who was trying to connect it in his mind to the debt-conversion plan. Then they told him there was a piece missing in the work they were doing—and that piece was a high school. The school would be in the neighborhood and would be created explicitly for students from the neighborhood, offering them a high-quality college-preparatory education. Munz, Foley, and Costello became more animated as they talked about the plan to open a high school. They described to Murray the enormous need in the neighborhood and the extensive research they'd done. They talked about the many difficulties facing young men and women in the neighborhood: overcrowded schools, high dropout rates, teen pregnancy, gangs, drugs, and crime.

Looking back on the meeting, Murray says, "It was clear to me that this was a group of people who got it. They understood the needs of the population they were trying to serve, and they had great intentions. It was clear, too, that they didn't have a very good sense of how they were going to do any of it."

The three Jesuits explained that the new school would educate two thousand students when it reached full enrollment—roughly the same number as Loyola Academy, the largest Jesuit high school in the United States, would have after opening its doors to women in the fall of 1995. The new school would make an effort to connect with the community and would respect the culture of the students and the parents in a way that most private schools—and almost every public school—seemed unable to do. It would offer classes in English and Spanish. And it would be tuition free.

"That's wonderful," Murray said. "Sounds like it would clearly benefit the people in the neighborhood. But I'm not sure why you're telling me all this. I mean, I'm not very well connected. I'm not very wealthy and couldn't even come close to paying for this kind of thing. I'm in the real estate business. I can probably help you find a site. I'm just not real sure what you want me to do, or what you're asking me to do."

"No, no," said Foley. "We're not asking you to do any of that. It's just that, well, it seems like you're clever with numbers. We're hoping you can help us figure out how we might be able to do this." It suddenly became clear to Murray. They were looking for an idea. His debt-conversion scheme must have impressed Foley. They wanted him to help them figure out how to finance this new school. Maybe he could help after all.

"Okay," he said. "That helps me understand."

Thanks to his work on a piece of legislation designed to restructure the tax system and education funding in Illinois, Murray had a rough sense of the cost per student in Illinois high schools. He ran the numbers quickly in his head. "Well, in very general terms, to run a school like this and keep it tuition free, you're probably talking about having an endowment of thirty million dollars. But that assumes you already have a building. If you don't have a building, the money you will need to get started is obviously going to be considerably higher. Do you have funds for an endowment that size?"

They shook their heads.

"Have you begun to identify donors who could make lead gifts toward an endowment?"

They shook their heads.

"Do you have a building?"

They shook their heads.

"Do you have the land that you'll put the building on?"

They shook their heads.

"Okay," Murray said, "let's try to get at this a different way. What do you have right now?"

Ted Munz reached for his briefcase. "Well, we've got a draft of a mission statement," he said. He handed Murray a copy of the document, much of which was taken from the feasibility analysis that he and Gartland had completed. Murray fought back a smile. "I can remember thinking, *These guys have been here for two years, and all they have is a mission statement.*" He took the document and flipped through it. It was "impressive," he admits, and much more than a three-line mission statement. "Well," Murray said to the three, "this is a great document, but you're going to need a lot more than this to get a school going. If you'd like me to think about this, just to see what I come up with—"

"Yes," Foley said, "that's what we want. Just think about it. See what you come up with."

"Okay," Murray said, "that's something I can do. But I'd like to ask you some questions about these students, about who they are, what they want, what they need." Munz suggested they discuss it over lunch.

Murray picked their brains over lunch at a small Mexican restaurant that had already become a favorite of the Jesuits. "What are these kids like?" he asked. "What are their hopes? What are their fears? What are their lives like? What do they do for fun? What are their homes like? What about their families?" Munz, who had done a great deal of research on the population and had reviewed all of Gartland's, fielded most of the questions.

A picture of the school's potential students began to emerge. They were the children of Mexican immigrants. They themselves, however, had very little memory of their homes or their parents' homes in Mexico. They didn't feel Mexican. But because of the color of their skin, they were not allowed to be totally American. They were raised in religious families but attended public schools. They spoke Spanish at home but were usually called on to speak English at school. Being bilingual was a hindrance to their education—although someday it might become an asset—because typically they hadn't mastered either language. Few of the students excelled in school. Those who didn't excel tended to drop out—often to take care of younger siblings or work to help their parents pay the bills. Sometimes they dropped out because they'd entered a gang and found they could make a lot more money selling drugs in an alley for a few hours than their parents made in a week of work.

These kids were generally poor. In some cases, their families relied on monthly welfare checks and food stamps. Others turned to the local church's food bank. These students, for the most part, didn't travel. In fact, some of them had never even left the neighborhood. The limits they experienced every day—educationally and economically—also extended into their futures. The high school–aged students in the neighborhood didn't speak of their futures in the way their peers in suburban schools did. The students in the neighborhood simply didn't know what else was out there. They didn't know there were opportunities beyond their neighborhood.

At the end of lunch, Murray said that he would set aside some time to think about options for the new school and would then report his ideas back to them. They walked back to Allport Street, where Murray had parked, and the Jesuits thanked him for coming. Just before Murray pulled away, he rolled down the window and said, "One last question. When are you guys planning on opening this place?"

Murray recalls now, "I was thinking ten years, five at the earliest."

"Next fall," Munz said, smiling.

"Okay," Murray said, nodding to them. He drove off, thinking, *They don't have anything ready—there's no way they can open a school like this in eighteen months.*

✺

They didn't want to open a school that would rely solely on charitable contributions [and] would not be sustainable for the long-term—one had only to look at the handful of Catholic schools closing their doors that very year.

Rick Murray had scheduled a block of five hours in his calendar to sit and think about how to pay for the new Jesuit school in Pilsen. It was an unseasonably warm day for early March in Chicago, so Murray donned a light jacket and took a calculator out to the deck behind his house in suburban Wilmette, where he would do his thinking.

To Murray, it seemed a shame that the Jesuits needed to open this school. It was indicative, he knew, of the struggles of the education system in America. The Jesuits were right; there was a very real need. But how could they meet it?

Munz, Costello, and Foley had made it clear they didn't want to open a school that would rely solely on charitable contributions. That type of school, they feared, would not be sustainable for the long-term. For proof, one had only to look at the handful of small Catholic schools set to close their doors that very year. Those schools had relied on charity, but they had gotten to the point where the charity of their parishioners and the small amounts of tuition they collected simply couldn't pay the bills.

One way around relying on charity was to create an endowment. The school would rely on charitable contributions only for as long as it took to raise thirty or forty million dollars. Once the school had that money, it would be able to offset the annual budget with interest income generated from the endowment. But the Jesuits didn't think they could raise that kind of money in the time they had. Murray wondered why they were in such a rush. Why did the school have to open in 1996? Why not 1998? All of this would be easier with more time. He didn't think they'd be able to pull it off, but he had to assume they would. Building a forty-million-dollar endowment in less than two years was out of the question.

An idea came to him. The school could have endowed faculty chairs, much like those at colleges and universities. He calculated what he thought it would take to fund a faculty position annually. Then he figured the endowment that would be needed to spit out that much interest income. The gift totals were under a million dollars, but not by much. And it was still an endowment. Then Murray thought about endowing student chairs instead of faculty chairs. Not a bad idea. And it would get the size of a gift down even further. But it was still an endowment. The Jesuits would still have to raise roughly thirty million dollars to make it work. And they didn't intend to do it that way.

Murray sat back in his chair and took in the backyard. Spring was just around the corner. The grass would soon turn from brown to green. Then, inexplicably, Robert Moses popped into Murray's mind.

Moses, who lived from 1888 to 1981, was largely responsible for building the infrastructure of modern-day New York City. Though Moses never held elected office, he was widely considered to be the most powerful man in New York City from the 1930s to the 1950s. His vision led to the creation of most of the highways—and bridges and tunnels—running into and out of the city. He's a controversial historical figure because he favored highways over public transportation and is sometimes blamed for the demise of the South Bronx and Coney Island's amusement parks and for the Brooklyn Dodgers leaving New York. But Murray wasn't thinking about all that. He knew a bit of Moses's story, and he knew that Moses funded many of his projects with revenue generated from tolls collected on the bridges and tunnels he'd built. Travelers were only paying nickels and dimes at the tolls, but there were millions and millions of travelers. Eventually, that meant millions of dollars.

Basically, Moses had developed a system that channeled countless small revenue streams into the same pot. Murray knew that to avoid having an endowment, the school needed some of Robert Moses's nickels and dimes. It needed revenue.

But revenue from what? Murray was in real estate. He had worked on scores of real estate deals and had seen all sorts of creative projects designed to generate revenue. Maybe the Jesuits could invest heavily in a building for the school that would have other uses, and the revenue generated from those uses could cover the annual cost of operating the school. He punched numbers into the calculator. Then he punched in more numbers. He concluded that, given the cost associated with developing a suitable piece of property in Chicago and the amount of capital that would be required to operate a school for two thousand students, there was no way they could finance it just with proceeds from a building.

Murray racked his brains. Nickels and dimes. Streams of revenue.

Where were the streams of revenue in a high school? Murray thought back to his years at the Roeper School in Detroit. That high school had been very different from what this one would be. It was small, and it catered to gifted children. Because of its economic and social diversity, it had been remarkably progressive for its time. The founders, George and Annemarie Roeper, were refugees from Germany. They had fled from the terror of Adolf Hitler's Third Reich and had opened a school in response to it. They wanted to do their part to ensure that a powerful minority with evil intentions would never again be able to so easily dominate an unchallenging majority. So they opened a school that would address the complex emotional and academic needs of gifted children. The school was located just outside of Detroit, where the Roepers lived.

Rick Murray had spent his sophomore, junior, and senior years at the school and says that it was "an absolutely extraordinary learning community." The school used block scheduling—in which students take longer classes but fewer each day—before anybody called it that and required every student to participate in service internships, known as "community duties." Murray worked as a teacher's aide, a carpenter, and a bus supervisor. He also held a for-credit internship in a stockbroker's office. "The internships," he explains, "were about forming a community and strengthening the community by giving the students a sense of ownership."

> Maybe the students at the new Jesuit school could work somewhere to earn their tuition. There were so many variables, but Murray figured that five students could hold down one full-time job.

Murray tried to refocus on the problem before him. He had set aside just a few hours to think about this, not two weeks. And then it hit him: the internships at Roeper. He'd often felt, looking back on his high school years, that some of his most important learning had taken place not when he was in a classroom but when he was working. It was an amazing experience to put what he had learned to use in a real-world setting and not just in another essay or paper. The experience had convinced him that there was great value in developing an understanding of one's talents and self-worth. In fact, that was just what Munz felt the students in Pilsen were lacking.

The internships at Roeper had been unpaid. There wasn't a doubt in Murray's mind, though, that he'd contributed something of value through his work. If students could add value to a business or a not-for-profit organization, they could ask for something in return.

Maybe the students at the new Jesuit school could work somewhere to earn their tuition. There were so many variables, but Murray figured that five students could hold down one full-time job. Each of the five would work one day a week. The five of them could probably earn twenty thousand dollars. If the Jesuits could get the cost per student down to around four thousand dollars, then they could just about offset the entire cost of running the school. Murray knew from his own experience that such a program would also offer enormous educational benefits.

But there was a lot Murray didn't know. First of all, was such an arrangement legal? And would businesses be willing to participate? He suspected they would, but he wasn't sure. He tried not to focus on those questions but instead contemplated the basic idea: exchanging work for tuition. He was still on the deck, thinking. He hadn't written anything down. Every so often he'd hammer a couple of numbers into his calculator to check the work he was doing in his head. By the time he stood up to go back inside, he was convinced he had a workable idea.

He called that night to schedule a meeting with Munz and Costello.

A Brilliant Idea   8

I N MID-MARCH, RICK MURRAY walked into one of the dining rooms at Chicago's swanky Union League Club—where John
Costello had a membership in order to entertain Jesuit benefactors—
to present his idea for the new school to Ted Munz, John Foley, and
Costello over lunch.

To most educators at the time, the idea of sending a fourteen-
year-old freshman with limited English skills—or any high school
student, for that matter—into corporate America would have seemed
completely off the wall. How could students work? They were supposed to be in school learning. Would they work after school? Before
school? They certainly couldn't miss days of school to go to work.
And what did it mean to say they were going to work? What would
they actually do?

Similarly, the idea of bringing a young student, likely one with
little if any previous experience, into the workplace and paying him
or her a hefty amount of money would have seemed outlandish, if not
downright stupid, to many businesspeople. How productive could a
fourteen-year-old really be? Who would pay the student's benefits?
What if the student got hurt—who would be liable? And who would
train the students? There was so much a student would have to learn
to be able to walk into a job—even an entry-level job—in the corporate world. And what if the student couldn't handle it? What if
the work was too hard and intimidating and the student was totally

To most educators at the time, the idea of sending a fourteen-year-old freshman with limited English skills—or any high school student, for that matter—into corporate America would have seemed completely off the wall.

undisciplined? What if he stole money? What if she couldn't speak English? Could the student be fired? These businesses weren't created to nurture wayward youths but to compete in an industry, to serve clients, and to generate positive returns for their stakeholders. There was no guarantee that bringing a student on board would help with any of that.

Murray didn't bring any diagrams or charts to the meeting; he hadn't written out anything. He just explained his idea. A number of issues and questions would need to be addressed, but he didn't focus on those. Instead, he explained exactly how his idea would work and how it would provide the needed finances. He talked a bit about how he'd benefited from his high school internships. By the time he was done with his presentation, Munz, Foley, and Costello were nodding their heads. There were hundreds of reasons to doubt that a program like this could ever work, but they didn't try to poke holes in his idea. He had made them believe it could work.

Munz, Foley, and Costello discussed the idea briefly at the table. Then, to Murray's surprise, Munz said, "We'd like to see where this goes. Can you do the research on this?"

Murray paused. He thought he had done his part. He had come up with an idea that the Jesuits liked. He was happy to be able to help them. But he understood better than anyone at the table what questions would have to be answered. There were a lot of them, and a few were particularly meaty. It would take a lot of work—work he unfortunately wouldn't be able to do, at least not for free. He explained all of this to the Jesuits, but Munz was not dissuaded. He said they'd like to hire Murray as a consultant and asked him if he'd be willing to work up a proposal detailing how much it would cost to research the idea further and determine for certain whether or not it would work. Murray was his own boss; he ran a real estate development firm. He could set aside time to do this work, and the project appealed to him—the school seemed like a great idea.

Less than a week later, Murray submitted a proposal. In it he estimated how much time he would need to complete the project. He named a price and asked for a desk and a phone in the Jesuits' Lincoln Park office. Though the province had already hired a fundraising consultant, they accepted Murray's proposal immediately. They were essentially betting all their chips on his idea. So far, it was the best idea they'd seen—really, it was the only even semiplausible idea they'd seen—and they had less than a year and a half to get the school up and running.

Days later, Murray showed up at the Jesuit Development Office, located at the corner of Sedgwick Street and Dickens Avenue in Lincoln Park, and was shown to a small square office with east-facing windows overlooking a row of Dumpsters. By the end of March, Murray had converted the space into a war room for the new school initiative and had determined—thanks to many hours in law libraries—that the idea was in fact legal. He had answered the first question.

Now he just had to tackle a couple hundred more.

※

APRIL WAS THE TIME for spring-cleaning.

Maritza was finally getting used to cleaning the basement apartment at the intersection of Twenty-first and Leavitt in Pilsen, where she lived with her mom, her mom's boyfriend, who Maritza had begun to call dad, and their two children, who Maritza considered her brother

Back in their homeland, her mom owned the house that Maritza had lived in. In the States, Maritza's family lived in a small dingy apartment in a neighborhood full of ramshackle houses. Sometimes gang shootings took place on the street outside.

and sister. The mop no longer intimidated her. She had figured out how to clean the floor, dust, and quickly do the dishes. But that didn't mean she liked it. In fact, she detested the work.

For six years, Maritza had wondered daily why her mom had left her behind in Mexico. Now that Maritza was finally with her mom in the United States, she had begun to wonder why her mom had stayed. Life in the United States was totally different from life in Mexico. Back in their homeland, her mom owned the house that Maritza had lived in with her grandparents. In the States, Maritza's family lived in a small dingy apartment in a neighborhood full of ramshackle houses. Sometimes at night, gang shootings took place on the street outside.

As Maritza silently swept beneath the kitchen cupboards, she wondered if she would ever go back to Mexico. Not that many months before, at the end of one of her mom's visits in Mexico, she had decided to take Maritza back to the States with her. It was what Maritza had always wanted, but there was no celebration. Her aunts, uncles, and cousins tried to convince her to stay. "Your mom is taking you up there so she can have a babysitter for her new kids," they told her. At that time, Maritza's mom and her boyfriend had two children. Maritza's aunts and uncles insisted that life was better in Mexico and she would be making a mistake if she left.

But Maritza wanted more than anything in the world to live with her mother. She was an extremely bright child who excelled in school. She was able to read and write with ease, and she could solve equations. But she had never figured out why her mom had left her. The reasons her mom gave didn't make sense. Moving to the States with her would give Maritza some answers. If not, it would at least allow her to be with her mom.

Maritza can still remember the anticipation and excitement she felt as the airplane to Chicago charged down the runway and lifted into the air. It took awhile for her to realize how life was going to change in her new home. Each realization was unpleasant. "Back in Mexico," Maritza says, "they had people—I don't like to call them maids, because we never got used to calling them maids. But these people helped take care of the house. I pretty much never lifted a finger; everything was done for me. And when I came to live with my mom, it was like, 'All right, if you want something, you have to do it yourself. And we're just gonna split everything and everybody's gonna help clean the house.' And it was just very frustrating, because first, I wasn't used to it. Second, I didn't know how. And third, I didn't want to."

Maritza had long been bothered by the way some members of her family in Mexico looked down on other people. She knew that the people who came every day to clean the house were poor and, in that sense, not their equals, but that was no reason for her uncle to treat them as he did. She loved the fact that when he wasn't home, her aunt would sometimes invite the help to eat with them in the dining room.

But when Maritza's mom put a mop into her hand, Maritza couldn't believe it. She had never cleaned a house. It wasn't her job, and she didn't want it to be her job. She pushed the mop back at her mom and shook her head. Her mom responded, "You're not living with your aunt, and you're not living with your grandmother anymore. The life you have here is different, and you've got to get used to it."

Maritza also learned that a check arrived every month from a place called "Welfare." Welfare sent money to people who were poor

> Whenever she encountered something difficult, she'd think of her grandma back in Mexico, who said, "You need a good education so you'll never have to depend on anyone else."

to help them get food and clothes and other basic necessities. The implication was that people on welfare couldn't get those things on their own. Maritza soon realized that she was now like the maids who used to clean her house. She had become one of the poor people.

The only upside to all of this was that things were going well at school. Maritza's mom had enrolled her second daughter at Ruben Salazar Bilingual Education Center. When Maritza arrived in January of 1995, in the middle of her fifth-grade year, she, too, enrolled at Salazar. All of her classes there were taught in Spanish. Though she had taken basic English classes and had access to private English tutors in Mexico, Maritza's English was limited to just a few sentences.

School became a refuge for her. She was comfortable there and continued to excel. Whenever she encountered something difficult or came up against a problem she didn't understand, she'd think of her grandma back in Mexico. Her grandma's schooling had ended after sixth grade, and her grandpa had received no schooling at all. When Maritza lived with them, they had stressed repeatedly how important it was to get an education. "You need a good education," Maritza's grandma had told her, "so that you'll never have to depend on anyone else."

While Maritza was getting a good education, she was learning very little English. At home, her family spoke mostly Spanish. At school, she spoke Spanish. In the neighborhood, she spoke Spanish. Unfortunately, she couldn't stay at Salazar forever. At some point she'd have to learn English.

❊

"Just a minute, Fr. Costello. I'll put you through."

Fr. John Costello was waiting to speak to Richard Notebaert, CEO of Ameritech, the company that was then providing phone service to millions of customers in the Midwest (Ameritech was later purchased by SBC, and SBC has since purchased AT&T and taken that name). It was one of Costello's first calls to a business leader about the new school's proposed work program. Notebaert had been named CEO of Ameritech a year earlier. At one point in his career, he'd been based in Indianapolis, where his children attended Brebeuf Jesuit Preparatory School, a high school opened by the Chicago Jesuits in the 1960s. Notebaert held the Jesuits in high regard and had supported the "Promises Kept" capital campaign for elderly Jesuit health care.

Costello's call, placed in June 1995, was the result of a recent meeting of the feasibility study team, which also included Rick Murray, Ted Munz, John Foley, and Sumner Rahr, a fund-raising consultant who had worked with the Jesuits on their health-care campaign and had been hired to advise on the new school project. The four of them had been meeting since April. The meetings were fast-paced brainstorming sessions. Murray would present his progress on the proposed work program and the business plan he was developing for the school. Munz, who was working with Elaine Schuster at the archdiocesan Office of Catholic Schools, offered updates about his progress. Most of the schools in the archdiocese were still adamantly opposed to the idea of a new Jesuit high school.

The group of educators and religious leaders Munz had assembled to explore curricular possibilities for the new school also continued their work. This academic committee was led by Sr. Judy Murphy, OSB, who had been hired as director of the after-school program at

St. Procopius. Brad Schaeffer hoped to eventually hire her as principal for the high school and wanted to keep her in the fold so she wouldn't take another job. There was little overlap between those on the academic committee and those continuing to work on the feasibility study team. It made sense that Murphy and her team of educators and community leaders would focus on the school's academics while the feasibility study team, made up mostly of businesspeople, would focus on the finances. But the complete separation between the two groups, however sensible, was a visible crack in the proposed school's foundation. And a crack in the foundation, no matter how small, can eventually bring down the house.

In May, Munz, Murray, Rahr, and Costello had decided they needed to determine if businesses would be interested in the idea of a work program. All along, they had assumed that Chicago businesspeople would want to get involved. But would they? Murray was excited to get moving on this question. He was becoming more and more confident that the model would work. But a couple of things worried him, and acceptance by businesses was one of them. The model would fall on its face if businesses didn't buy into it and wouldn't hire the school's students.

Murray, by that time, had refined the concept for the program enough that the feasibility study team could offer businesspeople a succinct explanation of it. Five students would job-share an entry-level clerical position in a Chicago business. They hadn't yet decided if the students would work ten, eleven, or twelve months of the year, but the business would pay a sum to the school—it would likely be around twenty thousand dollars—which would be used to cover tuition costs for the students. The business would not have to add the students to the payroll or provide benefits for them. It would simply pay the school, which would deal with benefits and tax issues. In return, the business would receive five energetic workers and the satisfaction of knowing it was helping these kids earn a solid education and a shot at a better future.

The team agreed to contact as many local businesspeople as possible—over the phone, at their offices, or even at cocktail parties—to ask what they thought of the idea. The response from Costello's first call—to Notebaert—was overwhelmingly positive. Costello remembers Notebaert saying, "It's brilliant. Anytime you put business and education together like that, you're doing a great service. That can benefit students and their communities, and the businesses where they work. We will help you with this. In fact, I know somebody else you should call right now: Art Martinez over at Sears." Notebaert gave Costello Martinez's number.

Martinez was Sears' CEO. Costello called him. He also called Bill Smithburg, the chairman and CEO of Quaker Oats. He talked to managing partners at law firms. He talked to bankers, traders, investors, and even an auctioneer, Leslie Hindman. He talked to John Buck, one of the most successful real estate developers in the country. Sumner Rahr, who, like Murray, lived in Wilmette, an affluent North Shore suburb, talked to his friends in the business world. Ironically, it was Murray and not a Jesuit who approached Loyola University about hiring students. The vast majority of businesses responded just the way Notebaert had. It was, at least in theory, a great idea.

An Uncertain Certainty   9

ARLY IN THE SUMMER of 1995, news reached the feasibility
study team that the provincial's consultors would consider the
project in the fall, likely in November. In the Jesuit governance structure, the consultors function both as advisers to the provincial and as
an informal check against provincial abuse of power. Brad Schaeffer
didn't technically need the approval of the consultors to open the
school. He did, however, need the approval of the superior general of
the Jesuits, Fr. Peter-Hans Kolvenbach, SJ, who directed the worldwide society from its headquarters in Rome. And Kolvenbach would
be hesitant to grant permission for the school if the consultors did
not sign off on it.

The team would have only until November to make a compelling
case for the school. The deadline didn't bother Murray. He was 95
percent certain the model would work. He, Munz, Foley, Costello,
and Rahr had already determined that businesspeople were interested
in the work program. That was one of the two problems Murray felt
had to be resolved. The second problem, though, continued to per-
plex him: taxes.

By that time, Murray had concluded that the new school and the
work program should be set up as two separate not-for-profit entities.
This separation was important, because it created a liability shield.
If something happened to a student at work that led to legal action
against the work program, it wouldn't put all the school's assets at

Executives in large corporations often don't have discretion over their company's charitable contributions. Those decisions are usually made by the company's foundation, and most foundations tend not to support faith-based organizations.

risk. Murray also felt it would be unwise for the principal to report to the director of the work program, or vice versa. Organizing two separate entities put the director of the work program and the principal on equal footing; both would report to the president.

Murray worried, though, that the Internal Revenue Service might not view the work program as a tax-exempt organization. The hang-up was the fact that the proposed work program would, in many ways, operate like a for-profit business.

Murray, Munz, Costello, and Rahr had learned that executives in large corporations often don't have discretion over their company's charitable contributions. Those decisions are usually made by the company's foundation, and most foundations tend not to support faith-based organizations. Numerous business leaders had voiced their support for the project, but they could help only if the school created an opportunity for a business transaction. The work program would do exactly that. By creating an opportunity for a transaction—services would be provided and payments made—the work program would move onto the operating budgets of its business sponsors and out of their foundations, where competition for charitable dollars was fierce. Essentially, the work program would function like a business.

When the work program collected its fees from the businesses, it would pay its employees (the students). The students would sign a contract agreeing to assign their earnings to the school, so the payments would be transferred immediately to the school's account. The application of any taxes to those payments, though, would significantly reduce the amount of money flowing into the school.

The Federal Insurance Contributions Act (FICA) requires that employers and employees pay 15.3 percent of earned income to Social Security and Medicare. That tax burden is split between employers and employees. The proposed work program would have to pay 7.65 percent of its payroll to the government. And each student would have to pay 7.65 percent of his or her income. The work program could minimize these payroll taxes by paying students minimum wage. Doing so, though, would generate earnings. If the IRS didn't recognize the work program as a tax-exempt organization—a substantial risk—those earnings would be subject to corporate tax rates, which would result in an even larger tax burden. In the best-case scenario, only 84.7 percent of the revenues collected by the work program would be available to offset its own expenses and the expenses of running the school.

Murray worried that the after-tax revenue might not be enough to sustain the school. The executives he and the feasibility study team had approached had expressed concern about paying high school students more than nine or ten dollars per hour—the equivalent of what they paid many of their rank-and-file clerical employees. They worried that regular employees would react negatively if student interns were being paid more. Murray's projections suggested the model could work at that rate—an annual fee of approximately eighteen thousand dollars—but it wasn't ideal. The margin for error would be tight.

Obviously, the proposed school couldn't break the law, but making it work would depend on finding a way to minimize the tax burden.

❋

THROUGHOUT THE SUMMER OF 1995, the feasibility study team began to grow. The first new member was Dave McNulty. After graduating from Loyola Academy in 1967, McNulty had entered the

Jesuit novitiate at Milford, Ohio, where he was a classmate of Brad
Schaeffer. McNulty left the Jesuits after four years and began what
would become a very successful career in banking. When he saw
that Brad Schaeffer had been named provincial in 1991, he called to
offer his congratulations. They started getting together for lunch and
talked often of the new school. In June of 1995, Schaeffer invited
McNulty to join the feasibility study team to help recruit additional
corporate sponsors.

In July, Tadas "Tad" Kulbis was hired by the province's development office to assist with the new school in Pilsen and the start-up of
a fund-raising initiative for Jesuit schools in post-Communist Latvia
and Lithuania.

In August, Tim Freeman was hired as the Chicago Province's
development director. John Costello, who had served previously in
that role, had recently been named provincial assistant for development and public information, a position akin to executive vice president for fund-raising, and had hired Freeman, a graduate of John
Carroll University, a Jesuit school in Cleveland, Ohio, to serve as his
development director.

Soon after McNulty, Kulbis, and Freeman came on board, the
feasibility study team received a tip that the consultors would likely
approve the plan for the school if the team could show by November
that it had commitments for all the jobs it needed to open the school.
If the school opened with 150 students, it would need thirty jobs.
Costello already had verbal commitments from a handful of businesses. The expanded team focused its attention on closing those
deals and securing the remaining jobs the school would need in order
to open. Costello and Rahr had kept a list of those businesses they'd
contacted and had notes about how different companies and executives had reacted. The new team members, especially McNulty, had

many additional contacts, and these were added to the list. For each company, the team members recorded their contact or contacts, the industry, the possible number of jobs, and the degree of commitment—soft, verbal, or written.

At the beginning of July, the feasibility study team had no written commitments. But the list was full of outstanding companies, such as Ameritech, Aon Corporation, Arthur Andersen, Bozell Worldwide, Chubb Insurance, First National Bank of Chicago, Heller Seasonings & Ingredients, Kraft USA, LaSalle Bank, Loyola University Chicago, Merrill Lynch, Paine Webber, Pan American Bank, Quaker Oats, Refco, Sears, Swissotel, Tellabs, Tribune Company, and True Value Hardware.

The team worked up a letter of intent and a folder explaining the nuts and bolts of the proposed work program and began calling on businesses. The majority of businesspeople they visited were excited about the school. Many said they loved the idea. Every meeting yielded more contacts, and the list grew. By the beginning of September, Costello and the other team members had secured numerous verbal commitments, many of them for multiple jobs. Richard Notebaert had said that Ameritech might be able to provide ten jobs—one-third of the entire need. A vice president at Loyola University had suggested that the school might be able to provide another ten. Many other businesses had said yes to one or two jobs.

Written commitments, however, proved elusive. Only one organization, the not-for-profit SOS Children's Village–Illinois, had signed the letter of intent. The team found that CEOs who promised jobs were reluctant to sign the letters. When it came time to put things on paper, they passed it down the food chain to their HR teams. The HR managers weren't always as enthusiastic about the program as their bosses.

Everyone was grateful for the first signee, but the team was pushing to get a marquee business on board. The written commitment of a company like Ameritech or Arthur Andersen or Aon or Quaker Oats would lend instant credibility to the program. "Big news," they wanted to tell their business contacts. "Such-and-such Fortune 500 company signed. And you should, too!" People in business tended to follow the leader. The school needed a leader.

✸

"I THINK I'VE GOT it," Rick Murray whispered to himself.

He was poring over the IRS tax code. For weeks, the tax problem had vexed him. Murray's initial projections were for a cost per student of $5,425. Roughly 10 percent of that cost would be financed by donations. The remainder would be financed by the work program and modest tuition payments from each family. If Murray couldn't figure out a way for the new school to minimize its tax burden, then the work program probably wouldn't be able to cover its portion of the cost. More of the financing would have to come from donors, and the Jesuits had said from the outset that they did not want to rely on charitable contributions.

Murray was reading through the section of the tax code dealing with unrelated income for a 501(c)(3), a tax-exempt organization. Murray worried that the profit generated by the proposed work program—if it paid its students minimum wage in an effort to minimize payroll taxes—would be considered unrelated business income. The IRS doesn't require not-for-profit institutions to pay taxes on their income, which is usually made up of charitable contributions. One exception, though, comes when the not-for-profit organization engages in business activities. This income is usually considered unrelated to the not-for-profit and is taxed at the regular rate. These taxes, Murray worried, could doom the school. To avoid rulings that could result in the removal of tax-exempt status or taxation on unrelated business income, the IRS Code said, it was necessary for an organization to examine "the relationship between the business activities which generate the particular income in question—the activities, that is, of producing or distributing the goods or performing the services involved—and the accomplishment of the organization's exempt purposes."

Murray stopped reading. He couldn't believe it. The answer was right there in a section of the federal tax code he'd read countless times. The school and the work program, while separate entities, shared the same purpose—educating students in Pilsen/Little Village. The income that would be generated by the work program wasn't unrelated at all. Even though the work program would function like a business, would generate earnings, and would be capable of financing much of the school's operations, it could still be a tax-exempt organization, because it, too, would be responsible for educating the students.

In an instant, everything clicked. If the articles of organization were created carefully and linked the work program directly to the school and its mission, then the work program would be able to get tax-exempt status and the school would be able to dramatically reduce its tax burden. Students would be paid minimum wage, which would minimize the payroll tax. At the end of the year, the fees collected from the employers, less expenses associated with running the work program, would be transferred to the school. These "earnings," though generated from business activities, would not be taxed because of the fact that they were directly related to the purpose of the tax-exempt school—educating the young people of Pilsen/Little Village.

"Hey," Murray called from his back office to Tad Kulbis, who had been working in the adjacent office for the last two weeks. "I think I figured it out. It was right in front of us the whole time."

❋

THE LATE-MODEL CHEVY SUBURBAN squealed around the corner of Forty-sixth Street and South Wolcott Avenue in Chicago's Back of the Yards neighborhood. The driver slammed his foot on the gas. He was chasing a small, beat-up sedan north on Wolcott. The driver of the sedan lived a few blocks north on Ashland. He was not a gang member, and he hadn't done anything wrong. He was just dropping off a toolbox at the home of one of his coworkers. He sped up and looked over his shoulder at the large black Suburban. He could see at least four people in the car, which was just inches from his back bumper. He wanted to get to Forty-third Street, and then to Ashland, where there would be heavy traffic and likely some police presence, which would put an end to this. If he could just get to Ashland, he'd be safe.

Leo sat quietly behind the driver of the Suburban, one of his cousins, who was a member of the Saints gang. This was Leo's first car chase, and while a bit scary, it was certainly exciting.

Since the age of eight, Leo had lived in the Two-Six gang's territory. When his mom, Teresa, enrolled him at St. Joseph High School, he reconnected with his cousin Junior. Most of the people in Teresa's family were Saints, the gang that controlled most of the Back of the Yards, a neighborhood located some fifteen blocks south of Pilsen. Leo's cousins convinced him he'd be safe in their neighborhood, so he had been hanging out there for most of his freshman year.

The driver of the sedan made a quick turn onto Forty-fourth Street, maybe out of fear that he'd be stopped at the light at Forty-third. He didn't know what the guys in the Suburban wanted. Were they going to rob him? Steal his car? Kill him? He accelerated. The old car sputtered as if it was going to stall and then rattled toward Ashland, just six blocks away.

Junior followed him around the corner onto Forty-fourth, whipping Leo's body against the back passenger door. Junior again pulled to within inches of the back of the sedan and flashed his lights. He chased the sedan until it made a hard left turn onto Ashland Avenue, forcing oncoming traffic to a screeching halt. Junior waited for the traffic to pass and then turned right.

They cruised slowly back through the neighborhood looking for someone else to chase out. If outside gang members came in, they'd chase them out, but usually they chased "regular" people. Leo says it was "just for the thrill of it."

By his own admission, Leo was now "all into the streets. Girls, the streets, all that stuff." As an eighth grader at Davis, he moved almost completely into mainstream classrooms. He attended parties regularly, started smoking marijuana, and discovered that "there are a lot of easy girls out there." He insists, though, that he never became a gang member, although he could have. Many of the students from Davis had turned Two-Sixes. The initiation was painful, literally. To enter the gang, a boy from the neighborhood had to subject himself to a two- or three-minute beating by three, four, or five of the gang members. They could only kick and punch—weapons were not allowed, and the head and groin were off-limits. The process was called a "beat in." Initiation for girls was worse, according to Fr. Sean O'Sullivan, SJ, a Jesuit priest and counselor. Young women were often required to have sex with a "train" of gang members. One after another, the boys and men would come into the room for their turn. The train could be made up of as many as ten members. If the girl could endure it, she could join the gang.

> "I was always scared of getting into the gang, 'cause me and my dad had a real good relationship and I was scared of losing that trust, you know?"

Leo was tough, and he knew he could handle the initiation. But he didn't want to join a gang. The reason was his father. "I was always scared of getting into the gang, 'cause me and my dad had a real good relationship and I was scared of losing that trust, you know? I could pretty much come and go when I wanted. He trusted me not to do anything real stupid. And I was always scared of losing that. So I never became a gang member. I would chill with them, but I was never in a gang. I don't know, it might sound like a dumb reason, but that's my reason, and I'm not scared to say it. I told everybody I met that's why I'm nothing, because of my dad."

By not having any sort of gang affiliation, Leo says he could pick his battles. If he was at a party and someone attacked one of his cousins, he'd be the first to jump in. But he didn't have to fight the gang fights. "That's not my problem," he says. "I could fight if I wanted, but I didn't have to. The guys in the gang, they have to fight." Leo's older cousin Junior, who was then a high-ranking Saint, also warned his younger brothers and cousins away from life in the gang. So Leo hung out with gang members, ate with gang members, and partied with gang members but managed somehow never to become one of them.

He was "nothing."

And in school he wasn't much more. Leo's mom, Teresa, had insisted he attend St. Joseph, a Catholic high school located just ten blocks south and twelve blocks east of their house. Teresa had come to the States because she wanted to be with her husband and wanted a better life. Both she and Leo's father worked long, hard days. In that time, Teresa had figured out that the key to a better life in the United States was education. She pushed Leo to St. Joseph because she hoped that a private school would give him the jump he needed. If Leo did well there, he could go to college and achieve things no one else in the family had. Leo was her only child, and she wanted more than anything to see him succeed.

> The feasibility study team decided to call the school Cristo Rey Jesuit High School. Cristo Rey was Spanish for "Christ the King." It was a bilingual name, which the Jesuits had wanted all along.

But school didn't matter to Leo. He knew he had to graduate eventually, or at least get a GED, so he could get a job in a factory or on a construction crew. "I wanted to finish high school, get a job, and have a kid by the time I was eighteen. I mean, it seemed like everybody was having kids, you know?"

Leo's primary aim was to get through school by doing as little work as possible and having as much fun as possible. For him, that was surprisingly easy. From day one, he made an effort to charm his teachers. If they liked him, they'd tell him when he was teetering on the brink of failure. "Then," he says, "I'd buckle up and do what needed to be done."

During his first few months at St. Joseph, that strategy seemed to be working.

EARLY IN THE FALL of 1995, plans for the new school in Pilsen began to accelerate rapidly. Work had continued at a hurried pace through the late summer and early fall, and there wasn't time to assemble a committee or conduct a survey on a name for the school. The feasibility study team simply decided, during one of its many meetings, to call the school Cristo Rey Jesuit High School. Cristo Rey was Spanish for "Christ the King." It was a bilingual name, which the Jesuits had wanted all along.

Team members gave more and more of their time to recruiting potential job sponsors—a remarkable feat, given that all of them, even the Jesuits, had other jobs and responsibilities. But by October 23, 1995, about a week before the plan for the new school in Pilsen was to go to the consultors, SOS Children's Village–Illinois was still the only sponsor who had signed a letter of intent.

A day later, J. Michael Heaton, a partner at the Chicago law firm O'Keefe, Ashenden, Lyons & Ward (today the firm is called O'Keefe, Lyons & Hynes), signed a letter of intent at his office during a visit from John Foley and Ted Munz. Heaton had grown up in central Illinois, lived in Wilmette, and sent his sons to Loyola Academy. Through his relationship with his sons' school, he'd developed great respect for the Jesuits. He says he "trusted" the Jesuits and knew "the school had to be a good thing if they'd put their name on it." He'd first heard about the new school months before from Chris Devron, SJ, a young Jesuit who, like Heaton, had graduated from the University of Notre Dame and was working in Chicago as part of an inner-city teaching program. "As soon as I heard about it," Heaton recalls, "I said, 'We're doing that.' I asked Chris to have the people at the school call me. Our office has always been one with a civic consciousness. The lawyers here try to give back to the city, to the community. All of us believe in education, and we contribute to Catholic education."

A few hours later, and just a few blocks north, Thomas M. Hayden, executive vice president and general manager of the global advertising firm Bozell Worldwide, signed a letter of intent at his office with Rick Murray and Tad Kulbis. The following day, Anthony B. McGuire, president of McGuire Engineers, signed a letter of intent at his office with Tim Freeman and Foley. McGuire, an engineer who has been honored with a place in the Chicago Area Entrepreneurship Hall of

Fame, had attended Regis High School, the tuition-free Jesuit school in New York City. He readily attributes much of his success to the education he received at Regis. He sent his children to St. Ignatius College Prep, the Jesuit high school on the Near West Side of Chicago. When he first heard from Foley about the new school, McGuire said, "I know these kids. I grew up with these kids. I'll do whatever I can to help."

Things were coming together. Everyone on the team knew that the written commitments combined with the more than thirty verbal commitments they had accumulated would look impressive when they were delivered to the consultors along with a copy of Rick Murray's "Cristo Rey Jesuit High School: Project Memorandum." The thirty-page document was, and is, remarkable. In a letter he included with the document, Murray said, "In only six months, a handful of committed and very talented individuals have worked to create a new high school from virtually nothing. Their progress is nothing short of amazing."

He was right. The team had started with nothing and was handing to the consultors a detailed plan for starting and running a school. The project memorandum, which was bound in a hard black leather cover featuring a black-and-white photograph of three Hispanic students sitting on a bench with textbooks spread open across their laps, included guidelines for enrollment, administration, the curriculum, and the work program.

A detailed section of the memo described how the school would be financed. Each student would contribute $3,325 to the cost of his or her education—money earned through participation in the school's work program less taxes. The student's family would contribute an additional $1,500 in tuition. While Murray's initial calculations had been geared toward creating a tuition-free school, the team decided in later conversations that there was value in collecting tuition. It would, they hoped, encourage parents to buy into the program and become involved in their children's education. Cristo Rey would make financial aid available to any student who needed it.

The funds provided by the students and their families would be supplemented by $500 per student of charitable contributions and $100 per student in activities and events revenue, which would be generated through car washes, bake sales and other student-led fundraising activities. It all added up to $5,325 per student. Opposite the revenues, Murray listed $5,325 worth of expenses. From the beginning, he projected a balanced budget. To achieve it, Murray and the founding team knew the school would have to exercise financial discipline. Murray's plan called for a lean college-prep school and curriculum. Cristo Rey Jesuit High School would be a no-frills operation designed to prepare the young women and men of Pilsen/Little Village for college.

In his project memorandum, Murray extended the budget over a twenty-year period. In that time, the school's enrollment would increase to a maximum of 516. To get the school off the ground and to sustain it once it was open, the school would need to raise money. Murray detailed various start-up costs—the interim site, a library, a technology center, and extracurricular programs—that he hoped could be covered by generous benefactors. He also detailed the expected costs of acquiring a permanent site for the school and outlined all the different options open to the Jesuits as they prepared for the purchase of land and, possibly, an existing school building. In addition, Murray presented an ambitious plan for using the work program surpluses he'd projected to fund the growth of the school's physical plant so that private donations would not be needed.

The final component of the memorandum was the College Plan, which Murray conceived as a way to further engage parents in the education of their children. He knew that sometimes parents could become an impediment to their children's education. It was easy for cash-strapped parents to think that everyone in the family would be better off if their children went to work instead of to school. By working, their kids could earn money that could be used to pay bills and buy food. By going to school, they merely generated more bills. And the payoff was so far down the line that parents might feel that education just wasn't worth it.

Murray hoped the College Plan he'd devised would help parents understand that their investment in their child's education would yield tangible returns. Through the plan, a student who completed college would be entitled to ten thousand dollars, nearly half a year's income for the average family in Pilsen. The student could use that money, which would actually exceed the total his or her parents had paid in tuition to Cristo Rey, to repay college loans.

Murray assumed that 70 percent of the school's graduates would go on to successfully complete college—a dramatically higher average than existed in the neighborhood. By deferring the payment until eight years after the student enrolled at Cristo Rey, the College Plan would allow the school to accumulate a small operating surplus. By the time Cristo Rey had to make its first payment, the sum of the payments would represent less than 5 percent of the school's annual operating budget.

"Think about what a program like that would do for alumni giving," Murray says. "Alumni giving is the lifeblood of many private schools. So here are these kids—they've just graduated from college and they're ready to begin their lives as professionals. They're carrying some debt from their studies. And then they get a letter from Cristo Rey that says, 'Congratulations on your graduation. We're proud of you. And we still care about you. In fact, we have ten thousand dollars waiting for you to help you repay your loans.' Talk about a great way to inspire loyalty among alumni." Murray says he expected that many of the school's students, grateful for the education they'd received and already gainfully employed, would refuse the money and allow the school to keep it. "It would be their first gift back to the school."

In the course of a few months, Murray had created a new model of education that would provide high-quality college-preparatory education to the young people of Pilsen/Little Village and would help them pay for their college education. The progress had been amazing. And just about all of it was contained in the tidy project memorandum that the team submitted with great satisfaction to the province's consultors on October 27.

The consultors would review the proposal the following week. But before they did, another review of the school hit the newsstands.

We're Opening This School 10

BRAD SCHAEFFER REGULARLY SAYS he wasn't the one responsible for the eventual success of Cristo Rey Jesuit High School, but rather the "good Lord" was. He means it and believes it. Obviously, it's a difficult claim to substantiate, but Schaeffer and some of the other Jesuits involved in the project's early days maintain that it is true. They point to certain events in Cristo Rey's development as evidence that a greater power was at work. One such event occurred on October 30, 1995, when the *Chicago Sun-Times* published a front-page story about Cristo Rey—which at that time hadn't been approved by the Jesuits or the archdiocese—under the headline "Catholic Students Could Earn While They Learn."

The story surprised everyone working on the project, and at first glance it seemed disastrous. The new school had been kept largely under wraps and the feasibility study team worried that the story might galvanize the opposition from other Catholic schools and maybe even diminish the chances of archdiocesan approval. The story got the attention of a lot of people, one of whom would eventually become one of the school's most valuable human resources.

GINNY KENDALL WAS WAITING for the downtown Metra train at the small station in Glenview, Illinois, when the headline on the *Sun-Times* caught her eye. She bent down in front of the blue newspaper box and read the text at the top of the paper tucked behind the smudged glass.

A unique Catholic high school giving students lower tuition for working outside jobs could open here as soon as next year.

The plan is raising concern among officials at some existing Catholic schools because they fear they would lose students if the school is approved by Joseph Cardinal Bernardin. The Jesuits are considering opening a high school in the Pilsen or Little Village neighborhoods, both of which are largely Mexican American. Students would pay lower tuition but would agree to work at a corporation or business for eight hours a week.

Ginny called her husband, Preston, from a pay phone on the train platform. "Buy a copy of today's *Sun-Times* and check out the story on the front page," she said. "The Jesuits are going to open a new school in Chicago, and it sounds like the kids are going to work in local businesses. I didn't have any change, so I didn't buy a copy. I don't know the rest of the story, but it looks like it could be perfect for you."

Preston Kendall had been thinking about a career change for a couple of years. After studying poetry as an undergrad at Northwestern University, he married Ginny, his high school sweetheart. Assuming it would be tough to make a living as a poet, he went to work for Washington National, the insurance company started decades earlier by his great-grandfather. After a year at the company, which had long since gone public and was no longer family owned, Kendall enrolled at Northwestern's Kellogg School of Management, where he completed an MBA. He spent the next nine years successfully climbing the corporate ladder. Then he hit a wall. The senior folks in his division had been at Washington National for years. They weren't going anywhere, and they told Kendall he wouldn't either while they were still there. He looked for different opportunities but didn't find anything very compelling.

On October 31, 1994, American Airlines flight 4184, an American Eagle flight from Indianapolis to Chicago, crashed in Roselawn, Indiana, killing everyone on board. One of the passengers, Joseph Begny, had worked at Washington National. Kendall had been on that same flight dozens of times, often with Joe. In the days after the crash, Kendall asked his superiors who from the company would be traveling to Ohio for Joe's funeral. "No one," they said. Not much was offered by way of an explanation. Kendall cashed in some vacation days and frequent-flier miles and made the trip himself. "That was kind of the last straw," he recalls. "I just couldn't believe the way Joe's death was handled. At that point, I said, 'I've gotta get out of this.'" The crash got Kendall thinking about his own mortality, about what he'd done with his life, and especially about what more he might do.

During a conversation with Ginny—who'd just completed a law degree at Loyola University Chicago and was going to work for the U.S. attorney for the Northern District of Illinois—about his frustration with work, she reminded him that he'd gone into the insurance business to support their family. Now that she was going to work, she could help shoulder the load. "Maybe it's time for you to look at something you really want to do." Kendall began researching how he could become certified to teach in Illinois. He hadn't yet signed up for courses when the story about the new Jesuit school ran in the Sun-Times. When he read it, he knew it'd be a perfect fit. He just had to figure out how to get in the door.

Leo Maldonado's plan was working perfectly. He knew his teachers at St. Joseph liked him. Just as he expected, they let him know whenever he neared the point of no return in any one of his classes. As the first quarter wound down, he was right where he expected to be—all Cs and Ds and not in great danger of failing any of his classes. Leo could do all the work; most of it was easy. He just didn't want to.

Just as Leo had figured out how to get by at St. Joseph, he started to hear rumors that the school might close at the end of the year. He couldn't believe it and asked his mom if the rumors were true. She told him they probably weren't, but he had a feeling they were.

Preston Kendall couldn't type the letter fast enough.

It was November 2, just three days after the Cristo Rey story appeared in the *Sun-Times*. After a bit of research, he'd learned that Fr. John P. Foley, SJ, was part of the team opening the school. Kendall and Foley had met in the summer of 1978, when Kendall and eleven of his Loyola Academy classmates had traveled to Peru for a six-week community service trip. The group helped build a school that would provide vocational training for young Quechua-speaking Peruvians whose skills were limited to farming potatoes on small plots of dry land that had been passed down from their parents. As the postage-stamp plots were divided generation after generation, it became almost impossible for the families to squeeze a living out of them. Many gave up and headed for the towns in the Peruvian Altiplano. But they had few marketable skills and almost inevitably ended up living in extreme poverty.

Kendall acknowledges that the group of students may have done some good during their brief stay, but he's more inclined to speak about how the experience affected him and his classmates. "It was a life-changing event. The poverty, injustice, and hope I saw there swirled around and percolated in my life for decades."

John Foley spent four weeks with the group from Loyola. Kendall found him captivating. He was a Loyola Academy graduate and was, like Kendall, from Chicago's North Shore. His family owned a car dealership, but he'd chosen to spend his life in Peru, where he had next to nothing and was working on behalf of people who had far less. When Kendall learned that Foley had returned to Chicago to work on the new school, he dashed off a letter to him. In the first paragraph he said, "While I have enjoyed my business experience, especially the more entrepreneurial responsibilities of my current position, I am drawn toward a position which will continue to challenge me while giving the added satisfaction of knowing my efforts will contribute to a cause with more evident meaning than simply increasing the corporate bottom line." He asked Foley to consider him for any teaching or administrative positions at the school. He mentioned that he was familiar with the language of business and with computer technology. As he typed the letter, Kendall was worried that he wasn't qualified to work in the school and wouldn't be taken seriously. So he added a PS about Loyola's '78 Peru trip, hoping that might tip the balance in his favor. He dropped the letter in a mailbox that night.

Two days later, moments after reading the letter, Foley called Preston and asked him to come in for a meeting. The meeting went well, though Foley didn't even mention a job. So Kendall went home and wrote another letter. "John," he began, "after our visit, I could not stop thinking about the program in Pilsen. It is really exciting and worthwhile. I jotted down some initial thoughts on the steps I would take and the questions/concerns that need to be addressed in the next (very few) months. These are just preliminary thoughts, so

> Because the idea was untested, the province reserved the right to pull the plug on the project if . . . the school wouldn't be able to accumulate the funding necessary to open its doors.

please excuse the lack of structure. I would like to be part of making this a reality for the community and the students."

The letter included a detailed "plan of action" and a list of "issues to consider." The carefully crafted four-page document arrived at Foley's office just a few days after their meeting. Foley knew that the feasibility study team currently working on the project wouldn't be the team to open the doors of the school. They'd begun to think about who could pick up where the initial team left off and take the school where it needed to go. It was a critically important role. Rick Murray had developed a brilliant plan, and the school needed a brilliant person to execute the plan. After reading Kendall's second letter, Foley knew Cristo Rey had its man.

❇

Days after Preston Kendall sent his letter to John Foley, Brad Schaeffer and his consultants approved the proposal for the new school. Because the idea was untested, the province reserved the right to pull the plug on the project if by January 1996 it appeared the school wouldn't be able to accumulate the funding necessary to open its doors.

A number of things happened fairly quickly in the wake of the consultors' approval. First, Schaeffer wrote to Fr. Peter-Hans Kolvenbach, the superior general of the Jesuit order, to request permission for the school. He then contacted Ted Munz and asked the feasibility study team to prepare for a transition of the school's leadership to a president, principal, and work director. He also asked the team to prepare some sort of public announcement about the new school.

Word came quickly from Rome: Fr. Kolvenbach had approved the plan for the school. Days later, Schaeffer appointed Ted Munz to serve as president of Loyola Academy and named John Foley the first president of Cristo Rey. Foley then hired Judy Murphy to be principal of the new school, and Murphy in turn hired Rosy Santiago to be the admissions director. In late December, Foley officially extended an offer to Preston Kendall to become the director of Cristo Rey's work program, which was now being called the Corporate Internship Program. The team planned a press conference at St. Procopius on January 18, 1996, while continuing to seek written commitments from Chicago businesses willing to participate in the Corporate Internship Program. The Tribune Company, the media conglomerate that owned the *Chicago Tribune*, WGN-TV, the Chicago Cubs, and numerous other media properties, had become the first marquee name to sign on. The company had signed a letter of intent in late November after John Foley and Dave McNulty met with Luis E. Lewin, director of human resources.

Foley and McNulty hadn't been too hopeful about the meeting with Lewin. Over the past six months, team members had made contact with numerous high-ranking Tribune executives, many of whom had attended Loyola Academy and were already friendly with the Jesuits. In every case, the team members had been referred to Lewin. They hadn't had much success with HR managers, to whom inviting high school students into the workplace seemed like asking for trouble, or at least headaches. Going into the meeting, Foley and McNulty knew that landing Tribune would be huge. "We had no idea what to expect," McNulty recalls. "We sat down across from [Lewin] and started telling him about the school. After a minute or two he put his hands up and waved. 'We'll do it,' he said. 'You don't have to tell me anything else. I went to a Jesuit high school. I know who you guys are. I know what you do. We'll do it.'" The Jesuit name was proving to be very helpful.

With approval from his Jesuit superior in Rome in hand, Schaeffer sought formal approval from the archdiocese. Both Joseph Cardinal Bernardin and Elaine Schuster liked the idea of the school, but other Catholic schools remained opposed to it. In an effort to quell fears that Cristo Rey would steal students from other Catholic schools, the Jesuits made the following commitments: they would not take freshman students in the school's inaugural year; they would never take transfers from other Catholic schools; and they would never offer an entrance exam on the same day the other Catholic schools in the archdiocese gave their tests. They also agreed not to accept any students until acceptance letters had been mailed by all the other Catholic schools in the diocese.

The concessions seemed insignificant to the team, given that there were literally thousands of high school–aged students in Pilsen/Little Village who weren't enrolled in Catholic schools. Cristo Rey's founders, though, had no idea how hard it would be to get those students into the school.

THE ROOM AT ST. Procopius was full of reporters, corporate sponsors, and supporters of Cristo Rey. Brad Schaeffer stood behind the podium excitedly explaining how the new hardworking school for hardworking kids would function. The work program, he explained, would help finance the school's operation and, more important, would help students "gain a sense of responsibility and pride by helping them pay for their own education."

Judy Murphy, John Foley, Preston Kendall, and Rosy Santiago sat behind Schaeffer. Cameramen from both English- and Spanish-language news stations filmed from the back of the room. Photographers snapped pictures in the front row. Reporters took notes behind them. Rick Murray and Ted Munz sat in the back of the room. It was, for the two of them, a jarring and somewhat bittersweet transition. The school was becoming a reality before their eyes. The project had been an intense labor of love for both of them, and as they listened to Schaeffer speak at the front of the room, flanked by Murphy, Foley, Kendall, and Santiago, it became abundantly clear that this was no longer their project.

During the conference, Schaeffer listed the various businesses that had by that time agreed in writing to participate in the first year of the Corporate Internship Program: Arthur Andersen; the Chicago Mercantile Exchange; Bozell Worldwide; McGuire Engineers; O'Keefe, Ashenden, Lyons & Ward; and the Tribune Company.

A few moments stand out as particularly important. The first was a comment made by Brad Schaeffer that appeared in the following day's *Chicago Tribune* as part of the paper's coverage of Cristo Rey's announcement. "We hope and we believe that this will be a national model for urban Jesuit education." Until that point, there had been little discussion of expanding the model on a national scale. The other memorable moment came during a question-and-answer session with reporters. The school's new leaders had made their entire presentation without ever addressing where the school would be located. At the time, they didn't know where it would be. But they tried to avoid talking about it for fear it would discourage potential students.

"When do you plan to open the school?" one of the reporters asked Schaeffer.

"This fall, in September."

"Where will it be located?" another reporter asked.

"We're still trying to find a suitable site," Schaeffer said.

"So you don't have a building?" the reporter asked, clearly surprised.

"No, we don't," Schaeffer said, adding quickly, before anyone in the room could laugh, "but we're opening this school." The message was clear: *Whether or not we're ready, we're opening the first new Catholic high school in Chicago in thirty-three years, and we're going to make it work.* Though Schaeffer never said it, he—and everyone else in the room—knew there was still a great deal of work to be done.

PART 2

Building a School from the Ground Up

———✤———

Early 1996–Summer 2000

What happens is that the viewer starts to lose the painted subject because of eye fatigue, the persistence of vision, and the way colors and contrasts are being used. When this occurs, a perceptual movement begins to take place, so that the surface of the painting appears to vibrate, fluctuate, and change. Then, if viewing time is increased, the subject matter starts to disappear as it seems to dissolve and transform itself beyond recognition into an energy field. In 1993, I coined the term "perceptualism" to describe this process. Much of it is based on the teachings of Don Juan Matus, a Yaqui Indian from Mexico. Don

Juan's teachings are geared towards being able to perceive other realities. It is in this spirit that I paint my current work, so that viewers can let go of the conditioned points of view which create their everyday reality.

Mario Castillo, the artist who launched the
Mexican mural movement in Chicago
with his 1968 work Metaphysics

A New School in Nine Months

11

THE DAY AFTER THE press conference was a busy one in Cristo Rey's temporary offices on the fourth floor of the gray stone rectory at St. Procopius. Throughout the day, the old fax machine cranked out letters of congratulations from people who had seen the news about the new Jesuit school that morning in the *Sun-Times* and the *Tribune* or the night before on one of many local newscasts. One letter came from the United Kingdom and another from Hawaii. Most of the letters, though, were from Chicago, and most of those were from alums of Jesuit schools.

The congratulatory faxes signaled the beginning of a new era. The feasibility studies were over. The school had been approved, and its founders had committed to opening it in just nine months. A tremendous amount of work had to be done in that time. Cristo Rey's founders had few guideposts; it had been thirty-three years since a Catholic high school had opened in the Archdiocese of Chicago and even longer since a school had opened in the center of the city. In addition to the usual business—hiring staff; acquiring books, desks, and equipment; arranging for food service; and buying basketballs and footballs—the Cristo Rey team had to focus on recruiting new corporate sponsors and formalizing the handshake agreements they had with many of the existing ones. They needed a plan for getting students to and from their work assignments. They also needed a program of some sort to train the students—they couldn't just send them into corporate America and expect them to figure it out. They still needed a building for the school and students to fill it. They also needed to raise many of the funds necessary to start up the school. Accomplishing all this in nine months seemed impossible.

Letters continued to roll off the fax machine during the next few weeks. One of them came from Steve Planning, a Jesuit from Maryland who was studying at the Jesuit School of Theology at Berkeley. He'd heard about Cristo Rey from one of his classmates, a Chicago Jesuit, and wrote to offer his services for the summer. Planning was still a couple of years from ordination and was, by his own admission, sick of being in school. During the three years between his philosophy and theology studies, he'd taught at a high school in Chile. He'd also spent time serving in Africa, and he was anxious to get back to ministry. That's why he'd joined the Jesuits in the first place.

Planning had wanted to be a priest since he was in eighth grade. He joined the Oblates of St. Francis de Sales after high school, but he left after two years, not yet ready for such a commitment. After finishing college, he still felt called to the priesthood and began to investigate the possibility of joining the Jesuits.

He knew a bit about the Jesuits because both of his parents had gone to Marquette University, a Jesuit school in Milwaukee. Planning set up a meeting with Fr. Jimmy Martin, SJ, who served as the associate pastor at a parish near the Planning family home in Virginia. "He was eighty-five years old. I remember thinking, *Oh jeez, what's this old man going to tell me?* Then he comes bounding into the room, full of energy. He joined the Jesuits in 1921 and served on the mission band and in the Philippines. He was almost hired to coach the Philippine Olympic swim team, but his Jesuit superiors denied him permission. He came back and founded the Loyola Retreat House in Faulkner, Maryland, among many other accomplishments. When he was done talking to me, he threw himself in the air, landed on his feet, shook my hand, said, 'Great to meet you,' and gave me the name of the vocations director. Then he walked out as quickly as he'd come in."

The dropout rates at the two public high schools serving Pilsen and Little Village were 55 percent and 73 percent.

In Fr. Jimmy Martin, Planning saw everything he'd hoped to find in religious life: energy, excitement, opportunities to serve, and abundant life. He entered the Jesuits in 1988. He was happiest in Africa and Chile, working with those who had little. When he heard about the new school in Chicago in December of 1995, it seemed to him exactly the sort of thing the Jesuits ought to be doing and exactly the sort of work he'd hoped to do as a Jesuit. He faxed a letter to Foley after the reports of the school came out in early 1996. The next day, Foley faxed a letter back and told him to come to Chicago whenever he could. They needed the help.

THE DROPOUT RATES AT the two public high schools serving Pilsen and Little Village were 55 percent and 73 percent. No one could explain with any certainty why these rates were so high. Each school principal, community leader, and parent had a theory. The schools were too crowded and the classes too large. Immigrant students struggled to learn English and to assimilate into mainstream American education. Schools failed to understand and respect the cultural heritage of their students. Gang violence scared away many of the serious students. Parents struggling to make ends meet often took their children out of school to work or to care for younger siblings. The only certainty was that many of the students in the neighborhood, for one reason or another, didn't value their education enough to show up each day. They simply didn't care about learning.

Judy Murphy, Cristo Rey's principal, wanted to change that. To do it, she'd have to build a school that students wanted to attend. She'd been thinking about how to do it from the moment she joined the project in the fall of 1994, and, in reality, for many years before that. Murphy had worked in education since entering the Benedictine order in 1960. She taught bilingual students at a Catholic boarding school in Colorado before coming to Chicago in 1974 to teach Spanish and religion at St. Scholastica, a high school for girls run by her order. Over the next twenty years, she earned a master's degree and served as the school's dean, principal, and president. Around 30 percent of Scholastica's student body was Hispanic. Twenty percent was African American and 10 percent was Asian. Many of the students came from immigrant families.

During her tenure at Scholastica, Murphy had tried to create a model school, one that offered an excellent education in an environment that was safe, healthy, and welcoming. Her passion was to provide high-quality education that was innovative and accessible, especially to children in need. This passion prompted her to accept the principal job at Cristo Rey even though she'd planned to spend a few years out of education after concluding her work at Scholastica.

From the outset, Murphy said that the traditional educational model in use at most college prep high schools—a rigid curriculum that called for a teacher standing at the front of a classroom and imparting knowledge through lectures—would not work at Cristo Rey. The other two Jesuit high schools in Chicago (Loyola Academy and St. Ignatius College Prep) used that model, but most of the students at those schools had attended excellent grade schools and had begun to develop some understanding of the value of education. The students from which Cristo Rey would draw its first class had, as a group, not benefited from high-quality middle schools, and tended to care less about school. To serve these students, Cristo Rey would have to be different. It would have to teach them to become learners and inspire them to learn.

Over the previous sixteen months, Murphy and the academic committee she directed had developed a vision for a school that could meet these challenges. Its classes should be small—around fifteen students each. The school, too, should be small, ideally with a total enrollment no higher than three hundred. This would enable teachers to provide the individual attention Murphy's committee believed was critical to the students' success.

Murphy said that the traditional educational model in use at most college prep high schools—a rigid curriculum that called for a teacher standing at the front of a classroom and imparting knowledge through lectures—would not work at Cristo Rey.

Because nearly all the high school students in Pilsen and Little Village spoke Spanish, the school should offer a dual-language curriculum. Unlike the bilingual education programs in use around the country that generally offered instruction in a student's native language only until he or she could handle instruction in English, Cristo Rey's program would offer continuous instruction in both languages. Students would take the usual English and Spanish classes, but they would take some of their math, history, and science courses in Spanish as well. By graduation, they would be equipped in both languages with strong reading, writing, and speaking skills. Mastery of two languages would better prepare the students for college and professional life, but that wasn't the only reason for the dual-language curriculum. Cristo Rey's founders were committed to respecting the cultural heritage of the school's students and families. Jim Gartland, in preparing his feasibility study, had spoken to many parents who said they didn't feel that the local schools understood them. They had expressed a desire for a school of their own—and that's what Murphy and her team would give them.

In January of 1996, Murphy began creating this dream school. It would prove to be a long and incredibly difficult process.

❀

THOUGH PRESTON KENDALL HAD worked for nearly ten years in corporate America, he was still taken aback by the lavish corner office of Ameritech's CEO, Richard Notebaert. Kendall and Foley were visiting Notebaert in early 1996 at Ameritech's Chicago headquarters to ask him to finalize his offer to employ Cristo Rey students. In the summer of 1995, when members of the feasibility study team were gauging interest in the project, Notebaert had said Ameritech might be able to offer as many as ten jobs to Cristo Rey.

Since starting work in January, Kendall had focused his energy on converting the letters of intent, handshake agreements, and verbal commitments obtained by the feasibility study team into formal contracts. He'd been working closely with Jack J. Crowe, an attorney at Winston & Strawn, a prestigious Chicago law firm. Prior to becoming an attorney, Crowe, a Boston College graduate, had been in the seminary of the Society of African Missions, had completed one year of an English PhD program, had volunteered as a teacher in Jamaica, and had worked as a concrete laborer. When he saw the October 1995 article in the *Chicago Sun-Times*—the same one that had attracted Preston Kendall to Cristo Rey—he immediately sent a letter offering to do anything he could to help.

Kendall called Crowe as soon as he started work at Cristo Rey and, just to be safe, asked for a second legal opinion on the proposed work model. Crowe and a team of attorneys from Winston & Strawn dissected the entire plan and drafted a thick brief that made numerous suggestions but concluded ultimately that Rick Murray's idea and model were fundamentally sound and legal. Kendall, Foley, Murray, and Dave McNulty began to meet regularly with Crowe and other Winston & Strawn attorneys. Murray had drafted a preliminary contract for the school's work program, and the attorneys at Winston & Strawn refined it.

Kendall and Foley were looking to get Richard Notebaert to sign ten of these contracts. By the time they went to see him, they had secured close to ten jobs. If they were able to get Notebaert to commit to ten more, they'd have enough for one hundred students. Then Kendall could turn his attention to figuring out how to operate the program. At the meeting, Notebaert said that Ameritech couldn't support ten jobs but might be able to do five. He directed Kendall and Foley to Ameritech's director of human resources to finalize things. When they finally saw her weeks later, they learned that there had been some miscommunication: Ameritech would only be able to offer one job for five students.

Kendall, Foley, and the rest of the team were now faced with an enormous task—they still had to find more than 60% of the corporate sponsors they'd need to open the school. Rick Murray had contacted Loyola University Chicago about employing students, and the early feedback had been so favorable that Cristo Rey's founders had at one point thought that Loyola might employ its entire inaugural student body. The plan, though, never came to fruition. In the end, Loyola opted not to participate, choosing instead to devote its resources to another proposed program that would bring at-risk high school students to the university to complete high school. By March of 1996, just six months before its opening, Cristo Rey had only half the jobs it needed.

❈

The small elementary school building seemed unfit to house a high school, but it did have a gym and a roller rink with a kitchen that could be used for a cafeteria.

DURING THE FIRST FEW months of 1996, the Archdiocese of Chicago announced the closings of a number of schools. Two of the closings—St. Stephen Elementary School and St. Joseph High School—would dramatically impact Cristo Rey's development.

Despite an exhaustive search—one aided by employees of John Buck's real estate development company and by Buck himself, who spent the better part of a day zooming around Pilsen in a limo with Foley searching for potential sites—the Cristo Rey team had struggled to find a suitable and affordable site for the new school in Pilsen or Little Village. St. Stephen sat at the corner of Cermak Road and Wolcott Avenue—in the center of Pilsen. The small elementary school building seemed unfit to house a high school, but it did have a gym and a roller rink with a kitchen that could be used for a cafeteria. It was better than any of the other options, at least for the short term. St. Joseph's wasn't in Pilsen or Little Village, but its closing meant that a few hundred students would be looking for a new Catholic high school. Within days of the archdiocese's announcement, Dave McNulty and Ted Munz had contacted St. Stephen Parish about leasing the space.

Leo Maldonado was midway through his freshman year at St. Joseph when the announcement came about the school's closing. He didn't know where he'd go for his sophomore year. He still thought school was a waste of his time. He planned to work in construction and have a baby when he got out of high school, and he knew he didn't need a high school diploma to do either of those things.

IN TWO YEARS, MAYRA'S interest in basketball had only intensified. She was ten years old and nearly done with fourth grade. She'd
emerged as a solid student and continued to put lots of time in at
home caring for her brothers and sisters. When Uncle Sergio came
by the apartment, Mayra always asked if they could go to the park
to shoot baskets. Her younger brothers and sisters had outgrown the
simple play lot near Juárez. There wasn't a jungle gym or swingset
there, just the busted-up patch of pavement with its battered backboard and rim. Mayra, though, longed for that court.

One day in the spring of 1996, aware that her love of basketball
wasn't a passing fancy, Sergio took Mayra with him to Barrett Park,
located near the intersection of Cermak and Damen in Pilsen, where
he went for afternoon pickup games before working the night shift as
an attendant at a local gas station. There was no one else at the park
when they got there, so the two of them played H-O-R-S-E. Soon
the other guys showed up and the game started. Mayra stood off to
the side dribbling a basketball and watching the game intently.

It was the beginning of her basketball education.

Throughout that summer, Mayra went to the park with Sergio
and played H-O-R-S-E or one-on-one with him until the rest of the
guys showed up. Then she watched. Standing off to the side, she
would try to replicate the between-the-legs dribbles and spin moves
she saw on the court.

❋

IN APRIL, THANKS TO the hard work of Dave McNulty and Ted
Munz, Cristo Rey signed an agreement to lease the soon-to-be shuttered St. Stephen grade school, including the classroom building, gym,
and parish hall/roller rink/cafeteria. The parish council had managed,
through hours of negotiations with Munz and McNulty, to insert a

clause in the lease ensuring that the parish would still be able to use the parish hall for bingo once a week and for its annual dances.

Finding a building, even one that was virtually uninhabitable as a high school, was a big step forward. The building, though, needed a lot of work. The fire department would require major changes to bring the new school up to code. The existing electrical system couldn't handle the number of computers the school needed. There were no lockers and only two usable, but very undersized, bathrooms. "We also knew," says Kendall, "that it was important to make a good impression to attract students. The school had to look good. It had to feel like a high school. Cloak rooms weren't going to cut it. We needed lockers."

Kendall, working with Winston & Strawn, had also managed to finalize the school's corporate structure. Cristo Rey Jesuit High School would be a licensed 501(c)(3) nonprofit corporation. The Cristo Rey Work Study Corporation would be a separate supporting organization.

Even with the building and the incorporation settled, the school was still struggling to make progress in other areas. Cristo Rey was still short on corporate sponsors. Without them, neither the work program nor the school would work. Sponsors who had previously made soft or verbal commitments to the school continued to drop out. Kendall and the feasibility study team, which had effectively become a recruiting team, continued to work tirelessly at finding sponsors, and Kendall still hadn't found time to figure out how the program would actually work or how he would train the students. Principal Murphy hadn't come close to finalizing a curriculum for the school—and she couldn't make a schedule, or buy books, until she knew what classes the school would offer. She couldn't make that determination until she knew what kind of students would enter

Cristo Rey in the fall. The school's admissions director, Rosy Santiago, was actively recruiting students, but none of them had signed up. And the school still hadn't hired a teacher, which was particularly problematic, since many teachers had already accepted offers at other schools for the coming year.

In early May, a realization of the sheer enormity of the task ahead slammed into Cristo Rey's offices like a locomotive. Foley, Kendall, and Murphy were gathered around a desk in their small office in St. Procopius's rectory when one of them said what all the others were thinking: "We're not going to be able to do this. There's just way too much to do." The others nodded. "So what should we do?" Kendall asked. "We've got to tell Brad." That afternoon, Foley called Schaeffer and told him that he, Murphy, and Kendall couldn't possibly open the school by the fall.

"Yes, you can," Schaeffer said.

"It's May," said Foley, "and we don't have students, teachers, a curriculum, or enough corporate sponsors. We don't have classes, a schedule. We don't have anything. We need another year."

"No, you don't. You can do it. The students will come," Schaeffer said. "And you're going to learn a lot more by getting the doors open and students in the desks than you would by spending another year preparing and planning."

That conversation set the stage for the heroic, albeit chaotic, push to open Cristo Rey by the fall of 1996.

Where Are Those Ten Thousand Students Now?

12

JUDY MURPHY AND THE curriculum committee she'd led for the previous eighteen months envisioned a ten- to twelve-hour school day for Cristo Rey. Students would come to school at 7:30 in the morning and take a full day of classes—at least an hour longer than the roughly six and a half hour-long school day offered by the local public schools—followed by two hours of mandatory extracurricular activities, a two- or three-hour study hall, and possibly an evening meal.

Murphy and John Foley, who together had more than fifty years of experience as educators in the United States and abroad, worried that teachers wouldn't be excited about the substantially extended hours. And Murphy wanted to attract the most dynamic and accomplished teachers possible. The school's success would depend on the ability of the teachers to inspire their students to learn—or at least to show up.

Because of the uncertainty about the curriculum and the academic model, Murphy and Foley had been slow to begin their formal recruitment of teachers. That changed after Foley's failed bid to delay Cristo Rey's opening. When Brad Schaeffer insisted they stay the course, it became clear that they needed to hire teachers in a hurry. They had received countless résumés from teachers around the United States who had read about the school and were interested in teaching there. Foley's first call, though, wasn't to one of the people who had sent in a résumé. Instead, he tried to track down Michael Heidkamp, a Loyola Academy graduate who was somewhere in Peru.

Heidkamp, described by just about everyone who has ever met him as incredibly bright and keenly thoughtful, had excelled in the classroom and on the football field as a student at Loyola Academy. He graduated in 1988 and enrolled at Williams College, where he majored in history and English and played football. After graduation, he spent a year working construction before returning to Loyola Academy, where he took a job teaching in the history department.

"I didn't know of any other profession," Heidkamp says, "where I could just walk into it out of college and have that level of freedom and control, not just in terms of what I could fashion myself into, but what I could explore." He thrived at Loyola—widely regarded as one of Chicago's top private high schools—where he taught mostly freshman history classes. He wasn't afraid to stray from the intense curriculum developed years ago and tweaked annually by Loyola's faculty. In an effort to cultivate critical thinking skills in his students, Heidkamp asked them to read chapters of Howard Zinn's *People's History of the United States* alongside their regularly assigned textbook readings. Instead of having them memorize the dates of the founding of the settlement at Jamestown, the Revolutionary War, and Kennedy's assassination, he asked them to think about how Zinn and the writers of their textbooks could have produced such radically different accounts of the same historical events. What had the textbook writers assumed? What had Zinn assumed? What did they, as readers, assume? How did their assumptions and perceptions of other people affect their interpretation of historical events? Was there one true interpretation of any given historical event, or did the interpretation of the event depend on the perspective from which a person considered it?

In addition to teaching, Heidkamp coached basketball and football. He was a favorite of Loyola students, and their affection and respect for him intensified as they moved on from high school and embarked on their adult lives and careers. Despite that, he quit after his second year. He says he enjoyed the work so much that he could see himself doing it for twenty-five years, just as many of his colleagues had done. "That wouldn't have been a bad thing by any means, but I felt that at some point other than the day I walked in to take the job, I had to consciously make a choice to come back to Loyola."

After leaving his job, he called Foley, an old friend of his father's, who had just returned from Peru. Heidkamp asked Foley about work and volunteer opportunities in Peru. The two met briefly, and Heidkamp made a favorable impression. Foley referred him to Fr. Fred Green, SJ, a California Jesuit then working in Tacna, Peru. Green told Heidkamp there was a need for English teachers. In the summer of 1995, Heidkamp enrolled in a Spanish class in Guatemala. Six weeks later, he flew to Peru. A year later, Foley was trying to find him. Foley thought he'd be the perfect teacher for the new school—if he could be convinced to return to the States.

※

THE FACT THAT THERE were ten thousand kids of high school age in Pilsen/Little Village, few of whom were enrolled in high school, had been cited repeatedly as justification for opening Cristo Rey. The Jesuits expected hundreds, if not thousands, of these kids to apply to their new school. But by the end of the 1995-96 school year, only a dozen students had completed the application.

A big reason for the low number of applicants was Cristo Rey's refusal to accept freshmen. Most new high schools start with only freshmen and build toward full enrollment by adding a new class of freshmen each year. Cristo Rey, however, would open its doors with seventy-five sophomores and seventy-five juniors. The school had also agreed not to accept transfers from other Catholic schools. By May it looked as if those policies might backfire. Rosy Santiago, the school's director of admissions, was promoting the school tirelessly to churches and community groups in an effort to find students who for one reason or another were looking for a new high school. But none of them were signing up.

Foley and Santiago worked with a team from advertising giant Leo Burnett to design a brochure for Cristo Rey that could be distributed to potential students. Foley, Murphy, and Ted Munz appeared on *Chicago Tonight*, a local PBS news show. In early June, Steve Planning, SJ, arrived at Cristo Rey just a day after submitting his final paper at the Jesuit School of Theology at Berkeley. "What can I do to help?" he asked Foley. Foley told him they needed students. Planning called local parishes and asked if he could speak to the congregations during Sunday Masses.

Santiago introduced Planning to Gustavo Rodríguez, who months earlier had become the first student to apply to Cristo Rey. Planning invited Gustavo—who, with his full mustache and tinted glasses, looked more like a middle manager than a high school junior—to help promote the school. They attended countless Sunday Masses in Pilsen and Little Village and developed a great tag-team routine. "I'd get up and speak at Mass," Planning recalls. "The message was always the same: 'This is going to be a great school. You should all come. We'll be outside with more information and to answer your questions.'" Then they trolled the sidewalks outside the churches for anyone who looked old enough to attend high school and handed out the brochures. Planning says most people would ask where the school would be located. "When we'd tell them St. Stephen, they'd frown and say, 'That crappy old place? Why there?'" A lot of them walked away after hearing that. But some stayed and asked questions. Some of the kids were with their parents. Some were alone. Gustavo and Planning didn't collect names and addresses. They didn't have time. But throughout June and July, applications trickled in.

They trolled the sidewalks outside the churches for anyone who looked old enough to attend high school and handed out the brochures.

Looking back, Judy Murphy says of the applicants' academic records, "Cs were infrequent, and anything higher than a C was really rare. I'd never seen grades like that." Cristo Rey's founders soon discovered that the only students who wanted to attend a new high school as sophomores or juniors were those who had dropped out, been kicked out, or were about to fail out of other schools. Gustavo was one of the few exceptions. He came from a family of devout Catholics, and when his mother heard about Cristo Rey—a Catholic school she could afford—she pushed him to apply. His grades were excellent.

Later in the summer, with the number of applications still well below expectations, Rick Murray convinced a local production studio to donate its services to make thirty-second radio and TV spots promoting the school. Foley recorded the commercials, which aired on numerous local Spanish and English stations. The phones in Cristo Rey's offices at St. Procopius rang off the hook every time one of the commercials ran. Applications began to flow in.

Murphy, Kendall, Foley, and Santiago insisted on interviewing every applicant to Cristo Rey—even though they accepted just about everyone. The only exceptions were those students who exhibited a serious deficiency—an inability to read, an obvious gang affiliation, or a profound learning disability. Cristo Rey could not be a school for students with special needs—it simply didn't have the resources necessary to meet those needs.

Even with the liberal admissions policy, by the end of June Cristo Rey was nowhere near its targeted enrollment of 150 students. Without enough students, the school wouldn't be able to generate enough revenue to cover its costs.

❈

CRISTO REY'S BOARD OF trustees, a group that would dramatically affect the school's development, first met on June 19, 1996. John Foley initially balked at the idea of a board, which had been brought to him by Brian Paulson, SJ, a sharp young priest who most guessed would eventually become the president of a Jesuit high school. Boards of trustees had come to play a critical role in all the Jesuits' high schools and universities, and Paulson told Foley that a well-chosen board would help Cristo Rey raise money and find jobs for the work program in addition to providing consultation on everything from curriculum to finances. But Foley wasn't sure he needed a board, or even wanted one. For thirty-four years, while working in Peru, he had run schools and had never had a board. The idea of ceding decision-making power to a group of outsiders didn't sit well with him.

Yet Brad Schaeffer had chosen Foley to be Cristo Rey's first president in part because he was in such a good position to assemble a board and to recruit donors. Despite having lived in Peru for most of his life, he had maintained contact with many childhood friends from his affluent North Shore neighborhood, many of whom had become part of Chicago's business and social elite. They were exactly the type of people needed to launch Cristo Rey.

Foley eventually accepted the idea of an external board at the school. The founding board he and Paulson put together was made up of the following people:

- Steve Baine, senior vice president of First Chicago NBD Corporation
- Daniel Cotter, president of Cotter & Company, which owned the True Value Hardware stores
- Rosemary Croghan, a civic leader and former nurse of Mexican heritage from the North Shore
- Jack J. Crowe, the Winston & Strawn attorney who had been providing pro bono legal services to the school
- Roberto Goizueta, an associate professor of theology at Loyola University Chicago
- Christopher G. Kennedy, executive vice president of Merchandise Mart Properties
- Peggy Mueller, associate program officer at the Spencer Foundation
- Fr. Ted Munz, SJ, who had conducted the second feasibility study for the school and had since been appointed president of Loyola Academy
- Luis P. Nieto. Jr., director of ethnic marketing and external relations at Kraft Foods
- Fr. Jack O'Callaghan, SJ, associate director of ministry at Loyola University Medical Center
- Fr. Larry Reuter, SJ, vice president of university ministry at Loyola University Chicago
- Trisha Rooney, president of R4 Services Inc.
- Marilee Stepan Wehman, another civic leader from Chicago's North Shore.

At the first meeting, the board elected Lou Nieto to serve as chairman.

The board was loaded with business and education leaders, prominent figures in the Hispanic community, civic leaders with ties to charitable foundations, and influential Jesuits. One of them would eventually lead Cristo Rey through its darkest hour. No one sitting at the table for that first meeting would ever have guessed it would be a diminutive woman without any business or educational experience.

✺

WHILE THE FORMATION OF a board of trustees was certainly an important step toward opening Cristo Rey's doors, hiring the school's founding faculty was a more pressing need. Throughout June and July, Murphy and Foley interviewed scores of candidates for teaching positions. Some of the early hires were handpicked, such as Germán (pronounced Hermán) Indacochea, a native of Arequipa, Peru, who had attended Colegio San José, where John Foley had been his fourth-grade teacher. Indacochea, who later came to be known to Cristo Rey's students simply as Mr. Indo, came to the United States to attend Loyola University. He eventually earned graduate degrees in mathematics, religious education, and computer science from Loyola. He chaired the math department at Quigley North, a local Catholic high school, before coming to Cristo Rey.

Murphy and Foley next interviewed Jim Wall, a 1964 graduate of St. Ignatius College Prep who returned to the school in 1970 to become an English teacher. He taught there until 1991, when he left to pursue writing full-time. At the time, he'd already seen two of his plays—*Parlor Games* and *Auschwitz Lullaby*—published and produced around the United States. "I learned a whole lot from the Jesuits as a high school kid. I learned from them at Loyola University. And then I really learned how to teach from a lot of the Jesuits I worked with," Wall says, explaining why he applied for a job as soon as he heard about Cristo Rey. Foley and Murphy made an offer soon after interviewing him. Like Indacochea, Wall understood Jesuit education. He'd experienced it as a student and as a teacher at one of the best Jesuit high schools in the country. Foley and Murphy hoped he would bring some of St. Ignatius College Prep's Jesuit tradition and academic rigor to Cristo Rey as the school's first English teacher.

Murphy and Foley also hired Sr. Frances Thibodeau, a Dominican nun with more than twenty-five years of teaching experience, to teach religion. Thibodeau had taught previously in Rome, Staten Island, and the South Side of Chicago. Mary Morrison, an artist and a teacher originally from Chicago but then living in Wyoming, was offered a job teaching art. Marjorie MacLean, who held a master's in education from Harvard and had taught American Palestinian students at an American Quaker school in Palestine, at University of Illinois at Chicago, and at Chicago's Quigley North with Germán Indacochea, was hired to teach science. Dave Galvan was hired to teach math and science.

Mike Heidkamp returned from Peru to interview for a job teaching history at Cristo Rey. When his parents had called to tell him about the opportunity, he was unsure of his plans for the upcoming year. He had fallen in love with a Peruvian woman named María del Rosario Pimentel and wasn't sure if they'd come back to the States or stay in Peru, but the job intrigued him. "I knew if I went back I probably wasn't going to fit at Loyola Academy. I wanted to explore avenues that would make my transition back to the States a little bit easier. Part of that was trying to find a community where I might be able to continue to learn Spanish. I was also looking for something that would allow me to continue this development I'd begun."

Upon his arrival in Peru, Heidkamp had found that despite six weeks of training, he couldn't really speak Spanish. Because of that, he couldn't create the one-on-one relationships with students he believed were necessary for effective teaching. He gave up the teaching job and wandered instead into a massive Habitat for Humanity building project on a large dusty tract on the outskirts of Tacna. That's where he met María—she goes by the nickname Charo—who was helping build a house for her mother. He spent most of his time in Peru building houses and trying to woo Charo with a mix of broken Spanish and physical comedy. He also held an informal reading group at the house where he stayed for students trying to learn English.

Heidkamp's experience in Peru contributed to the development of his unique approach to education, which would eventually play an enormous role in Cristo Rey's development. "My time there forced me to abandon the idea that my experience was universal," he says. "Whether it was my lifestyle or my experience of education, I realized that other people not only approach education differently but are treated differently by educational institutions, social institutions, and governmental institutions. In Peru, I wrestled with that fact and started to realize that it's not only that people are treated differently, but that different values are placed on people based on who they are culturally, racially, socially, economically. It isn't just that we're all different. Certain differences are privileged.

"I think this made me more aware of the politics of education. Education doesn't function the same way for all kids and all communities. I'm not just talking about resource allocation. That's part of it, but there's also the fact that part of education is teaching people to assimilate. Part of education is developing a common culture. But what does it mean if you're starting from the outside and moving in? What do you have to check at the door at various stages along the way? Compare that to the person who's starting at the center, the person who already owns that common culture. That person doesn't have to compromise nearly as much and I believe will have a very different educational experience. For me the question became how can I rethink and rework education in a way that doesn't ask people to deny parts of themselves?"

In hiring Cristo Rey's first-year faculty, Murphy says she was looking primarily for experience. She wanted teachers who had spent many years at the front of a classroom, ideally a classroom full of students like the ones who would enroll at Cristo Rey. She also wanted teachers who were experienced at teaching in both English and Spanish.

Mike Heidkamp didn't have any of the above and was much younger than the other teachers Murphy had hired. But he impressed both Murphy and Foley during his interview. At one point, he talked about his belief that education is crucial to sustaining a vibrant democracy. He understood that education was about more than just teaching children to read and write; it involved training them to be citizens, learners, and thinkers. Remarkably, he seemed to share Murphy's vision of education. He knew that education—and Cristo Rey in particular—could be more and do more. He was an idealist, and a highly intelligent one at that. He was exactly the type of teacher who could help make Cristo Rey a truly revolutionary school, so Murphy and Foley made him an offer.

Heidkamp and the rest of Cristo Rey's founding faculty showed up for their first full day of work together on August 5, 1996 (at one point, earlier in the year, this had been targeted as opening day for the school). The small elementary school building that would eventually house the school was nowhere near ready, and there still weren't enough students enrolled to fill it. During the first day of meetings Murphy presented a sketch of the typical Cristo Rey student to the

> Heidkamp's experience in Peru contributed to the development of his unique approach to education, which would eventually play an enormous role in Cristo Rey's development. "My time there forced me to abandon the idea that my experience was universal."

new faculty members. Most of the students were poor. The average family income in the neighborhood was around twenty thousand dollars, and the average family size was five. Most of the students were being raised by recent immigrants who spoke Spanish at home. While the students could carry on conversations in Spanish or English, they lacked advanced writing and reading skills in both languages. Generally, they struggled in school. Often they were ostracized or treated differently because of cultural differences.

"With those issues in mind," Murphy recalls, "I asked the teachers to come up with what they thought should be the curriculum for this new school in their area of expertise." It was a remarkable challenge, Foley says: "From day one, Judy told the teachers, 'No one has figured out how to teach center-city kids. We need to.'" Teachers were usually handed a curriculum and told what to teach. Murphy, however, demonstrated from the start that she was a different kind of school leader and that she was serious about wanting to create a different kind of school. She was asking Cristo Rey's teachers what should be taught and, just as important, how it should be taught.

The teachers jumped at the chance to participate in the creation of a new and better curriculum. Heidkamp says they tackled innumerable curricular questions in the four weeks before the students were scheduled to arrive. They discussed optimal class size and debated whether the classrooms should be set up with traditional desks or with tables that fostered group work and collaborative learning. They shared ideas about how teachers could connect on a personal level with students and inspire, challenge, and cajole them to do more than what was required. Most high schools usually used forty- or forty-five-minute class periods. Cristo Rey's teachers considered class periods of sixty, eighty, or ninety minutes. The teachers brainstormed ways to connect the content in different classes. They spent days exploring how the curriculum could develop the students' reading, speaking, and writing skills in both English and Spanish. They debated how to discipline students and talked seriously about not implementing a disciplinary system at all. It's hard to imagine a school without one, but Cristo Rey's faculty was operating from the assumption that what had been done previously for the students in Pilsen had not worked. If it hadn't worked, then it could—and probably should—be changed.

"Any of the topics we were covering could've been a doctoral dissertation," Murphy says now, "and we were working through a half dozen of them a week. We could've spent six weeks on each one." For Heidkamp, the experience was exhilarating. At Loyola Academy, he'd enjoyed having control over his classroom. At Cristo Rey, he and nine other faculty members were literally shaping the school. And it was shaping up to be a new kind of school.

But it was still a school that didn't have enough students.

❋

DURING ONE OF THE hectic days leading up to Cristo Rey's opening, the post office made an unexpected delivery. Slipped into a thick pile of official school mail and junk mail was a telephone bill. Up to that point, the Chicago Province had funded all of Cristo Rey's operations. The Cristo Rey team had not yet seen a single bill.

Steve Baine, one of Cristo Rey's founding board members and a well-traveled financier and corporate strategist, points out many similarities between the Jesuit effort to open Cristo Rey and one of the methods used to fund start-up companies. "In the business world, we'd say the Jesuits provided venture capital," Baine says. "They made an initial donation. They invested capital in this idea. And they also took some of their best guys—Jim Gartland, Ted Munz, and John Foley—and assigned them to develop the idea and to think about ways it could be successful. That's what venture capital investors do. They turn ideas into sustainable, profitable ventures by contributing their finances and their expertise to the idea."

In the business world, venture capitalists make these investments in exchange for some percentage of ownership in the venture. If the business is successful, the owners will eventually sell it, either to another company or to public shareholders through an initial public offering. When the business is sold, the venture capitalists get their percentage of the proceeds.

Just like venture capitalists, the Jesuits wanted their new venture to be sustainable, maybe even profitable. The phone bill that arrived in the mail that summer represented a step toward sustainability. All of Cristo Rey's bills had been going directly to the Jesuits. Aware that the school would soon have a revenue stream, the province began to send the bills on to the school. The first bill, though, surprised Foley and Murphy. Both had led schools, and both had employed large faculties and staffs, but it had been decades since either of them had even thought about paying a bill. Other people had done that work. So Foley and Murphy stuffed the bill back into the envelope and took it over to Preston Kendall's desk. "Preston, do you believe it?" Foley said. "We just got a bill. What should we do with it?"

Some might find it alarming that neither Foley nor Murphy could deal with a simple phone bill. But both of them had made the decision early in life to enter religious orders, where the personal accumulation and management of money simply wasn't a priority. As a young Jesuit completing collegiate studies, Foley had been given allowances from his superiors for train and bus rides, and he was expected to return the change. While understandable, the school's leaders' unfamiliarity with money would, over time, negatively affect Cristo Rey's development. As for the bill, Kendall, the director of the Corporate Internship Program, said he'd pay it. To do so, he would have to open bank accounts and have checks printed. What he didn't know was that by paying that first bill, he would become the school's chief financial officer and effectively double the size of his job. It would eventually prove to be far too much work for one person.

Opening Days   13

T HE FIRST LONG BLACK Chevy Suburban with darkly tinted
windows rolled up to Cristo Rey just after sunrise on August
26, 1996. The second one arrived moments later. The doors opened
in unison, and half a dozen Secret Service agents clad in suits climbed
out onto the cracked asphalt at the corner of Wolcott Avenue and
Twenty-second Place, in front of the St. Stephen Church. In just a
few hours, First Lady Hillary Clinton would officially open Cristo
Rey Jesuit High School.

Her visit was the result of a dogged letter-writing campaign
mounted by Fr. John Foley, who fourteen months earlier had seen
President Clinton along Chicago's lakefront while both men were
out for morning jogs. When Clinton passed Foley, who had stepped
aside to let the throng of reporters and Secret Service agents get by,
Foley called out, "Hoya saxa!" ("What rocks!"), the Greek and Latin
motto for Georgetown University that was long ago used as a cheer
for defensive linemen on Georgetown's football team. Clinton had
graduated from the school in 1968, and Foley had studied there as
well for a year before entering the Jesuits in 1954. Clinton looked over,
nodded, and shouted, "Hoya saxa." Most folks would've gone home,
content with their good fortune, and told all their family and friends
about their chance encounter with the president. But Foley saw an
opportunity. That night he wrote a letter to the president in which he
recounted their "meeting" and then explained that the Jesuits would

be opening a new school the following autumn in Chicago—though at the time the school wasn't close to being fully approved. Foley described how the school would work, based on what was then a very rough plan for the work program. Then, noting that the new school's opening would coincide with the Democratic National Convention in Chicago, he invited the president to formally open the school.

Days later, Foley started checking his mailbox, fully expecting to find a letter from the president accepting his invitation. It was months before a note from the White House did finally arrive. It was from a staffer and stated that the president wouldn't be able to participate. Foley wasn't willing to settle for a brush-off from a staffer and tracked down a Jesuit priest from the New Orleans province who had gone to Yale Law School with the Clintons. The Jesuit forwarded Foley's request to the president, and weeks later Foley received a letter from the White House stating that the First Lady would be there to open the school on August 26. Foley knew her visit would lend immediate credibility to the school and would garner substantial media attention. He began referring to her visit as the day Cristo Rey would receive its "birth certificate."

The visit went off without a hitch. The First Lady toured the grounds and spoke to a group of Cristo Rey's students, teachers, and corporate sponsors, as well as a contingent of community leaders and local politicians. Reporters from Chicago's major TV stations and newspapers were there. Foley had sent the First Lady everything he had in writing about Cristo Rey, and it was clear from her remarks that she'd read it. She spoke about the importance of the school's dual-language program and the innovation of the work program. It was, Foley felt, a perfect way to open the school—if only the school were ready to open.

By that time, Foley and Murphy had already pushed the opening date back a month, to early September. They were still far from the initial target enrollment and had scaled that back, too, to a more reasonable target of one hundred students—fifty sophomores and fifty juniors. Thanks to the faculty, who had spent an August weekend literally recruiting high school students off the street at the neighborhood's Fiesta del Sol festival, they had almost one hundred students. But they didn't have anywhere to put the students, because the rehab of St. Stephen was far from complete.

Foley received a letter from the White House stating that the First Lady would be there to open the school on August 26. Her visit would lend immediate credibility to the school and would garner substantial media attention.

"The building still needs a lot of work," Br. Dave Henderson, SJ, Cristo Rey's director of facilities, told Foley after Clinton's visit. Henderson had entered the Jesuits after serving in the Marine Corps and working for Ameritech. As a Jesuit, he had been a guidance counselor at Loyola Academy and had worked in missions in Alaska before returning to Chicago to serve at Cristo Rey. He'd made a heroic effort to tidy up the campus for the First Lady's visit, but he'd been telling Foley for weeks that the rehab of the school building would not be ready by September 5, and might not be ready by October 5.

"We'll figure something out," Foley assured him.

✳

EVEN IN THE TIE and well-worn white button-down shirt he wore to Cristo Rey on September 5, 1995, Leo Maldonado was an intimidating-looking fifteen-year-old. His head was shaved on the sides, and the hair on top, which he pulled straight back, reached past his shirt collar. As he strolled into Cristo Rey on the first day of school, Leo knew he looked like a gangbanger, and it didn't bother him at all. In fact, he kind of liked it. In Leo's world, gangbangers had

Some of the incoming students had literally never left their neighborhoods. Some had never been downtown, never been in an elevator or on an escalator. Cristo Rey was asking its students to go into a world about which most of them knew very little.

power, and power meant safety and security. It wouldn't hurt for people to be afraid of him.

Already on that first day, Leo knew how he would get through his sophomore year. "My plan was to only deal with the people and the teachers I had to go to class with," he says. "I didn't need anybody else. But with those people I did have to deal with, like the teachers, I couldn't get on their bad side. You have to think smart, you know. I knew I'd have to be cool with those people."

He didn't know exactly what to expect on the first day of school. He knew he was going to be in a school building for little kids, and he didn't like that at all. And he knew he'd have a job. He thought that was cool, even though he'd never had a job before. He hoped he'd get to work on a construction site. That's what he wanted to do when he got out of high school.

Preston Kendall knew that Cristo Rey's students would eventually learn a lot from their jobs. But they couldn't learn everything on the job. During admissions interviews, Kendall, Judy Murphy, and Rosy Santiago learned that some of the incoming students had literally never left their neighborhoods. Some had never been downtown, never been in an elevator or on an escalator. Cristo Rey was asking its students to go into a world about which most of them knew very little. Going into corporate America, with its plush offices and immaculately dressed professionals, would be a culture shock for the students, and quite likely a scary one. In order to learn from that world—or just survive in it—they'd need to be prepared.

They'd have to look people in the eye and stand up and shake hands when they were introduced to new people. They'd have to speak confidently and clearly. They'd have to know how to get around the city. They'd have to be able to use a fax machine. They'd have to know which fork to use at an upscale restaurant in the event that they were taken to lunch. They'd have to answer phones, make copies, and understand the basics of a filing system. And they'd have to be able to use computers. Kendall had weeks, maybe months, of material he needed to cover with the students before they went to work.

All that material proved to be a godsend. School was scheduled to start on September 5, the day local public schools started, but the school building wasn't yet ready. So instead of attending classes, the students would go through an intensive job-training program off-site. The new students welcomed the news that they wouldn't have to go to classes for the first three weeks of school. Even better was the fact that much of the training would take place downtown at Loyola University Chicago's Maguire Hall.

The first day started with an assembly. Folding chairs were set up in the gym, which was housed in the low slung building across the street from the school. Leo sat with a few of the kids he knew from St. Joseph's. The gym was small. It didn't feel like a real high school. Leo recognized the white-haired priest with glasses—John Foley—who had come to tell St. Joseph's students about Cristo Rey. Foley was the first to speak to the students. He gave a speech, half in Spanish and half in English. He talked about how they were creating a brand-new school together. He said there was no other school like it, and they'd be the first high school students in the country to earn their own tuition. And then he talked about dreams. This was a school, he said, that would help the students make their dreams come true. He challenged them to dream big dreams. Leo, like most of the other students, listened quietly.

After the rest of the teachers introduced themselves and the assembly concluded, Cristo Rey's ninety-seven students spent the rest of their first morning learning how to introduce themselves and shake hands. No textbooks were distributed and no notes taken. The whole thing seemed kind of silly to Leo. But when he showed up for work for the first time and didn't know what to do, he'd default to the behavior he'd learned in his job training. Looking back on the experience, Leo says, "I still keep it in mind. In fact, when I shake somebody's hand, the eyes still stand out. You know, when somebody's approaching you to shake your hand, I still think, 'Okay, stand up.' And then I shake their hand, and I always look at them in the eyes."

❀

"Oh my Lord, Preston, it's almost time for lunch," John Foley said, rushing toward Kendall. "What are we going to feed them?"

During admissions interviews, many parents had asked Foley, Kendall, Murphy, and Santiago what would be served for lunch at the new school. The frequency of the question surprised them. Their standard answer was "We don't know that yet, but we'll take care of it." By 10:00 a.m. on the first day of school, they still hadn't given it much thought. Eventually, they would use the back half of the roller rink as a cafeteria, but the kitchen there wasn't yet functional. Between recruiting students and teachers and trying to get the classroom building and the curriculum ready, no one had thought about the lunch menu.

Kendall literally ran out the door. "I'll be right back," he yelled over his shoulder to Foley. He jogged to Swordsmen Pizza, the storefront pizza place across the street from Cristo Rey. The owner was a Mexican immigrant named Joe Treviño. He and his wife, Maggie, ran the tiny place, which had an impossibly small kitchen outfitted with a mammoth pizza oven and a small seating area with half a dozen tables and mismatched chairs in the front. On most days it appeared that Treviño, who usually wore his long white hair in a ponytail, served more coffee than pizza. Many in the neighborhood joked that he had a daily pizza quota and

Between recruiting students and teachers and trying to get the classroom building and the curriculum ready, no one had thought about the lunch menu.

that when he met it, he'd close up shop and go home. Sometimes the store was open until eight or nine at night; sometimes it was closed at two in the afternoon. No hours were posted. Most of Joe's business was selling slices, hot dogs, and cheeseburgers, although he did occasionally dish up a full-size pie. He also sold deep-fried pizza puffs, two of which, thanks to a remarkable preservative lacquer, were mounted on the wall next to the cash register.

When Kendall pushed the door open, Joe and his wife were planted in the far corner of the kitchen watching a small black-and-white TV tucked between two Pepsi coolers. "Excuse me," Kendall said. "Hello."

"Hey, buddy," Treviño said, coming to the front of the store. "Watchu need?"

"Twenty pizzas. In about an hour. Can you do that?"

"Sure, buddy." Treviño smiled, not sure if this manna from heaven was real or some kind of cruel joke. "Pepperoni?"

"Some cheese," Kendall said. "Some pepperoni. Some sausage. Will you take a check? I'm with the school across the street."

"Sure, buddy."

Cristo Rey served pizza from Swordsmen and Pineda's Pizza for the rest of the year.

First Day at Work 14

O N MONDAY, SEPTEMBER 30, 1996, students from Cristo
Rey Jesuit High School went to work for the first time. That
morning, Preston Kendall called roll nervously in the assembly area
and offered last-minute advice. Then he and the group of twenty students who would be going to work instead of class on every Monday
for the rest of the school year rushed through the rain to the bus,
car, and van that would shuttle them to their jobs. Kendall drove the
small bus. His days had been starting around 6:30 or 7:00 a.m. and
rarely ended before 8:00 p.m. He was working hard, and he'd taken
a huge pay cut to do it. And he'd never been happier.

But he was on edge that first morning as he piloted the bus through
the rainy Chicago streets. He couldn't help but wonder if the students
were really prepared. During Corporate Internship Program (CIP)
training, Kendall had driven the students into the city and walked
them to the front doors of their offices. But that was all he could do.
The rest was up to them. This, he knew, was the moment of truth.

"We were so scared the first day the kids went to work," John
Foley recalls. "I say now that I wanted to hide under the desk.
When Preston left, I thought they might be back in twenty minutes.
I thought the supervisors would call and say, 'Are you out of your
mind? What do you want us to do with these kids?'"

Kendall expected them to call, too. It wasn't that he didn't trust
the students, or didn't think they could handle it. The whole idea was

"We were so scared the first day the kids went to work. I thought they might be back in twenty minutes. I thought the supervisors would call and say, 'Are you out of your mind? What do you want us to do with these kids?'"

so . . . far-fetched. The absurdity of the enterprise—sending high school kids into the Tribune Company, Ameritech, Aon, Bozell Worldwide, Quaker Oats, and some of the city's best law firms—became perfectly clear as he drove the students to work. Doubt came crashing down on him. What had Cristo Rey's founders been thinking? It could never work. After dropping off the last student, Kendall rushed back to school. He wanted to be there to personally answer the calls.

The calls did come—the first one no more than thirty minutes after he returned to the office. Then another call came. Then a third. "I remember Preston coming into my office," Foley says. "He said, 'The sponsors are calling.' He paused for a while and let me think it was bad news. We were both worried that they'd call, but then Preston said, 'To say thanks. They're calling us to say thanks for sending in the kids.'"

❀

MARITZA'S SEVENTH-GRADE ENGLISH CLASS was reading *Charlie and the Chocolate Factory*. It was early in the school year and one of the first times she had been asked to read aloud in English. The Ruben Salazar Bilingual Education Center, Maritza's old school, where she'd taken most of her classes in Spanish, went only to sixth grade, so she'd enrolled at the Galileo Academy, a Chicago public school that at the time offered almost all of its classes in English. She was struggling.

In Mexico, she'd come to love the peace she could find in the pages of a book. She'd always enjoyed being a student, and school was her main connection to Mexico, almost the only part of her life that was the same. But when she moved to Galileo Academy, school became different, too. She knew it the first time she said the word *chocolate*. She was reading slowly and carefully, sounding out the words as she went. She thought she'd gotten the word right until the student next to her giggled. When she came to the word a second time, she tried to say it more quickly. More people laughed. Unfortunately, *chocolate* appeared two more times in the passage she was reading. By the fourth time she said it, it seemed that everyone in the classroom was laughing. The teacher did nothing.

Everything at Galileo was harder because Maritza couldn't speak English well. It was harder to understand the teachers, and it was almost impossible to make friends. Everyone made fun of the kids who couldn't speak English, and no one wanted them as friends. Many days, Maritza just wanted to stay home and read a book. When she started to feel like quitting or taking it easy, though, she would think about what her grandmother had told her so many times: "Concentrate on your studies, *mija*, so you'll never have to depend on anyone else, so you'll be able to take care of yourself."

Maritza repeated her grandma's advice to herself as she struggled with the nuances of English, and in the mornings when she stood with her bag waiting for the bus. She knew her grandma would be disappointed if she stopped going to school, so she vowed to stick with it and to get As in her classes. It was all she could do.

❊

THE FIRST DAYS AND weeks of Cristo Rey's Corporate Internship Program were chaotic, but they paled in comparison to the first few weeks of classes, which also began on Monday, September 30. During the first week, two of Cristo Rey's students plowed a minivan into a parked car in front of the school. They left the scene of the accident and hid behind a nearby grocery store. A fight over a girl erupted between two boys in the cafeteria. Gang signs were found on the bathroom stalls despite the insistence of faculty and staff that the school would not tolerate any gang activity.

In the midst of all this, though, something else was happening, something very good. Cristo Rey's students, few of whom had ever experienced great success in school, were showing up for class every day.

The school opened with twenty-two juniors and seventy-five sophomores. The plan had been to open with roughly fifty juniors and fifty sophomores, but the faculty determined that many of the students who'd applied to be juniors at Cristo Rey hadn't really completed the necessary credits to begin as juniors, so they were placed in the sophomore class. The decision was made just before the faculty members finalized the course offerings for the year. Judy Murphy had asked them to study the academic backgrounds of the incoming students so they could make an effort to tailor classes to their needs.

Murphy was unique in insisting that Cristo Rey's curriculum be custom built for its students. Curricula are often based on the expertise of a school's teachers or are borrowed from another school with a similar mission. Murphy's student-centered approach was a departure from the model in use at most Jesuit high schools in the United States. Some may have viewed it as a risky departure, given that each year 95 percent of graduates from Jesuit high schools enrolled at four-year colleges and universities, often the best ones in the country.

As it turned out, Murphy was well ahead of the curve. Late in the spring of 1996, she was given a copy of a manuscript called *Breaking Ranks*, which was scheduled to be published in the fall by the National Association of Secondary School Principals. The fruit of a groundbreaking study by leading educational thinkers, *Breaking Ranks* set forth a strategy for reforming and improving high schools in the United States. Two of the central recommendations in the book—that high schools be small and offer more personalized instruction—confirmed that Murphy's instincts were correct.

While Cristo Rey's first students went through their job training, Murphy and the faculty divided them into five classes—one junior class and four sophomore classes. Each day, the students in one of the five classes would go to work. The others would come to school, where they'd take five eighty-minute classes. The long classes were designed to allow teachers from different subject areas to collaborate and co-teach. The faculty believed that important connections between different subject areas were often lost because classes were taught in separate rooms by separate teachers and for shorter class periods. They hoped that Cristo Rey students would see how the subjects they were studying were connected to one another and to their lives. Instead of giving eighty-minute lectures, teachers would develop experiences, group work, and special projects designed to foster active learning. While there was certainly still a place for lectures, they were a means to an end rather than an end unto themselves.

When classes started on September 30, Cristo Rey's students encountered a truly cutting-edge educational experience. In the course of just a few months, Murphy and her faculty had come remarkably close to building a model *Breaking Ranks* school.

Few of the students were aware of the innovation. "I just remember thinking how small it was," Leo says. "St. Joseph's, where I was

> Murphy and the faculty divided Cristo Rey's first students into five classes—one junior class and four sophomore classes. Each day, the students in one of the five classes would go to work.

at high school, wasn't all that big or anything, but it was a real high school. At Cristo Rey we were in a grade school and we were having classes in the gym, on the stage, and in the cafeteria."

Because Cristo Rey's building still wasn't ready, the first classes were held in the "roller rink building." Located directly south of St. Stephen, the roller rink had once been the center of parish life. The building also housed a small gymnasium with two basketball hoops, a stage, and an adjoining "social room," replete with a long oak bar and a cooler big enough for kegs. The roller rink, which had a large kitchen, became Cristo Rey's cafeteria and assembly hall. Until the building was ready, the school used different corners of the roller rink and the gym as classrooms. One class met on the stage. The bar—the only room with doors that could be closed—was used as a "media room," because it was the only room dark enough to show movies or PowerPoint presentations. Until the school building was ready, teachers used whatever space they could find in the small building that once served as the St. Stephen convent—essentially a small single-family home—for offices.

It wasn't exactly the setting Murphy and her teachers would have chosen for the unveiling of their student-centered approach to education. Three and sometimes four classes were held simultaneously in the roller rink/assembly hall/cafeteria. At lunch, students pulled their chairs out of the corners to the middle of the room, where the pizza was served.

Sr. Frances Thibodeau, who had nearly three decades of teaching experience, taught religion near the cafeteria kitchen. Jim Wall taught English on the floor of Cristo Rey's gym, which wasn't air-conditioned or particularly well heated. Rolling chalkboards were brought in and folding chairs were set up.

"I'll never forget the first day," Wall says, "standing there watching these kids walk into the school. I thought to myself, *My God, what the hell have I gotten myself into?* They all had their street faces on. There was only one kid, José Lopez, who smiled. All the rest of these kids looked like they'd stab you in the back and steal your last penny."

According to Mike Heidkamp, Cristo Rey's students fell into three basic groups. "The big thing was that none of these kids had given up on education, because they were all still there. But they did have different kinds of relationships with schools. The students who had recently arrived from Mexico were very formal. They were well-dressed and respectful and traditional in their approach to school. Then there were a few kids who really saw Cristo Rey as a chance to get to college. And then there was a group of kids who seemed wary of the school. They seemed to be sitting back in their chairs and saying, 'You claim to be all these things. Prove it. Show me why I should show up on a daily basis. Show me why I should care.' For me as a teacher, it was an amazing challenge. There was this sense of urgency. How do we keep this relevant? How do we keep the kids coming? We knew that just opening our doors in the morning wasn't going to be enough."

Teaching in the gym didn't bother Jim Wall at all. But he did struggle with the lack of discipline and obedience from students. "I remember after the second or the third day, I was driving home, and I thought to myself, *I should quit. I should just get the hell out of here. I don't think I can do this.* I was behind a truck and I was doing about two miles an hour and I suddenly got this feeling. *I don't give a damn what kind of faces they're wearing. I'm not gonna let some group of high school kids drive me out of a place where, at least right now, I want to be.* I had to strengthen my resolve."

> "I'll never forget the first day, standing there watching these kids walk into the school. I thought to myself, *My God, what the hell have I gotten myself into? They all had their street faces on.*

The students had no idea they were experiencing a radical departure from traditional pedagogy. But after three months, most of them were still showing up, which suggested that things were working. Not everyone made it, though. Some students simply refused to do any work. Cristo Rey's teachers, reluctant to throw anyone out of school, worked with the administration to develop performance contracts. If a student was put on contract, he or she agreed to meet certain benchmarks over the coming weeks or months. If, after being put on contract, the student still refused to work, he or she was asked to leave the school. No student was dismissed from the school before faculty members were given an opportunity to argue on his or her behalf. In many cases, Murphy, Foley, and Kendall deferred to the faculty. A handful of students were dismissed, though, for ties to gangs or major disciplinary problems at school or work.

One student was fired by his Corporate Internship Program sponsor, a bank, after security cameras caught him stealing money from the drawer at the end of the day. When confronted about it, he admitted to taking the money and explained that he planned to repay it. The bank fired him anyway, and he was expelled from school. The next day, his parents showed up at the bank with the money and pleaded with those in charge to take him back. They didn't, and neither would Cristo Rey.

STEVE PLANNING, THE JOVIAL Jesuit from Maryland who had volunteered to recruit students in the months leading up to the school's opening, called John Foley in the fall of 1996 to ask if he could come back to Cristo Rey in January. Most of his fellow students at the Jesuit School of Theology at Berkeley would be staying to take intersession classes. Planning wanted to work.

"Of course you're welcome to come back," Foley said. "We can certainly find something for you to do." On Planning's first day back, he was asked to substitute for the gym teacher, Dan Bowden, who was home sick. Due to a scheduling conflict, gym classes were being held in the basement of the school building instead of in the gym. Planning's job was to run a study hall, which meant "keep them busy and make sure no one gets hurt."

When Planning introduced himself to the students as Mr. Planning, many of them looked surprised. "How come you're a Mister and not a Father?" one of them asked. It was a fair question. Planning had not yet been ordained, but, like most Jesuits in training, he wore a black shirt and the traditional Roman collar. While Planning was trying to deliver a watered-down explanation of Jesuit formation, one of the kids in the back of the room asked, "Why you want to be a priest? What about all the honeys, the ladies? You don't get to be with the ladies, right?"

The student was Leo Maldonado. Planning's first thought was that Leo was a punk. "He was ghetto," Planning says. "That's probably the easiest way to describe him. His hair was long, like a long rat tail. He just looked like a thug."

At first Planning laughed at the question. It was the easiest thing to do. But when he looked at Leo, he sensed it was a genuine question. And he saw something more in Leo, something beyond the tough demeanor: his eyes were smiling. Though Leo would never let the rest of his face betray him, he couldn't control his eyes.

Planning spent the next fifteen minutes attempting to explain to the gym class his vocation as a Jesuit. He told them about grace and that he felt God was calling him to a life of priestly service. Yes, there were sacrifices. But the sacrifices didn't seem all that important. A life of service, he told them, was profoundly rewarding.

That conversation was the beginning of a friendship that would dramatically alter the course of Leo's life.

❊

FOLEY AND KENDALL DIDN'T let themselves celebrate the work program's initial success for long. This was wise, because it wasn't long before they started to encounter bumps in the road. The first crisis happened on a rainy October afternoon in just the third week of the work program. Kendall was picking up students from work. The days were starting to get shorter, and it was already dusk when he pulled up to the first stop. The students clambered up the steps of the bus, their jackets and backpacks wet. Kendall counted heads as they passed. Seven. There should have been eight. He stood up and counted everyone on the bus. "Who's missing?" he asked.

"Edgar."

"Where is he?" The students shrugged. Kendall sat down and waited. Five minutes passed. He still had two more stops to make. Another five minutes passed. He had to pick up five other students who were standing out in the rain. Five more minutes passed, and he finally left, his heart pounding. Once he'd dropped off all the students at school, he turned around and drove back into the city. He double-parked the bus near Edgar's office, got out, and started looking for him. He walked the streets, calling Edgar's name.

Finally, Kendall called Rosy Santiago on his cell phone, and she found Edgar's home phone number. When Kendall called the house, Edgar's mom said he was home and had been for hours. Kendall asked Edgar why he hadn't waited for the bus, and Edgar said, "It was raining. I didn't want to wait, so I took CTA [Chicago's public transit system] home."

Kendall made the first of many, many mental notes: *We need a better system.*

A few weeks later, Kendall was calling each of his corporate sponsors to check in. He had planned to call much earlier, but things had been so busy that he'd never been able to get to a phone during regular business hours.

Until he called Refco, the trading firm at the Chicago Board of Trade who'd hired students, the reports from the sponsors had been overwhelmingly positive. And the conversation with Frank Rizzo started out much the same way. He said, as most of the sponsors had, that he was thrilled to have the students and that they'd proven to be a wonderful addition to the office. "But," Rizzo said, "we've all been wondering what happened to Erubiel*, the Tuesday student. We haven't seen him since the first week."

Kendall flipped quickly to his attendance record. "Erubiel? I've dropped off Erubiel every Tuesday. I've actually watched him walk into the building. And we've picked him up each day as well."

"Oh, that's not good, because he definitely hasn't been in the office since the first day."

Later in the day, Kendall found Erubiel. It was true; he hadn't been to work. Erubiel and the other Cristo Rey students at Refco were working as runners on the floor of the Chicago Board of Trade, where they were responsible for delivering orders to traders. When a customer calls and says she wants to buy one thousand soybean contracts, an order is put on a ticket and given to the runner. The runner takes it to a broker, who attempts to execute the trade. If he can, the

---

*Not his real name.

broker fills the order and gives it back to the runner. If he can't, he keeps the ticket, and the runner comes back periodically to see if it has been filled. The Board of Trade is not a place for the meek. The floor is big, loud, and chaotic, and people don't talk there—they yell. When you screw up, they yell louder. Profanity-laced tirades are common. The whole place scared Erubiel, a timid and reserved student, so much that he told Kendall that he "just couldn't go back."

"But I watched you walk into the building," Kendall said.

"I just went into the lobby until you were gone and then I left again."

"Where'd you go?"

"All over the city," Erubiel said. "I just walked around until it was time to come back and wait for the bus."

Kendall made his second mental note: *Taking attendance from the driver's seat of the bus won't cut it. I need to verify that students are actually going to work.* He and Rosy Santiago began to call sponsors every day to confirm that students had gone into the office. They made the calls until Kendall developed a time-card system. The students had to fill out a card stating when they arrived, when they went to lunch, when they returned from lunch, and when they left work. If the students didn't come back to school with a time card signed by their supervisors, they didn't get credit for working, and they had to pay one hundred dollars for a missed day of work.

Erubiel was the only student who had skipped out on work, but some of his classmates confessed that they, too, were struggling with their work on the floor of the Board. So Preston asked Rizzo if there were any other places at Refco where the Cristo Rey students might be able to work. Rizzo assured him that everyone wanted to continue working with the students and suggested they move into office services.

"That's perfect," said Kendall.

Working Out the Work Program 15

Cristo Rey's first year was marked by numerous triumphs, challenges, and changes. One group of students, led by Gustavo Rodríguez, excelled both in the classroom and on the job. "Cristo Rey really hit a home run with Gustavo," says Mike Heaton, the partner at O'Keefe, Ashenden, Lyons & Ward who had championed Cristo Rey's cause at the firm. Pat Jiganti, who managed the Cristo Rey students at O'Keefe, says Gustavo quickly demonstrated he was capable of more than making copies and filing; soon Jiganti had him delivering documents around the city and filing official documents at city offices. At the end of the year, O'Keefe hired him for the summer. "That's really all you need to know about how well the program worked," Heaton says. "We're not in the business of giving money away here. If the students weren't pulling their weight, we wouldn't hire them over the summer."

Heaton says the students did more than just help out with the day-to-day work at O'Keefe. "I think the kids made me and the other lawyers sit back and think about how precious education is. Those students, and the ones we employ today, are willing to do a lot and sacrifice a lot for their education."

Leo Maldonado had a similar experience at Katten, Muchin & Zavis, the law firm where Paula Kendall, Preston Kendall's sister, had hired ten Cristo Rey students. Leo couldn't believe the size of the building, or the size of Katten Muchin's office, or the fact that he had a job there. "On my first day on the job, they gave me a full tour of the office," Leo says. "But when we got to floor sixteen—we were going down the floors—we stopped. The sixteenth floor was where I was going to work, in the copy center. And I met my supervisor, and he was like, 'We're kind of busy here. Can you help? We'll finish the tour later.'" Leo rolled up his sleeves and jumped in. He was given quick instructions for operating one of the small copy machines. Hours later it was time to go home. Over the course of the year, he learned how to use the bigger machines and how to bind documents. He learned how the work flowed through the copy center. He delivered urgent documents throughout the firm. He took copy orders from attorneys. "I loved my job from the first day," Leo says, "but to this day I still haven't gotten my tour."

Some students, though, struggled at work and were asked to leave. "This was a huge problem," Kendall says, "because losing a student meant losing revenue. I hadn't expected us to lose many, and I didn't have anyone to replace them. So I had to go to our sponsors and offer to give them their money back." Not a single sponsor accepted the reimbursement.

The first year just about drove Kendall to a nervous breakdown. He sensed that there was far more at stake in this job than he'd first realized. Midway through the year, he worried that the whole thing might come unglued because of one sophomore class in particular. The class was full of troublemakers, or at least trouble finders. Despite the efforts of their teachers, these students were consistently underperforming. The vast majority of complaints from corporate sponsors were about this group. Meanwhile, Kendall was barely keeping his head above water. He was managing the school's books, which had more money going out than coming in, and trying to run the internship program. Rosy Santiago, the school's admissions director, had been helping him, but she needed to focus on recruiting students for Cristo Rey's second year. Kendall knew he should be meeting one-on-one with each of the students in the group, but he didn't have time.

The school's budget didn't allow for an additional employee to run the Corporate Internship Program, but in the middle of the second semester, Kendall put an ad in the paper. He needed help. Carlos De La Rosa, a Chicago native and a recent graduate of the University of Chicago, applied for the job. The youngest of twelve, De La Rosa had come to the States with his mother as a seven-year-old undocumented immigrant in 1978. He eventually became a citizen and enrolled at Whitney Young High School, a magnet school in Chicago. He later attended the University of Chicago, and after graduation took a job with the Little Village Chamber of Commerce. He then started his own consulting business, which had not succeeded.

Kendall couldn't believe his good fortune when De La Rosa showed up for the interview. He spoke fluent Spanish, was great with computers, and had run his own business. He was articulate and professional. But most of all, he knew what it was like to grow up as an immigrant in the United States. Kendall had no doubt that De La Rosa would be able to connect with Cristo Rey's students in a way Kendall could only hope to.

❁

SOON AFTER DE LA Rosa took the job, he and Kendall took the troublesome sophomores through a team-building ropes course. It was a turning point for the group, and the school. Looking back on the first year, Kendall says he thinks the sophomores could have torpedoed the internship program and the entire school. "One of those students was working at each of our corporate sponsors, and almost every one of them had encountered problems. But we couldn't afford to lose many sponsors. In fact, we were already in the process of recruiting new sponsors because we planned to double enrollment in the coming year."

The ropes course was a hit with the students and an epiphany for Kendall. "At the end of the day, the students were all climbing this wall, and I remember one of the girls looking up and saying, 'I'm not going.' I said, 'I won't force you. But you should try. I'll go up there with you.' I thought it'd be a piece of cake.

"We climbed the wall, and when I got up there, I started looking down. I kept telling myself I was safe—I was strapped into a safety harness and wearing a helmet—but every part of my body was telling me I wasn't. My legs were shaking and my heart was pounding. It was really scary. I only realized then how much I'd been asking the students to do. All year I'd been telling them they had nothing to be scared about at work. Standing up on the ropes course, I realized how I hadn't been aware of their fear. When we came down, the girl looked up at the wall and said, 'You know, Mr. Kendall, I never thought I could do that, but I did.' She was just gazing up at the wall. And that's when I realized that this was the best thing we'd done all year. I wanted every one of our students to be able to say, 'I never thought I could, but I did.' "

The sophomores turned it around. Twelve of the seventeen original corporate sponsors eventually agreed to participate in the program the second year. Watching the students at the ropes course, Kendall also realized that the experience fit beautifully into Jesuit education. Jesuit schools all employ the Ignatian Pedagogical Paradigm, a teaching method based in large part on the spirituality of St. Ignatius of Loyola. "Basically," Kendall says, "the paradigm instructs you to give kids an experience and then ask them to reflect on it. Use the reflection to come up with a plan of action. Then take action. That's the next experience. Then you reflect again. It's action, reflection, and transformation."

In the wake of the ropes course experience, Kendall and De La Rosa rebuilt the entire Corporate Internship Program training. They developed experiential training exercises and recruited corporate sponsors to lead many of the activities. They ditched the lecture model they'd used in the first year. "Our teachers were exactly right. The students learned more from trying these things than from hearing us lecture about them." The end result was a new three-week training program loaded with challenging exercises and interactive activities designed to get students to take action, reflect, and—their teachers hoped—be transformed.

During the inaugural year, Cristo Rey's teachers put forth a herculean effort on behalf of their students. The founding teachers all say they've never been part of another school where the faculty cared so much about the students. The teachers were handcrafting the curriculum as they went—a labor-intensive process—and met regularly to evaluate their own work as well as the progress of each student. When students didn't do their homework, the teachers called home. Teachers were available for tutoring before and after school. When the school finally moved out of the gym and into the classroom building, the teachers were given a small windowless room in the basement (formerly used for storage) as an office. A desk for each teacher was crammed into the room. Not one teacher uttered a single complaint, and the room soon became the center of life at the school. Students lingered outside the door waiting to ask questions or for help on assignments. The small office was usually abuzz with activity until ten

In the wake of the ropes course experience, Kendall and De La Rosa rebuilt the entire Corporate Internship Program training. They developed experiential training exercises and recruited corporate sponsors to lead many of the activities.

The teachers were handcrafting the curriculum as they went—a labor-intensive process—and met regularly to evaluate their own work as well as the progress of each student.

or eleven at night and then again before seven in the morning. Teachers had keys to the building and were there on Saturdays and Sundays. It was incredibly exhausting work, but seeing students begin to fall in love with learning was worth it.

EVEN WITH HER BACK turned, Charo could sense that she was being watched intently by the clerk at the front of the convenience store. It made her uncomfortable. She'd been in the United States for almost six months. When her boyfriend, Mike Heidkamp, left Peru to take a job teaching at Cristo Rey, the two of them had agreed that she would come to the States as soon as she had all the necessary papers. She had arrived in November of 1996, a day before Thanksgiving. It had taken her awhile to settle into life in the United States, but by the time spring rolled around she was visiting DePaul University to inquire about enrolling in classes. She thought she might become a teacher. At the moment, she was buying lunch in a store across the street from campus.

At the checkout counter, when she tried to pay with a credit card, the clerk exploded. "What's the matter with you? Can't you read? Don't you speak English? We don't take credit cards." He pointed to a small paper sign behind the counter that said No Credit Cards.

"I'm sorry," Charo mumbled, putting the credit card back in her wallet. She didn't have any cash.

"You better be sorry. You took all these things off my shelves and now you're not going to buy them. You better find a way to buy these things, or else you better go put them back where they came from."

Then the clerk spotted two police officers standing across the street. He went outside and waved for them to come to his store.

"Hey, I've got a problem in here." The officers jogged across the street. Charo didn't understand what was happening, what she had done wrong. She saw the man from the store talking to the police officers and pointing at the store. Then the three of them walked inside, and the clerk pointed to Charo and said, "That's her."

The police asked Charo for her ID. She handed them her Illinois state ID card. They inspected it closely and then handed it back to her. They asked the clerk if everything else was okay. He explained that she'd taken things off the shelf that she didn't intend to buy. When it became clear Charo had done nothing wrong, the police left.

Later that night, shaking, she recounted the day's events to Mike, who offered to take the following day off work to go back to the store with her. She shook her head quietly, before giving Mike a detailed explanation about why she didn't want him to go to the store.

"Charo was basically saying to me that if I wanted to enter into a relationship with her, I would have to be comfortable with a level of frustration and complexity I'd never experienced as a white man living in the United States. She was reminding me that my experience is only one way of understanding the world and that if I was going to be connected to her—a person who experiences as oppressive the institutions that are familiar and affirming to me—I needed to be willing to understand her perspective."

Charo's experience as an outsider in the United States and Heidkamp's devotion to her changed the way he approached his role as a teacher. He began to ask himself a question he found very difficult to answer: "What are the most important things I can teach?"

❈

"START-UPS ARE SUPPOSED TO lose money," says Steve Baine, one of Cristo Rey's founding board members, who was then an executive vice president at First Chicago NBD. "There are start-up expenses and inefficiencies that exist at the beginning of any kind of initiative or venture like this one."

When the dust settled after Cristo Rey's first year, the school had lost eighteen students and nearly $850,000.* Losing those students didn't help the bottom line—they represented almost 20 percent of the school's revenue stream. The work program was unable to cover its own expenses in its first year of operations and ran at a deficit.

But there was much more to the problem. Cristo Rey assigned five students to each corporate internship, and those students together earned $18,000. Each family was also asked to pay $1,500 in tuition. Each group of five students thus generated $25,500 in revenue—assuming that every family paid full tuition, which few did. If Cristo Rey's revenues were to cover expenses, no more than $5,100 could be spent per student.

In its first year, Cristo Rey spent $15,420 per student. The revenue per student, when taking into consideration those who couldn't pay full tuition, was only $4,931. Thus, the school had lost $10,489 per student. Jack Crowe, the board member and attorney from Winston & Strawn who had continued to serve the school on a pro bono basis, joked that it would have been cheaper to bus the Cristo Rey students to the Latin School of Chicago, a high-priced private school on the North Side of the city.

---

*There are two ways of recording the transactions of a business—accrual accounting and cash accounting. The difference between the two methods is in the time in which a sale is credited to an account or a purchase is debited from it. In accrual accounting, a sale or purchase is accounted for when it happens, even if money hasn't yet changed hands. Cash accounting only recognizes revenue and expenses when cash is received or paid. It does not recognize promises to pay or expected payments. Accrual accounting is the standard accounting practice for most companies. Many start-ups and small enterprises use cash accounting, which is what Cristo Rey did in its early years. This book focuses primarily on figures generated using cash accounting.

Rick Murray says he saw it coming: "There was a lack of discipline regarding spending." Cristo Rey had hired far more people than he'd allowed for in the initial projections. The school had also started with fewer than 100 students when the plan had called for 150. Murray knew the school would lose money in its first year, and it rankled him. But he, like Baine, was a businessman and knew that start-ups were expected to lose money.

"All the spending decisions were made because John, Judy, or the faculty felt the students needed certain things. It wasn't frivolous or wasteful spending in that sense. But it was money the school didn't have."

Murray became more and more discouraged, though, over the course of the first year as spending mounted and departing students strangled the school's revenue stream. "All the spending decisions were made because John, Judy, or the faculty felt the students needed certain things. It wasn't frivolous or wasteful spending in that sense. But it was money the school didn't have." Murray felt that Cristo Rey's administrators were bungling the implementation of his model. It was becoming clear to Murray that the school, as it was being run, would likely never generate the profits he predicted it could. Nor would it ever be able to help its graduates repay their loans. Murray regularly made his feelings known to Foley. But the school's administrators, Foley says, "didn't think Murray's plan was realistic given the population they were trying to serve." Around that time, the school began to part ways with Murray.

The board, which was responsible for the financial stewardship of the school, met quarterly. By the time the third meeting took place, in early February 1997, the school was clearly in financial distress. Baine and Crowe, board members with financial acumen and extensive business experience, advocated ramping up the school's enrollment as quickly as possible in an effort to boost revenues. Peggy Mueller, who'd spent her career working as an educator and for foundations and not-for-profits that supported education, felt that dramatically increasing enrollment could compromise the quality of the education being offered at Cristo Rey.

Today Mueller says, "I knew that one of the greatest challenges in this city, and in the nation, were the high schools, because we're failing at that level of education pretty dramatically." The talk of increasing the size of Cristo Rey alarmed her. At different times, people had raised the possibility of the school growing to one thousand or even two thousand students. She and Judy Murphy, though, had advocated for keeping the school much smaller. "We needed to take into account new knowledge about what size high schools work most effectively for urban children as well as what programs are needed to support their learning," Mueller says. "A school of 1,000 or 2,000 students could potentially compromise the ability of the school to serve students who needed a setting in which they were well-known by teachers and where their linguistic, cultural, and academic assets and needs were constantly addressed."

On the other side of the table, Baine argued that Cristo Rey had certain fixed costs—utilities, rent, salaries, and benefits for administrators and staff—and that more students meant a lower fixed cost per student. Members of the board's finance contingent were pushing to expand the enrollment to 750 or even 1,000—anything less, they believed, would result in the school continuing to hemorrhage money.

In the wake of the January board meeting, the board's academic affairs committee and facilities and finance committee both conducted studies about how the school could increase enrollment. At the April 1997 board meeting, the academic affairs committee cautioned against rapid growth and stressed the need for maintaining an academic program that could respond to the unique academic and cultural needs even as enrollment grew. They strongly recommended that class sizes at Cristo Rey not exceed twenty-five students and total enrollment be grown slowly and carefully.

The facilities and finance committee looked closely at the school's financial situation and determined that the school couldn't be sustainable with fewer than five hundred students. And because of student attrition, the committee believed it was better to have *more* than five hundred students. In its report, the committee recommended that the board create a building subcommittee and grant it fifty thousand dollars to conduct a study of how Cristo Rey could expand its physical plant to accommodate the needed increase in enrollment. The building subcommittee would be charged with looking at expanding the current school, purchasing an existing facility in Pilsen that could be converted into a school or building a new school somewhere in Pilsen/Little Village.

The minutes from the April 28, 1997, board meeting exhibit growing tension between the academic and financial players on the board. It was becoming clear that they had very different—and often conflicting—approaches to building and managing Cristo Rey. Representatives from the board's finance committee had sparred with those from the academic contingent in the February and April meetings about the amount of time Cristo Rey's teachers spent in the classroom. The finance side felt the teachers didn't teach enough. The academic side argued that some of the faculty's most important work actually happened outside the classroom, when they were designing a curriculum that their students would find engaging. Following is an excerpt from the board meeting minutes on the academic committee's report:

> Faculty is learning how to do integrated curriculum; the students are learning a new way of being, and those things require a lot more attention. The present schedule even though appearing thin is not, because the time the teachers are not teaching serves for planning and working together in integrated curriculum, dual language, etc.

The finance committee saw something else, as illustrated in its report:

> We need cost-saving ideas. The morale is extraordinarily high, and that is very positive. But everything is fragile; you can only push things so far. We must work toward operating in the black. . . . Two things that need to be kept in mind is that if we went to a comparable bilingual setting we would find that they are more expensive than regular programs. Block scheduling requires a 23 percent increase of the cost for teaching staff over traditional teaching.

The academic affairs and facilities and finance committees wanted the same thing—for the school to serve its students as well as it possibly could—but they had different ideas about how to do that. The situation was further complicated in May 1997 when Lou Nieto, Cristo Rey's board chair, stepped down. His decision had nothing to do with the school's performance in the first year. He was an executive

Joseph "Joey" Garcia

Mayra Hernandez

Billy Holiday

Audelio "Leo" Maldonado

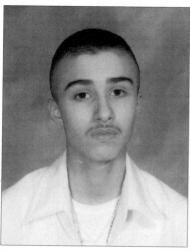

Frank Rojas

Maritza Santibáñez-Luna

Left: A view of downtown Chicago from Cristo Rey, which is located on the Lower West Side of the city

Below: Blue Island Avenue just south of 18th Street, the heart of Pilsen, a neighborhood populated primarily by Latino immigrants since the 1960s

Above: During the initial feasibility study for the school, Fr. Jim Gartland conducted scores of formal interviews and many more informal interviews like this one with residents of Pilsen.

Right: During Phase II of the feasibility study, Fr. Ted Munz determined that the Jesuits should open a high school, but he struggled with how to fund it.

Right: In January, 1996, Fr. Brad Schaeffer, the Provincial who'd led the Jesuits into Pilsen, formally announced that the Jesuits would open Cristo Rey Jesuit High School . . . in nine months. At the time, the school didn't yet have a building, a teacher, or a registered student.

Below: Rick Murray, the management consultant who dreamed up and designed Cristo Rey's Corporate Internship Program

On August 26, 1996, then First Lady Hillary Clinton formally "opened" Cristo Rey, a few weeks before the school opened its doors to students.

Above: Cristo Rey held its first classes and sent its first students to work on September 30, 1996.

Right: Germán Indacochea has served as math teacher and dean of students and is one of the two original faculty members who still teach at Cristo Rey.

Above: Fr. Steve Planning, Fr. Lou Busmeyer, Fr. John P. Foley, and Br. Dave Henderson, the Jesuits who opened Cristo Rey

Right: Original Leadership Team: Jeff Thielman, Fr. John Foley, Sr. Judy Murphy, and Preston Kendall

Cristo Rey Students at Work

Left: Nora Perez searches for blueprints at McGuire Engineers.

Below: A Cristo Rey student on the floor of the Chicago Board of Trade, a job that proved short-lived

Left: Wester Camacho worked at Loyola Press (the publisher of this book) while a student at Cristo Rey. Today Wester continues to work at Loyola while pursuing an undergraduate degree in accounting. Loyola is one of the seven original corporate sponsors who continue to employ students today.

Right: A Cristo Rey student working at JPMorgan Chase

Right: Jim Wall, an English teacher shown here overseeing Cristo Rey's yearbook staff, was part of the school's founding faculty.

Below: Cristo Rey students examine a crime scene during the Active Learners capstone experience, a forensic investigation and trial.

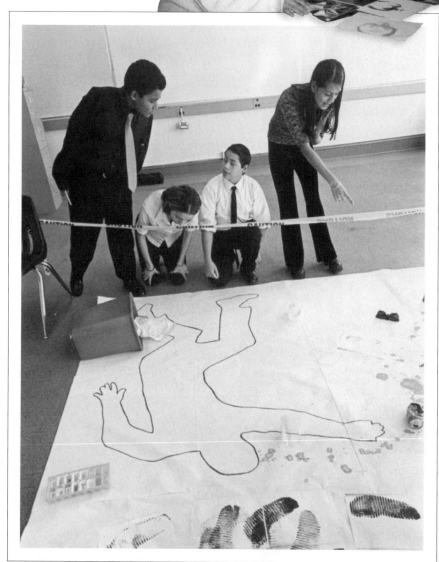

Mike Heidkamp, who returned from Peru to become a member of Cristo Rey's founding faculty

© Steve Donisch

© Steve Donisch

Sr. Frances Thibodeau, a member of Cristo Rey's founding faculty, continues to teach English and religion at the school.

© Root Studios

© Steve Donisch

Cornerstone laying ceremony for Cristo Rey's new classroom building. (L to R) Tony McGuire, board member and corporate sponsor; Jeff Thielman, development director; Fr. John Foley, president; Sr. Judy Murphy, principal; Rosemary Croghan, board chairperson; Fr. Larry Reuter, board member; Preston Kendall, CIP director and executive vice-president; and Peggy Mueller, board member

Fr. John Foley and Jeff Thielman with venture capitalist B. J. Cassin, who with his wife, Bebe, created the Cassin Educational Initiative Foundation to support the replication of Cristo Rey

(L to R) Rosa Sánchez Walke, who has taught English and Spanish at Cristo Rey since 1997; Carlos De La Rosa, who joined Cristo Rey midway through the first year and is currently the school's CIP director; Patricia "Pat" Garrity, Cristo Rey's current principal

Fr. Jim Gartland returned to Cristo Rey as a faculty member in 2000. He currently serves as president of the school.

with Kraft Foods and had been tapped for a promotion that required he move to Los Angeles.

At the conclusion of its first year, Cristo Rey had lost close to one million dollars, was without a board chair, was preparing to nearly double the size of its faculty, was faced with the prospect of massive budget cuts, and would close in a few years if it couldn't boost enrollment in a hurry.

Deeper into the Red 16

CRISTO REY NEEDED MONEY.

Little attention had been paid to fund-raising during Cristo Rey's first year because the school's aim had been merely self-sufficiency—and because there was so much else that needed to be done. Rather than hiring a full-time fund-raiser, the board had created a development committee whose members frequently wrote checks and encouraged their friends to do the same. Aside from a newsletter assembled by some of Cristo Rey's first employees and a Christmas appeal letter, there was little in the way of an official fund-raising operation. At the beginning of the school's second year, aware that Cristo Rey was already in a precarious financial position, the Chicago Province Jesuits pledged up to two million dollars to help make ends meet.*

---

*Many wonder how the Jesuits, a religious order with a vow of poverty, can be in a position to give away two million dollars. The fairly simple answer is that individual Jesuits take vows of poverty and can't accumulate money. The order, though, can and does accumulate funds for operating its ministries, educating its new members, caring for its older members, and providing for international ministries. The funds come from benefactors and from the income of individual Jesuits. When Jesuits work in ministries that can afford to compensate them for their efforts—high schools, hospitals, and colleges—they are paid. Their income, though, goes to their community, and most of the surplus goes to the province. At the time, the Chicago Province had two very successful authors—Fr. Mark Link, SJ, and Fr. John Powell, SJ—and the millions of dollars of income they generated coupled with the generosity of benefactors resulted in a strong financial standing that allowed the Jesuits to make such a substantial gift.

The Jesuits had set out to create a school that wouldn't have to rely on charity, yet after just one year they found themselves making a charitable contribution to keep the school afloat while John Foley and the board began to work out ways to raise money. The realization that Cristo Rey needed a fund-raising office came at a retreat attended by board members during the summer of 1997. "I remember thinking, 'Oh, a retreat—that will be nice,'" says board member Rosemary Croghan. "Then I got the agenda and saw that the retreat was being held at a law firm. That's when I figured out we weren't going to a spiritual retreat. We were going to be working."

※

BY THE END OF the retreat, the academic affairs committee had agreed to take one hundred freshmen for the 1997–98 school year and had signed off on a rough draft of a plan to increase enrollment to six hundred students. Their principal goal was to "reconcile academic goals with financial realities." The facilities and finance committee formalized its plan to expand Cristo Rey's physical plant to accommodate the increased enrollment. A new ten-classroom building would be constructed adjacent to the existing building.

In order to build, the school would have to purchase and demolish a number of homes. The entire process would be enormously expensive and equally complicated, and no one expected the revenue generated by Cristo Rey's students to cover the cost of construction. Instead, Cristo Rey would launch a capital campaign to raise the needed funds. The board members didn't settle on a number at the retreat but talked about a target of three to four million dollars. Everyone present knew that the school needed a professional to raise that kind of money. They set a goal to hire a fund-raiser by September 15, 1997, and to launch the capital campaign by early 1998.

In addition to pushing the school toward sustainability, reining in expenses, recruiting corporate sponsors, and overseeing the development of a radically innovative curriculum, the board would have to manage the acquisition of property and the construction of the new building. The new board chair would play a critical role in all of this. That's why Foley's pick for the job surprised everyone.

Despite the fact that the board had a number of business and educational leaders, Foley turned to Rosemary Croghan, one of only three board members without experience in schools or business, to chair the board. Croghan, a diminutive, soft-spoken mother of six who had worked for ten years as a nurse, hardly seemed the dynamic leader needed to steer the school through challenging waters over the next few years.

Croghan's father, Joseph Anderlik, was born in Pilsen to Bohemian parents and baptized at St. Procopius. In 1918, Anderlik, a pianist who'd been sent to Mexico City by the piano business he worked for, met and fell in love with Maria Rosa Diez. They married in Mexico and had their first child there. In 1924, they returned to Chicago and settled in a neighborhood on the northwest side populated by Irish, German, and Polish immigrants and soon had three more children. "My dad spoke and wrote Spanish beautifully," Croghan says. "My parents spoke to each other in Spanish. My mom talked to us in Spanish, and Dad talked to us in English. We talked among ourselves and back to them in English." Croghan attended Immaculata high school on the city's north side and the St. Francis Hospital School of Nursing. In 1954, while working, she met John Croghan, who was visiting his father in the hospital. She and John married less than a year later.

When Croghan and her husband, a Chicago investment mogul, first heard about Cristo Rey in 1995, it was still just an idea. But it was

an idea they both liked, and they asked their parish priest to introduce them to Foley. The Croghans were already generous supporters
of a number of Catholic charities and virtually every Jesuit institution in Chicago, and soon after Foley first visited them, he invited
Rosemary Croghan to join the Cristo Rey board. Her cultural heritage combined with the couple's track record of philanthropy made
her a logical choice. Most boards of trustees are made up of people
who can do at least one of three things: provide substantial financial
support, encourage friends and family to do the same, and provide
legal, business, academic, or strategic counsel. Ideally, a board member could do all three. Rosemary Croghan could definitely help with
the first and probably the second. Many wondered, though, if she
was the right person to chair the board at Cristo Rey, with its many
pressing needs.

That autumn, the Croghans pledged one million dollars to the
silent phase of the upcoming capital campaign. Croghan then set
about encouraging other board members and friends to lend their
support to the school. Another family pledged one million dollars. Other board members made gifts of $500,000, $250,000, and
$100,000. By the end of the year, Croghan had helped amass more
than two million dollars in additional pledges—most of which came
from the school's board.

✸

CRISTO REY'S FLEDGLING FUND-RAISING effort got a jump
start in the beginning of the school's second year when a Chicago
businessman and friend of John Costello pledged nearly seven hundred thousand dollars to help start up a fund-raising operation at
the school. Foley knew the gift would be enormously helpful, but
he still hadn't found the development director who would be able to

put the money they had raised to good use. That changed when Jeff Thielman visited Chicago.

Thielman and Foley had first met in Tacna, Peru, in October 1985. Five months earlier, Thielman had graduated from Boston College, where he majored in political science and philosophy and served as president of the student body. He'd grown up in a largely unreligious family, though his grandparents had always taken him to Mass. In his years at Boston College—during which he met many Jesuits—Thielman found himself drawn to the church and more interested in attending Mass, which had seemed like a chore to him when he was a child. During his senior year, in the midst of applying to law school, he realized that he wanted to do something with the church, something faith-based, something, he says, "that mattered."

At that time, Boston College ran an international volunteer program that sent students to volunteer in Jesuit ministries in Peru, Egypt, Belize, and Jamaica. On the day his first law school acceptance letter arrived, Thielman applied to the volunteer program. Days later, Fr. Julio Giuletti, SJ, the charismatic Jesuit who ran the program, called and offered Thielman a position in Peru. "Why don't you come into my office, and I'll tell you about it."

"I didn't know exactly where Peru was," Thielman says, "so the first thing I did was look at a map." At their meeting, Thielman told Giuletti he was excited about the opportunity and planned to defer law school for a year. Giuletti told him that wouldn't work. "It's a two-year program, and the school year in Peru doesn't start until March."

"So I'd be there for three years?" Thielman asked. Giuletti nodded. Thielman was hesitant. He'd already been accepted to the law schools at George Washington University and the University of Connecticut and still planned to become a lawyer. Three years was a long time to wait. Ultimately, it was a conversation with Fr. Robert Drinan, a Jesuit priest who had served in the House of Representatives and was then a law professor at Georgetown University, that convinced Thielman to go. "Jeff, you've got your whole life to practice law," Drinan said. "Go be a volunteer." Thielman accepted the offer and was assigned to teach English at Colegio Cristo Rey, a private Jesuit high school in Tacna, Peru. When he talks about his first few months in Peru, Thielman says things like "culture clash," "trial by fire," "lonely," and "lost." (He offers an amusing, heartwarming, and informative account of his experience in his book, coauthored with Fr. Raymond Schroth, SJ, *Volunteer with the Poor in Peru*.)

A couple weeks into classes, it became clear to Thielman that despite more than a month of training, his Spanish was awful. Students were laughing at him. His class was a joke. He worried that none of the students were learning anything. He was frustrated— and angry. He wanted to go home; he'd left a girlfriend back in the States. On an afternoon in late March, he was sitting on a bench in Tacna feeling sorry for himself and considering dropping out of the program and going home when a small boy offered to shine his shoes. Thielman knew all about the working kids in Tacna—they were desperately poor and lived on the streets. They shined shoes, washed cars, and sold newspapers. Most of them had come to the city from smaller, rural towns. Often their parents, who struggled to feed and clothe them, sent them into the city so there would be one less mouth to feed. Plus, the children usually earned a bit of extra money.

Thielman, who'd been staring at the dirt beneath his feet, remembers looking up at the dusty face of the boy, who he suspected was no more than eight years old. "I thought, *I've got a hell of a lot of nerve feeling sorry for myself.* And then I started thinking maybe I could do something to help these kids." He went back to Colegio

Cristo Rey and asked his students to think about ways they could help the working kids as part of their required social service project. They organized a soccer game at the high school field for the working kids, and scores of them showed up. Playing soccer was nice, but Thielman knew these kids had literally nothing and knew he could do much more. That was the start of the Centro Cristo Rey del Niño Trabajador, the Cristo Rey Center for the Working Child.

Over the next three and a half years, Thielman worked tirelessly on the project. He managed to acquire a small building in Tacna, which he used to establish the center. It served essentially as a home for the working children. The building had no beds, but the children were welcome to congregate there during the day, play games, clean up, and eat. The center was always crowded—too crowded. After a year of relentless campaigning, negotiating, and fast-talking, Thielman convinced the local government to give him land on which to build a bigger center. He returned to the United States for what proved to be very fruitful fund-raising trips.

In 1989, Thielman left Peru and returned to the United States to attend law school—by that time, he'd stayed in Peru for a year and a half beyond the end of his volunteer commitment and the center he'd started was flourishing. Soon thereafter, John Foley assumed direction of the Cristo Rey Center for the Working Child, which had become an official ministry of the Peruvian Jesuits. Today the center occupies a 7,200-square-meter piece of property on the outskirts of Tacna and also runs an overnight shelter in the city center. Between these two campuses, the center offers the working children a health center, a legal aid clinic, an eight-classroom building with a cafeteria, a library, a chapel, and four rooms for technical training. Each year it serves three hundred children and their families; since its inception in 1986, it has offered services to roughly six thousand working children. There are currently ten people on staff, including a Jesuit brother who serves as the director, social workers, staff for the overnight shelter, and a group of Peruvian volunteers. The health center is staffed by an independent group of alumni from Colegio Cristo Rey and serves both working children and local families. Since leaving Peru, Thielman has continued to promote the center and each year travels to a handful of Catholic parishes in the United States to make appeals on behalf of the center.

In August, 1997, Thielman was in Chicago for the Jesuit Development Office's annual donor recognition dinner. At the time, he was an agent at Northwestern Mutual Life Insurance in Boston. After returning from Peru, he'd studied law at Boston College and gone into private practice. Months after passing the bar, he argued his first trial, which involved defending his boss in a sexual harassment suit. Thielman, who worked nonstop on the trial, unearthed inconsistencies in the plaintiff's story and, he says, "destroyed her" in his cross-examination. On the trial's final day, he vomited in the courthouse bathroom and then delivered a compelling closing argument. He won, but the experience soured him on the law, so he left and took a job at Northwestern Mutual Life.

Thielman had been invited to the Jesuits' donor recognition dinner because he had made a substantial gift to the Chicago Province Jesuits for the center in Peru. Before the dinner, he and Foley went for a walk along Chicago's lakefront. Foley told him about Cristo Rey, and Thielman spoke about his work as an attorney and his work at Northwestern Mutual Life helping individuals build retirement plans. "Things are going okay," he said. "I'm pretty happy."

"But, Jeff," Foley asked, "what are you doing for the kingdom?"

Thielman knew exactly what he meant; the Jesuits used that language all the time. They talked about building the kingdom of

God on earth. He didn't have an answer. "I don't know," he said. Looking back, Thielman is grateful for the question. "He was asking me, 'Is this it? Are you doing what you're called to do?'"

"But, Jeff," Foley asked, "what are you doing for the kingdom?"

Then Foley asked Thielman if he'd think about coming to Chicago to be the development director at Cristo Rey. "I hadn't planned on asking Jeff to take the job," Foley says. "He didn't have any formal fundraising experience. But as we were walking along the lake, the idea came to me, and I just felt it would work. I thought Jeff would be great."

"I thought about John's question a lot," Thielman says. "It was really a great question. I started to think I was being way too cautious. I shouldn't waste ten years of my life trying to pay off my bills. I should just do what I love to do." Six weeks later he called Foley and told him he'd take the job. Foley was ecstatic, though he knew it would be tough to explain to the board that the "professional development director" he'd hired had two weekends worth of fundraising experience, had never applied for a grant, and had never managed a large-scale special event,

When Thielman arrived in January 1998, the board was still debating how much money they wanted to raise. They agreed that $12 million dollars would just about cover the cost of the building and might result in enough left over to start an endowment, but many on the board, especially those who had served or were currently serving on other boards, didn't think Cristo Rey could raise anywhere near that much. Thielman's hiring didn't help. He didn't know a soul in Chicago. He'd never raised money on this scale. The school didn't have any alumni. The parents weren't in a position to make gifts. Twelve million dollars, many of the board members said, was simply out of the question.

The uncertainty about the campaign goal didn't stop Thielman from getting to work. Remarkably, not knowing anyone in Chicago didn't seem to hinder him at all. In fact, it may have been one of his greatest advantages. Because he didn't know anyone, he wasn't afraid of anyone. As soon as he showed up in Chicago in January, he started making a list of donors. He got names from board members, from Foley, from anyone who'd give them to him. Then he invited the people on the list to come to the school so he could "show them the product." His focus, though, wasn't on raising money to cover the school's operating expenses; the work program would eventually do that. He was there to raise money for a building.

Thielman's office was located in the modest rectory adjacent to Cristo Rey. He lived in a small basement apartment in the building and worked between twelve and fourteen hours each day. He remembers the work as thrilling. "There was enormous potential. Lots of people were already supporting the school when I got there. At that time, every single one of our grant requests to local foundations had been approved. That's unheard of. When I got there, I just started stumbling around. It was all about seeing people, calling them, getting in front of them, talking to them, showing them the product, and selling the idea."

Rosemary and John Croghan hosted a dinner at a downtown club to introduce Thielman to some of their friends, friends who could certainly help finance a building. Steve Baine hosted a lunch. Thielman documented everything he did, each visit and each request for funding. The donor whose gift was financing Thielman's work wanted to see proof that it was really happening and that his money was being put to good use. It was; in Thielman's first six months at the school, he raised close to two million dollars. All told, the capital campaign, including the silent phase that predated Thielman and the pledge from the Jesuits, had already raised nearly seven million dollars.

Jack Crowe says, "On the board, we started to wonder if we'd somehow hired the Michael Jordan of fund-raising."

✳

THE REDESIGNED CORPORATE INTERNSHIP Program (CIP) training launched by Kendall and De La Rosa at the beginning of the second school year was a smash. The CIP training had proven so valuable the year before that all new students were required to attend a similar three-week training program in August, before school started. Kendall and De La Rosa hired a local carpenter to replicate many of the challenges they'd seen at the ropes course. Every incoming freshman spent a day and a half working in teams on various "challenge exercises" facilitated by the CIP staff, a handful of teachers, and corporate sponsors who volunteered to help. There were also classroom exercises, though Kendall and De La Rosa tried to make them more interactive. Students practiced their handshakes and introductions, studied maps of Chicago, took basic computer classes, and practiced sending faxes and making copies.

The new CIP training was just one of many changes evident at the start of Cristo Rey's second year. The faculty had grown to accommodate the student body, which had expanded to include a freshman class of eighty students and a sophomore class of thirty-nine students. With a seasoned first-year faculty to anchor the school, Murphy hired younger teachers in year two. Rosa Sánchez, who had spent two years teaching in Peru after graduating from Carleton College in 1995, would teach Spanish and English; Brent Dexter, a twenty-two-year-old graduate of Grinnell College who'd completed the Urban Education Program offered by the Associated Colleges of the Midwest, was hired to teach global issues and other social studies classes; Julie Minikel-Lacocque, a twenty-five-year-old Carleton College graduate who had focused on

English as a second language (ESL) in the Urban Education Program and had taught Spanish in public schools in Milwaukee and Chicago, would teach ESL and Spanish; Jeff Susor, a twenty-six-year-old who'd spent two years teaching in Micronesia as part of Jesuit Volunteers International and two years clerking at a law firm in Chicago, would teach English; Chris Nanni, a thirty-one-year-old Notre Dame alum who'd volunteered in Portland, Orlando, and the Dominican Republic before becoming the director of a community center for Latinos in South Bend, became the assistant principal; and Bridget Rush, a twenty-seven-year-old with an MA in theology from Loyola University Chicago who'd just completed a year of service as a Claretian Volunteer at a Latino parish in Chicago, would be the school's second religion teacher. Murphy hired as many bilingual teachers as possible in an effort to create a faculty capable of executing the school's dual-language curriculum.

The combination of new teachers and veterans created a sort of "dream team" faculty remarkably well equipped to continue the design and implementation of the school's innovative student-centered curriculum. Just as they had in the first year, the teachers gathered at Cristo Rey in early August to prepare for the start of school. The ten new teachers moved into the already cramped faculty room in the basement of the school. Bridget Rush says the lack of space didn't matter and that from day one, being at Cristo Rey was "invigorating." "I was ecstatic to be there. It was a godsend to be with those coworkers in that environment."

Julie Minikel-Lacocque, who is now pursuing a PhD in ESL and bilingual studies at the University of Wisconsin–Madison, echoes Rush's sentiments.

"Cristo Rey was different in so many ways. The first thing that comes to mind is the collaboration and support between teachers. It was a one-of-a-kind atmosphere, especially for the first two years I was there. I'd worked in five or six schools before I got to Cristo Rey. I'd never seen that spirit of collaboration before, and I've never seen it since. Part of it may have been the fact that we were all in that crappy room. In a lot of schools, you have your own room. You eat lunch in your room. You go to your room during your free period and grade papers. But we all had our desks in that one small room. It forced us to share the space and ideas. But it was more than that. The faculty had made a conscious decision not to divide ourselves into departments. That had nothing to do with physical space."

> "I'd worked in five or six schools before I got to Cristo Rey. I'd never seen that spirit of collaboration before, and I've never seen it since."

During the second year, Cristo Rey's growing faculty grappled with how best to institutionalize this unique collaboration. The block schedule afforded the teachers the flexibility to make connections between different subject areas and classes, to sometimes teach in teams, and to regularly straddle a number of subjects. Even when they weren't formally team teaching, the teachers shared ideas. Because of their physical proximity to one another, religion teachers talked to social studies teachers, and math teachers talked to science teachers. They were learning from each other. At faculty meetings, they continued to check their progress against benchmarks laid out in *Breaking Ranks*. It was routine for teachers to stay at school until eight or nine at night preparing for the following day's classes. But there were no complaints, at least not that year. The experience of

personally shepherding struggling students was so intensely rewarding that the teachers were, without exception, thrilled to do it.

❀

LEO SHOOK HIS HEAD as Sr. Frances Thibodeau handed out copies
of *The Killer Angels,* a novel about the Battle of Gettysburg. Thibodeau,
a longtime teacher blessed with seemingly unending patience, set the
book on Leo's desk and continued down the aisle, distributing the
already worn paperbacks to the rest of the class. Before coming to
Cristo Rey, she'd taught exclusively at middle schools. Her first class
at an international boarding school run by the Dominicans in Rome
had included twenty-five students of twenty-two different nation-
alities. She had taught the children of Irish Catholic immigrants in
a parish school on Staten Island before moving to St. Thomas the
Apostle, a predominantly African American parish on the South Side
of Chicago.

At Cristo Rey, Thibodeau discovered that high school students
were often more obstinate than middle schoolers. A handful of students at Cristo Rey—Leo was one of them—simply refused to do
their homework. Thibodeau knew when she set the book on Leo's
desk that he had no intention of reading it. But she knew, too, that
behind all his bravado, Leo was like many of the other students she'd
taught: he was essentially a good child who lacked direction or motivation or some combination of the two.

Thibodeau assigned roughly ten pages per night from the book.
Leo didn't read any of it and failed all the quizzes. During his sophomore year, Leo hadn't failed any classes. And Thibodeau knew he
probably wouldn't fail her class. At the end of the semester, he'd
manage to ace the test and get a C or a D in the class. Or just when
he was about to reach the point of no return, he'd start handing in

assignments. But she knew he was capable of much more, and she wasn't willing to stand by and let him do nothing. So, at the end of class one day, after Leo and a few of his classmates had bombed a quiz, Thibodeau told them to return to the classroom at lunch.

"What for?" Leo asked.

"We're going to work on the book."

"Man, I hate this book."

"You're not even reading it," Thibodeau said. "You couldn't possibly hate it."

Leo and his classmates showed up during the first half of their lunch period, which was generally reserved for study hall. Thibodeau sat at one of the student desks with a tape recorder and a recorded version of *The Killer Angels*. She sat the boys down and started the tape. They listened, their faces blank. Thibodeau told them they'd have to return each day until they finished the book. The next day they showed up, listened for half an hour, and promptly left for lunch. This continued for over a week.

Halfway through the second week, Thibodeau shut off the tape recorder when the half hour was up. "Wait," Leo said. "I wanna see what happens. I'll skip lunch if you'll keep playing it."

"Are you enjoying the story?" Thibodeau asked.

"I just wanna see what happens."

"Then why don't you take the book to lunch and read it."

"Don't push it, Sister," Leo said, smiling. Then he went to lunch. But Thibodeau knew something had happened, something momentous. For the first time in his life, Leo had expressed a desire to learn something. He'd discovered the joy of story. It was a baby step, but it was, unquestionably, a step forward.

❈

THE PACE OF CURRICULUM development became a bone of contention between Cristo Rey's faculty and board during the school's second year. The board was anxious to put the curriculum down on paper, which would facilitate planning and budgeting. Murphy and the faculty weren't ready to make that kind of commitment. They were still trying many new techniques and didn't yet have a firm grasp of what worked and what didn't.

At the same time, a group of teachers—including Mike Heidkamp, Dave Galvan, Mary Morrison, Rosa Sánchez, Alex Basson, Jeff Susor, and Germán Indacochea—were discussing the possibility of a new class that would help Cristo Rey students catch up with their peers at other college-preparatory schools. The teachers were voluntarily dedicating substantial chunks of time before and after school and on the weekends to work on the idea. The question they asked themselves was what could Cristo Rey do to accelerate college preparation for its students? As incoming freshmen, most of Cristo Rey's students were well behind their peers. This group of teachers believed that it wasn't enough to simply give the students information they were expected to know when they got to college.

"There was a question," Heidkamp says, "about teaching knowledge for the sake of knowledge. We all wondered how well that works in terms of what students actually take with them. We felt that in order for many of those early students to be prepared for college—and given how much ground needed to be covered—they were going to need to take a greater amount of ownership over their education than, say, I needed to take when I was their age. Because of this, we wanted to develop a course that would address attitudinal aspects of their education. Instead of pretending we could, in four years, teach them everything they needed to know, we wanted to equip them with the ability to constantly learn what they felt they needed to know. We wanted to foster in them the belief and confidence that not knowing something was okay as long as they were capable of seeking out the answer, as opposed to simply having it given to them. We wanted them to know this was a natural part of the educational process.

The first graduation was a triumph for the school. Thirteen of the nineteen graduating seniors would enroll in college in the coming fall.

Once the faculty had figured out the best way to prepare their students for college and life, they would formalize a curriculum. Until then, they were willing to custom build classroom experiences based on the needs of their students. Designing and redesigning classes was labor intensive, but the faculty gladly accepted the responsibility—and most of the teachers enjoyed it. In light of this, they were somewhat perplexed by the board's desire to have a curriculum formalized so quickly. They weren't being paid extra for their efforts, and they enjoyed the work, so what was the rush?

❋

CRISTO REY'S SMALL GYM was abuzz with activity on June 19, 1998, the day of the school's first graduation. Br. Dave Henderson and the maintenance crew had shined the stage, mopped the gym floor, and set up lines of folding chairs. Families, corporate sponsors, and donors filled the seats. Most of the freshmen, sophomores, and juniors were also there. News cameras lined the back wall, and reporters from the local papers were in attendance.

The first graduation was a triumph for the school. Thirteen of the nineteen graduating seniors would enroll in college in the coming fall. Gustavo Rodríguez had been accepted to Xavier University, a Jesuit school in Cincinnati, and offered a presidential scholarship. Other Cristo Rey students had been accepted at Barat College, Benedictine

University, Concordia University Chicago, DePaul University, Dominican University, Lewis University, Loyola University Chicago, Marquette University, Rockhurst College, Saint Louis University, Saint Peter's College, Saint Xavier University, and University of Detroit Mercy, among others.

Leo, a junior at the time, remembers that all week there had been talk about the graduating seniors who were going on to college—about the opportunities they'd earned and how great it was that they would be able to continue their studies. But Leo couldn't imagine why anyone would want to study more. The school had printed programs for graduation that included a list of the different colleges and universities the seniors would be attending. Leo thought it was funny, listening to the other kids talk about the colleges. The names meant nothing to him, but the other kids in his class seemed to think college was a big deal. They all talked about wanting to go to college, too, and about where they wanted to go. Leo just kept quiet. He'd never been to a college, and he didn't want to go to one. He just wanted to finish the last week of school so he could go work full-time in the copy room at Katten, Muchin & Zavis. His corporate sponsor had hired him for the summer, and he had an opportunity to make almost $70 a day. That was $350 a week, $1,400 a month, and over $3,000 for the summer. Why, he wondered, did all these kids want to go to college when they could go to work and start making money?

Many of the parents cried as their children accepted diplomas during the graduation ceremony. In many cases, these were the first members of their families to graduate from high school and the first to go on to college. At the end of the ceremony, the teachers gathered spontaneously near the back of the gym to applaud the students as they recessed from the stage, diplomas in hand.

The week after graduation, final exams were given to Cristo Rey's freshmen, sophomores, and juniors. At the end of the school's second year, the financial results were worse than those posted in the first year. Between tuition and sponsor contracts, Cristo Rey had generated $887,000 in revenues. Its total expenses, though, were $2,138,000—a loss of $1,251,000. The cost per student fell slightly because there were more students over which to divide the total, but the fact remained that the school was spending too much money—or wasn't generating enough revenue.

Cristo Rey was able to meet its short-term capital needs thanks to the gift from the Jesuits. The hope, though, had been that most of the money the Jesuits had pledged could be used for the new building, and not to offset annual operating deficits. Thielman and Foley had, despite the skepticism of some board members, convinced the board to approve a twelve-million-dollar capital campaign, and Thielman wanted to put as much of the annual appeal as possible into it.

On one level, Cristo Rey was working splendidly. Students were coming to class and going to work. Teachers were developing classroom experiences that engaged students, and the students seemed to be learning. But the school was proving to be a financial disaster, regularly spending far more than it was able to earn.

What Am I Going to Do in College?

17

ARITZA SANTIBÁÑEZ-LUNA, WHO HAD unsuccessfully applied to public magnet school Whitney Young, was one of the 107 freshmen students who enrolled at Cristo Rey in the fall of 1998. Maritza's mother, Socorro, was astounded when she heard about such a cheap private school in the neighborhood. She had refused to send Maritza to Farragut, having heard so many bad things about the school, and was thinking about sending her back to Mexico. Cristo Rey seemed like a perfect alternative. But Maritza didn't want to go to a private school. She agreed to apply only after her grandmother called from Mexico to urge her to. Like almost everyone else who applied that year, she was accepted.

❄

MARITZA'S SCHEDULE INCLUDED SOMETHING called Active Learners. The class was the result of hours of discussion and research undertaken by the small informal committee of faculty members seeking better ways to prepare Cristo Rey's students for college. No class like it was being offered anywhere in Illinois or, quite likely, anywhere in the country. The semester-long classroom experience would last three hours each day and would be managed by two teachers. It would not be lecture based but instead would require students to participate in a variety of activities.

"Our goal was to create a gateway course that accelerated the pace at which the students would be prepared for college by doing three key things," Heidkamp explains. "First was explicitly communicating that expectations would be very high by placing much greater responsibility on the shoulders of the students for their own learning. We tried to create a classroom environment in which students were consistently in leadership roles. Second, the course attempted to teach students *how* to learn rather than merely *what* to learn. We wanted them to feel comfortable teaching themselves and teaching one another in the future. Third, we tried to encourage students to have a different relationship with, and attitude about, school. We wanted them to see it as a place where the outside world constantly interacted with the classroom space."

Active Learners wasn't organized around one discipline such as math, science, or social studies. Rather, the teachers had designed a course in which a particular question or project would challenge the students to think critically and creatively. Over the semester, students became architects and worked in teams to design homes for their teachers after conducting extensive interviews to determine their tastes, needs, and preferences. Students also worked as reporters and editors, assembling a series of small newspapers chronicling the events in their school and neighborhoods. Through the activity, the Active Learners students were forced to confront the same choices that editors and reporters at major newspapers faced on a daily basis. The students presented their final products to local editors and newspaper staff, including the editor of *La Raza*, a local Spanish-language newspaper. As part of their assessment, students were put in the position of having to clearly explain and defend the choices they made, often in front of an audience of professionals. "The purpose of the exercise," Heidkamp says, "was to encourage students to understand the process of news construction from the inside out so that they would be much more critical consumers of the news and be better equipped to participate meaningfully in civic life."

Every Active Learners student also took part in a lengthy unit on chess. Heidkamp says the game of chess beautifully integrated elements from language, math, social studies, and science courses. Some say chess isn't a game, but rather an art or a science. Either way, it is incredibly complex and requires tremendous thought, foresight, and strategy. For students who were so often unable or unwilling to imagine what their lives would be like five years down the road, chess presented an unfamiliar mode of thinking.

Once the students learned the basics of the game, the teachers would start to turn the tables on them, literally. Midway through a game, they'd ask all the students to stand up and switch places with their opponent, forcing them to attempt to understand their opponent's strategy. Next, with games under way, players would be moved to different tables. The player who could more quickly assess the implications of the situation on the board would be more successful. The teachers also created a life-size chessboard and divided their classes into two teams. Next to the life-size board was a regular board. Before making a move, teams could congregate at the regular board and strategize. Sacrificing a pawn was a little different when you had a crush on him or played basketball with her after school.

Instead of a multiple-choice exam, the Active Learners capstone experience involved a forensic investigation and a criminal trial complete with a crime scene, depositions of witnesses, and a trial against opposing counsel before a judge and jury. The experience—one so complex it required participation from nearly all the school's faculty members—began a month and a half or so before the end of the semester. Students were taken to an empty classroom. On the floor

Instead of a multiple-choice exam, the Active Learners capstone experience involved a forensic investigation and a criminal trial complete with a crime scene, depositions of witnesses, and a trial against opposing counsel before a judge and jury.

was the chalk outline of a body. "This," the students were told, "is a murder scene." Everything in the room was considered evidence, and they were required to collect and document all of it. Later they would conduct scientific analyses on the samples they collected. They were required to take extensive notes and encouraged to diagram the crime scene, because it would be gone in a few days.

The murdered man was Felix Navidad, and the scene of the crime was his beachfront home. Four of his friends had been at the house the night he was killed. Active Learners students interviewed each of them. The teachers who played the different roles were given only loose guidelines and, as a result, often gave conflicting information to different groups. This was okay, Heidkamp says, because "there was no right answer in the traditional sense of a preset response that all students needed to give in order to be correct. Rather, it was more demanding, in that students were evaluated in their ability to analyze the information they received and fashion it into a clear and compelling argument."

In this final project, the students learned the difference between civil and criminal trials and learned what attorneys do; teachers generally tried to bring in guest speakers who worked in law to explain these concepts. Then the students set about creating their arguments. They were divided into teams and were required to prosecute or defend various suspects. Actual attorneys came to Cristo Rey for the trial, and Cristo Rey teachers sat on the jury. The students made opening statements. They questioned and cross-examined various witnesses, and, as the trial concluded, they made closing statements.

They weren't given an answer about who had committed the crime, but they were graded on how well they'd pleaded their respective cases. "They were expected to demonstrate mastery of the material," Heidkamp says. "To do well, they had to think clearly, create arguments, and present them effectively. It's a different approach than offering a multiple-choice exam.

"Traditionally, we think of students as absorbing the knowledge of the teacher. We wanted to teach the students to actually create knowledge, to become producers of knowledge. When you think about research, it's literally going out, gathering information, making sense of it, and then adding it to the knowledge base. Asking students to present knowledge to a challenging audience and asking them to know it so well that they could defend their position would be a powerful learning experience. It goes back to our fear that we could never get these students fully caught up or fully prepared for college. But if they had these skills, we figured they'd be able to tackle pretty much anything at the college level."

Many on Cristo Rey's faculty shared Heidkamp's sentiments. Almost every teacher on the faculty volunteered to participate in Active Learners activities. Murphy, the principal, was a huge advocate and lauded it on a public radio news program. In the first days of Cristo Rey's third year, Thielman and Foley began bringing donors and potential donors to the Active Learners class. They sang the praises of Cristo Rey's faculty and the dynamic, innovative, and responsive curriculum they were creating. Active Learners attracted the attention of a local bank, which offered to fund its continued development with a fifty-thousand-dollar grant.

But not everyone thought it was a good idea. "There were a number of things we did there," says Jim Wall, one of the two most senior teachers at Cristo Rey, "that I thought were a little crazy." Wall remembers the day when Heidkamp presented the plan for Active Learners to the faculty. "It sounded great. He wanted the students to be active learners and not passive learners and he wanted to prepare them to be active citizens in our democracy. And I remember thinking to myself, *Isn't that what four years of high school and four years of college are for?*"

At the time, Wall wasn't happy that traditional history classes would be dropped from the freshman curriculum to make room for Active Learners. "For urban kids living in gang-infested city neighborhoods where they were recruited with the notion that *this* neighborhood is your world, your territory, your family, and you have the right to kill for it, sell drugs in it, and die for it, it seemed incredibly important to me that these students be given a sense of their citizenship in a much, much wider world going all the way back to ancient times." Looking back, Wall isn't shy about saying he "had problems with a lot of the untraditional, unfounded glitzy ideas that people came up with. Active Learners was an incredible program on paper but had absolutely no merit to it at all. None whatsoever. There was no content to the course. None."

Wall, though, was a distinct minority, and his opposition to Active Learners didn't slow it down. Midway through the first week of Cristo Rey's third year, Maritza found herself sitting around a table with three other students trying to figure out a way to turn the pile of plastic straws in front of them into a cantilever—a one-day exercise Heidkamp and the other Active Learners teachers used to help foster basic creative and critical-thinking skills. She didn't understand why she was taking the class or why she needed to know how to build a cantilever. It was a strange class. And she wasn't sure she liked it.

She did, however, love the ritual of school: the books, the classes, and the learning. She enjoyed it even more because she'd become fluent in English, even though at Cristo Rey she'd also get to take classes in Spanish. By the end of her second week in high school, Maritza was doing two to three hours of homework each night, far more than most of her classmates.

❋

No one ever said it, but during Cristo Rey's first two years many of the teachers wondered how long it could last. Everything at the school was so good. Teachers got along well with administrators. While the progressive faction and the more traditional and conservative faction of the faculty sometimes butted heads, their discussions were always respectful. Nearly everyone who taught there during the first two years says it was by far the most supportive faculty community they've ever been a part of. Outside school, they were all friends. Nearly every weekend one of them would have a party, or they would all go out together. Everyone believed deeply in the school's mission, and all the teachers shared a desire to see the students succeed. Just as important, they were all willing to work hard—much harder than was expected—to make it happen. Early in the third year, though, it became clear how easily this delicate balance could be upset.

Members of the faculty gathered in autumn for the first of a series of meetings that would come to be known as the Grass Roots Movement. Cristo Rey's teachers were not unionized and created the Grass Roots group as a way to unite their voices, because they had become concerned about the direction of the school. "That fall," Brent Dexter recalls, "the number of preps, classes, and class sizes all went up." Preps are the different classes a teacher must prepare each day. A history teacher who teaches five freshman history classes has much less work to do than a teacher who teaches a Spanish class, a freshman history class, and a sophomore history class. During the school's first two years, Cristo Rey teachers had willingly taken on two and sometimes three preps. By the beginning of the third year, three preps were becoming the norm. There were also more students in most classes. Dexter says he "could hardly move around" in the junior-year social studies class he taught to thirty-one students. The large class sizes were a clear break from everything the founding faculty members had wanted—a small school providing small classes with intensely personal instruction.

The conspicuous absence of a cost-of-living pay increase for faculty between the second and third school years was also an issue. Julie Minikel-Lacocque, by then a second-year Spanish and ESL teacher, recalls, "Members of the administration came to us at the beginning of the third year and said, 'We dropped the ball on your pay increase.' Our reaction was, 'Well, then pick it up.' But that was the end of the discussion. We weren't getting a cost-of-living increase, which is pretty standard practice. And the cost of health insurance had gone up again." The cost of gasoline had gone up, too, as had the cost of milk. Many of the teachers had college loans to pay off and were barely making ends meet. They had poured themselves into the school during the previous year. To a person, they knew they'd done far more than had been asked of them. And they weren't getting anything in return.

The teachers had also begun to express frustration about the messages CIP was sending to students. From the outset, Cristo Rey students were charged one hundred dollars for missing a day of work. There was no charge for missing class, and students often missed classes around the holidays and at the end of the year to attend holiday parties at their jobs. The teachers were pleased that the corporate sponsors wanted to include the students, but it didn't sit well with the faculty that students were missing classes to attend Christmas parties a couple of weeks before finals.

At the first meeting of the Grass Roots Movement—which was closed to members of the school's administration—the teachers discussed all these topics. They talked, too, about whether or not they were fulfilling their mission. They discussed their general feeling of disconnection from the school board; it seemed that the board was making many significant decisions about the school and that the teachers' interests were not adequately represented at the meetings. By the end of the first Grass Roots meeting, the teachers had written out their concerns on a dozen or so sheets of pink copy paper. The "pink sheets," as they came to be known among the faculty members, were eventually cleaned up and submitted to the school's administration with the hope that they would eventually be shown to the board.

The honeymoon was over.

❈

IN MID-SEPTEMBER 1998, JUST weeks into Cristo Rey's third year, the school broke ground on its new seventeen-classroom building. Jeff Thielman had proven to be a fund-raising wunderkind. In the spring of 1998, he had hosted Cristo Rey's first annual ¡Viva! fund-raiser, which had raised $120,000 for the school. He'd also brought in numerous gifts in excess of $50,000 for the new building. Each month he made it a goal to see ten people who were capable of making gifts of $10,000 or more. And he wasn't shy about asking for their money. In large part because of Thielman's success, the board had, over the summer, expanded the goal for the capital campaign to fourteen million dollars.

In addition to his major gifts work, Thielman led a remarkably successful campaign for capital from charitable foundations. Most organizations are thrilled if 25 percent of their requests to foundations result in grants. On Thielman's watch, Cristo Rey went nearly

> The general contractor had commissioned a study of the ground to make sure they could put in a deep basement, but the subcontractor had faked the report. Just days after it started, construction on Cristo Rey's new building ground to a halt.

a year without being turned down. Nearly 40 percent of the school's income came from foundations—an unprecedented feat in the fundraising world. People liked the idea of students earning their own education. They liked the idea of a school that would be able to support itself, even though at that point it couldn't begin to do so.

The goal was to have the new building ready for the start of school in the fall of 1999. But days after the formal groundbreaking—which was attended by two bishops; a state senator; a Chicago alderman; the new Jesuit provincial, Richard J. Baumann, SJ (Brad Schaeffer's term had ended in 1997); board representatives; a teacher; and two students—the construction crew made a disturbing discovery.

When they tried to excavate the land—made available by demolishing the rectory that housed the development office and the internship program and by purchasing and razing a number of houses adjacent to the rectory—they slammed into a thick layer of bedrock. The general contractor had commissioned a study of the ground to make sure they could put in a deep basement, but the subcontractor had faked the report. Just days after it started, construction on Cristo Rey's new building ground to a halt. Without the building, Cristo Rey wouldn't be able to increase enrollment for the next school year.

LEO'S PATH OF LEAST resistance was working perfectly until Steve Planning started to interfere in the fall of Leo's senior year. Unlike most of his classmates, Leo could see the future. He wanted to get out of school and get a full-time job. Working in the copy room at Katten, Muchin & Zavis, he'd learned he could do a job and do it well. He'd learned he could make money. And he knew he could make a lot more of it if he didn't have to sit in a classroom for seven or eight hours each day. He wanted to get out of school as soon as possible so he could start working construction; that's where the big money was. Many of Leo's classmates had begun to talk about college. Cristo Rey's college counselor and the teachers were asking everyone where they would apply. Leo didn't pay much attention to the conversations, and when people asked him where he was going to apply, he either told them he wasn't applying or tried to change the subject.

But it was different when Mr. Planning asked. When he came back to Cristo Rey in the fall of 1998 after completing his theology studies, the kids had asked him if he was Fr. Planning yet. He wasn't. He wasn't scheduled to be ordained until the following summer, so he had a flex year of sorts. Jesuits with an extra year are generally encouraged to use it for additional study. But Planning, who'd already enrolled in a master's program in school administration and supervision at the University of San Francisco, says he "was sick of school." He wanted to work, ideally at Cristo Rey, which seemed to him exactly the type of school the Jesuits should be running. His provincial, though, wanted him to finish his degree. So he cooked up a plan that let him do both. He took classes at Loyola University Chicago's Mallinckrodt Campus in Chicago's North Shore and became Cristo Rey's new assistant principal.

Midway through the fall semester, Planning asked Leo where he was applying to college. "I'm not gonna apply anywhere," Leo said.

"Why not?" Planning asked. The question surprised Leo. Most people usually just nodded and accepted the fact that he wasn't going to school. He wasn't a good student. He always seemed to be on the verge of getting in trouble, and he'd been thrown out of school for a day on the suspicion of selling drugs. (He and his parents were able to convince the school that he hadn't done anything wrong, and a day later he was readmitted.) Leo didn't stand out in academics or in sports. Of all the students in Cristo Rey's senior class, Leo seemed least likely to go to college.

But Planning knew there was more to Leo. He was bright, whether he understood it or not. "Leo, why aren't you going to apply to college?" Planning asked again after Leo tried to change the subject. "It doesn't hurt to apply."

"Man, what am I going to do in college?" Leo asked, laughing. But Planning knew that underneath the laughter lay a serious question.

He explained that college would open up more opportunities, more choices. "To get a good job today," Planning said, "you need to have a college degree."

"I don't need a degree to work construction."

"A lot of people in construction have degrees. If you get a degree you can become a manager. You can do much more. And who knows? You might like college."

"I don't think so."

"Well, you should apply. You should work next quarter to get your grades up, and then you should apply. Good grades during the first semester of your senior year will show a lot of colleges that you want to go to college."

"But I don't want to go to college."

"But you should still apply. You might like it. You don't know. If you apply and get in, you'll have a choice, and choices are good. You don't have to go just because you apply."

Over the next few weeks, Leo replayed the conversation in his head. He didn't discuss it with anyone—not with his friends or cousins or parents. He tried to picture himself in college but couldn't. He had never set foot on a college campus.

He knew he wouldn't go, but he did start to work a little harder at school.

❀

THE MEETING OF CRISTO Rey's administrative team—John Foley, Judy Murphy, Preston Kendall, and Jeff Thielman—was heated. It was the middle of February 1999, and they were up against a deadline. By the following day, they had to submit to the board of trustees their proposed budget for the 1999–2000 school year. Everyone in the room knew that for the third year in a row, they would lose money—this time it looked to be just shy of one million dollars. This couldn't continue, at least not for the long term. They had enough money in the bank—all of which had come from charitable contributions—to cover their working capital needs for one full school year.

When Thielman made requests for major gifts, he always explained how the gifts would support Cristo Rey's plan to become sustainable. Thielman, though, felt that the budget they'd created was far from sustainable. Yet they couldn't find anything to cut. Pulling funding from CIP would be a mistake; it was already understaffed. Plus, it was the school's lifeblood. It paid the bills—or would eventually. Neither Murphy nor Foley wanted to cut anything from the academic side. They didn't want to run an average school—they wanted to run a great school, a school that could get the children of Pilsen caught up and prepared for college. They wanted a school on the cutting edge of educational research and development. Their untiring vision was of a school that addressed the specific needs of its students, a school that had a top-notch physical plant, that fairly compensated its teachers, and that provided counselors to help students address emotional trauma from gang violence or abusive families.

Cristo Rey had been working closely with a Catholic nun, Sr. Kim Mis, who ran United Stand Family Center, a not-for-profit organization that provided counseling services to many low-income schools in Chicago. United Stand had conducted a survey of Cristo Rey's students and produced an extensive report detailing the various issues they encountered on a daily basis. Death was high on the list. Every week or two, a young person was killed in Pilsen or Little Village, usually as a result of gang violence. Alcohol and drug abuse also plagued many homes.

For as long as she'd been involved in education, Murphy had been a firm believer in counseling. Cristo Rey could educate its students only if they felt safe in school and could concentrate. Both Murphy and Foley had devoted their lives to serving others, often underprivileged children, through education. Together, they had a hard time saying no to anything that would enhance the students' ability to learn. Whether it was a safety fence around the school's parking lot, a larger faculty, a new series of math textbooks, or expensive field trips, Murphy generally said yes.

Thielman and Kendall, though, were concerned about the budget. At the strategic planning meeting the year before, the board and members of the administration had agreed to try to trim the budget deficit by half over each of the next four years. Thielman knew the proposed budget wouldn't do it. Murphy and Foley, though, wouldn't budge. They insisted there wasn't anything that could be cut without adversely affecting the students. After meeting with the board's finance committee, Kendall and Thielman reluctantly agreed to submit the report to the full board.

Everyone on the board seemed to know that the budget was a turning point, though no one was really saying it. The board members knew Cristo Rey's revenues wouldn't come close to covering the proposed expenses. By approving such a budget, they would essentially be giving up the dream that Cristo Rey could in fact sustain itself. They would be shifting the long-term responsibility for maintaining the school from students and families to donors—exactly the model the Jesuits had wanted to avoid.

One by one, the board members signaled their approval of the budget. In the end, it was a Jesuit, Fr. Ted Munz, who put his foot down. Munz had been on the board since the beginning but had been pretty quiet. Because he'd been so involved in the formation and founding of the school, he tried not to involve himself in any of the day-to-day operational issues. "I never had any illusions that everything would go according to plan," he says. "But sometimes decisions were made, and I said, 'Hmmm, I wouldn't do it that way,' but it wasn't 'mine' anymore. I had to step back and let those decisions happen. I couldn't meddle."

He knew, however, exactly what the proposed budget meant and couldn't let it pass. "I can't vote for this budget," he said. "This school can be fiscally responsible and has to be fiscally responsible if it's going to survive." Other board members quickly reversed their votes and joined Munz. The proposed budget was rejected. Foley, Murphy, Thielman, and Kendall were back to square one and faced the prospect of creating an entirely new budget or else trimming costs substantially on the current one. Without an approved budget, the school wouldn't be able to open in the fall.

No one knew exactly what to do or where to look. Expectations for Rosemary Croghan, the board chair, were low. While she'd done a nice job managing the board and moderating occasionally touchy discussions, she'd never faced a challenge like this, and she didn't have any experience with cutting costs or facilitating turnarounds.

But Croghan had something few others on the board had. She understood the validity of everyone's perspective. She was the mother of six and, at the time, grandmother of twenty-six. She'd worked as a nurse. She'd grown up the daughter of an immigrant in a Spanish-speaking household. She understood the importance of education and the desire of the academic representatives on the board to provide the best education possible to Cristo Rey's students. But Croghan, whose husband was a successful businessman, also understood the perspective of the businesspeople on the board.

The businesspeople were right. The educators were right, too. The businesspeople had spent their careers making hard financial decisions, minimizing costs, and maximizing returns. The educators had spent their careers caring for and serving others in schools and foundations. The bottom line for them wasn't on a balance sheet but in the hearts, minds, and futures of their students. Unfortunately, the educators thought the businesspeople were clueless about what really went on in the school, and the businesspeople thought the educators were financially unsophisticated.

Croghan knew these perceptions were crippling, and she also knew there was common ground. Her husband, John, was the perfect example. In 1967, after working in several investment firms, he founded Lincoln Partners, which eventually became Lincoln Capital Management and was then sold to the investment bank Lehman Brothers. He served as chairman of the company until his retirement. He now manages Rail-Splitter Capital Management, a Chicago-based hedge fund. But Croghan's life wasn't then, and isn't now, just about finance. He's devoted much of his personal wealth and a great deal of his time to a variety of religious and educational causes. He sits on the board at Northwestern University. He is the vice chairman of the Archdiocese of Chicago's Big Shoulders Fund. He and his wife are donors to numerous charitable and civic organizations in Chicago.

Rosemary Croghan knew that some businesspeople—like her husband and the members of Cristo Rey's board—cared deeply about education. They just contributed to it differently. The school needed their business acumen, and she knew she had to figure out a way to get the two sides to listen to each other, work together, and come up with a solution. She was, quite possibly, the board member best suited for the job.

Over dinner the night the board rejected the budget, Croghan confided in her husband that, while she understood the problem, she had no idea how she—or anyone else—could solve it.

Enter the Consultants 18

WHAT ABOUT GETTING A consultant to come in and help you?" John Croghan asked his wife days after the board rejected the administration's budget. "Maybe McKinsey."

The suggestion surprised her. "What would McKinsey do for Cristo Rey?"

John Croghan had been in business for decades, and during that time he had sat on the boards of many public and private companies. On numerous occasions, he'd seen consulting companies come in and provide valuable strategic advice to their clients. Thriving companies and struggling companies alike often turned to consultants for guidance. They helped conduct market research, develop strategies for entering new markets or launching new products, cut costs, or look for ways to incorporate new technology into a company's operations. In other words, their business was strengthening other businesses.

Rosemary Croghan wondered if a global consulting company like McKinsey would be able to work with a small start-up like Cristo Rey. It seemed like two worlds colliding. But those worlds had long ago collided when the Jesuits turned to local businesses to help fund their new school. She agreed that it couldn't hurt to learn more.

So John Croghan called Mike Murray, a straight-talking partner at McKinsey & Company, and asked if Murray and McKinsey might be willing to do some pro bono work for Cristo Rey. McKinsey has been in business since 1926 and has become the world's premier management consulting company. Today, with ninety offices in fifty-one countries, McKinsey serves three of the five largest companies in the world and two-thirds of the Fortune 1000. The company also has a thriving nonprofit practice. Murray, a graduate of Boston College High School and Boston College, both Jesuit schools, had been working for McKinsey since 1967, had been in the Chicago office since the early 1980s, and had served for ten years as the managing partner in Chicago.

Murray knew all about Cristo Rey—the Chicago office was half-way through its first year as a corporate internship sponsor—and said that he and McKinsey would be glad to help.

That night Rosemary Croghan called Mike Murray. "What's the main problem?" he asked her. She explained that Cristo Rey's expenses were far outpacing its revenues. "I had a vague sense," Murray says, "that the place was financially out of control. My conversation with her confirmed it." They talked a little bit about where Cristo Rey needed to go and how quickly it needed to get there. By the time they got off the phone, Croghan was convinced that McKinsey could help Cristo Rey.

Weeks later, a team of four McKinsey consultants descended on the school. They interviewed Preston Kendall and Carlos De La Rosa about the Corporate Internship Program. They interviewed Judy Murphy and John Foley, most of the faculty and staff, and a group of students. They gathered every piece of financial data they could find: receipts, expense reports, invoices, payroll records, budgets, and the record of charitable contributions. They asked for reports of class sizes. They wanted to know how many hours a day teachers actually spent teaching. They spent a great deal of time analyzing Cristo Rey's schedule, which was no easy task. It usually took new teachers a couple of weeks to get comfortable with the schedule, which included classes of varying lengths and different classes on different days because of the fact that one-fifth of the students were at work on any given day. In each of its first three years, Cristo Rey had offered an entirely different schedule.

Through this extensive research, McKinsey was trying to get a handle on two things: how Cristo Rey worked and where all the money was going. After two full weeks of on-site research, the consultants retreated to their downtown offices.

Four McKinsey consultants descended on the school. They interviewed Preston Kendall and Carlos De La Rosa about the Corporate Internship Program. They interviewed Judy Murphy and John Foley, most of the faculty and staff, and a group of students.

❀

JOEY GARCIA SAYS HE knew his life was spinning out of control, but he didn't care. It was early March of 1999. His mom, Dolores, had died on January 23, just a couple of weeks after Joey submitted his application to Cristo Rey. She'd heard about the school and made him apply—she just knew it was the type of place where he could shine.

"My mom filled up my whole life," Joey says. "She was my motivation, my everything. She gave me love no five parents could give one child." But then she was gone. She died at Saint Anthony Hospital. Joey was there for most of the day. The doctors wanted to put his mom on a respirator, but she refused. Joey's aunts, Susie and Connie, tried to change her mind. Over and over she shook her head. They prodded Joey to ask her. He did, but she again refused.

That night Joey fell asleep at the hospital. Eventually, Connie took him to her house, where he slept on a sofa in the living room. In the middle of the night, he woke with a start. "I remember an ice-cold shiver running down my back," he says. Uneasy, he wrapped himself tightly in a blanket and tried to fall back to sleep. A few miles away, his mom had taken her last breath. At the time, she'd been in her mother's arms. Moments before she died, she said to her mother, "Tell Susie to make sure to take care of my Joey." Susie, who had four children of her own, was the youngest of Dolores's eight brothers and sisters.

When Joey woke up the next morning, his grandma and his aunts were at Connie's, and they were all crying. They told him his mom had died. "I didn't even know what to feel," Joey says. "I didn't really cry, because I felt like she was there with me, making me feel like it was okay. To this day I believe I woke up the instant she died. I've always felt that she let me know when it was her time to go. I think that's why she said no to the machine, because she knew God was telling her it was her time to leave."

Later that day, while Joey's aunts and grandma were planning his mom's funeral, he went up to the apartment he and his mom had shared. He flipped on the small radio in the kitchen, which was tuned to 104.3, his mom's favorite oldies station. She had listened to it when she was cooking and cleaning, or just sitting and resting at the kitchen table. When he heard the words and the upbeat music, the memories flooded in. He went into the bathroom and stood before the mirror. He could still hear the music. And he could see his mom standing at the stove. He could see the two of them sitting at the table, and lugging groceries up to the third floor. He saw her face, laughing and smiling.

"That's when I just let it out," Joey says. "I don't think I ever cried so hard in my life. I was in there for a good hour. I remember just letting all my anger, my frustration, my sadness, just everything that I ever had in me, out. It got to a point where no tears were coming out and my chest hurt so bad." He washed his face and went into the living room, where he sat down on his mom's bed. He ran his hands back and forth across the blanket. She was gone. He couldn't believe it.

Dolores's wake was held at the Zefran Funeral Home, just a few blocks from Joey's apartment. After the wake, her casket was taken to St. Paul's, the neighborhood church, for a funeral Mass. Joey remained after Mass, kneeling near the front of the church. He didn't notice when the doors at the back of the church opened, and he didn't hear his classmates from Irma C. Ruiz file in. All eighty-five of them were there. So were the eighth-grade teachers. "I couldn't believe it," Joey says. "It was the most moving thing that anyone could ever do for me." It helped to know he had friends and that people cared about him. But it wasn't enough.

In the days following his mom's death, Joey moved his stuff downstairs to his grandma's apartment. Every morning he walked the same two blocks to Ruiz, but it wasn't the same. He couldn't get as excited about his homework, and his teachers let him slide. Joey spent a lot of time at Susie's house, where one of his cousins introduced him to video games. He started skipping homework assignments to play them.

A year earlier, as a seventh grader, he'd won a school-wide poetry recitation contest. His teacher, Mr. McGuire, had been so impressed that he had entered Joey in a larger contest. Joey can't remember all the specifics, only that it was held somewhere "fancy" and that he recited a poem by Walt Whitman. Mr. McGuire "had opened my mind to all these new things and people like Whitman. I love Whitman." During seventh grade and the first half of eighth grade, Joey had begun writing his own poetry.

But when his mom died, it all stopped. Everything went dark. He disappeared into video games and their faraway worlds of colored pixels. Using nothing more than his thumbs, he could kill the bad guys and slay the dragons. But when he wasn't playing games, he couldn't do anything. He didn't really care whether or not he got into Cristo Rey, but Susie took him to the interview. He wore a shirt and tie. He didn't like wearing ties and didn't really want to go to a school where you had to wear ties, but his mom had wanted him to go there.

The people at Cristo Rey wanted to know what had happened to his grades. Until the third quarter of his eighth-grade year, they had been perfect. But in the third quarter, he had Cs and Ds. Susie explained that he'd lost his mother.

A few weeks later, he got a letter telling him he'd been accepted.

❋

MAYRA KNEW SHE COULD play basketball. That's why she didn't quit. Most of the girls on the José Clemente Orozco Community Academy basketball team who didn't get to play all the time quit after the first couple of weeks. But Mayra knew she was as good as the girls who were playing, and maybe even a little better. She'd played scores of games at the park since the day in the summer of 1997, before her sixth-grade year, when only seven people showed up to play in Sergio's usual Barrett Park pickup game. Even though she was ten years younger and six inches shorter than anyone else on the court, they asked her to be the eighth.

The first time she got the ball, she made a panicked pass that was easily stolen. She didn't see the ball too often for the rest of the game. When she did, she made a point of making good passes to people who were open. At the other end of the court, she played fierce defense. A couple of weeks later, they needed her to play again. Within a year, she'd become a regular in the games. She was never the leading scorer, but playing with grown men helped her develop strong skills in passing and handling the ball. And it taught her how to play tough defense. She didn't get to take too many shots during the playground games. She didn't score too often during the tryouts for her seventh-grade basketball team either. Once she made the team, she didn't score much during practice, so she spent most of her time during the games on the bench.

She was never the leading scorer, but playing with grown men helped her develop strong skills in passing and handling the ball. And it taught her how to play tough defense.

But Mayra never said a single word to her coach at Orozco about playing time. Nor did she ever skip a practice or a game. Mayra's mom didn't complain—she was glad Mayra played basketball, mostly because it meant one less body in the family's small apartment after school. By the time Mayra was in seventh grade, her mom had eight kids—she'd given birth to Lalis in May of 1997—and was pregnant with her ninth. Mayra's dad was the father of all the children, but his relationship with the family was stormy. He was rarely there, and when he was, he was often drinking and sometimes violent. He couldn't hold down a steady job, and Mayra's mom didn't have time for a job. They got by on welfare checks and food stamps. In the Hernandez family, Mayra's basketball career meant very little.

To Mayra, though, it was everything. She loved it all: the feel of the ball in her hands, the squeaking of gym shoes on the wood-floored court, and, most of all, the feeling of making a jump shot. She loved the sound of the ball tearing through the net. It sounded different—maybe better—on the playground, where the nets were made of chains. Mayra still went to the park with Sergio and sometimes to Harrison Park to practice by herself. She worked on her layups, spin moves, and jump shots. By sheer force of will and the plain power of repetition, she was becoming a solid basketball player.

❁

THE APPLICATIONS TO MOST top colleges and universities were due sometime in January. Leo didn't submit any. February came and went, and Leo still hadn't applied anywhere or even requested an application from the college counselor. He'd discovered during his junior year that his parents were splitting up, and their separation wasn't going smoothly. Somehow college had gotten lost in the mix.

Then, in the spring, Cristo Rey's college counselor asked Steve Planning, who got along well with the students, to drive a group of juniors to Marquette University in Milwaukee. Planning found Leo and told him, "You should come along and see if you like it."

Leo agreed to make the trip—in large part so he could get away from home—even though it meant giving up a Saturday.

After the trip, Planning asked Leo what he had thought of the school.

"It was cool, I guess."

"Do you think you'll apply anywhere?"

"I don't know. I don't know where to apply. Plus, I think it's real expensive."

"The counselor can get all your application fees waived. All you have to do to apply," Planning said, oversimplifying things a bit, "is write a page about yourself and fill out some forms."

Leo shrugged and looked away. "Why not just do it?" Planning asked. "What do you have to lose?"

Minutes later, they were in the small college-resource room paging through the viewbooks of local colleges, trying to figure out whose deadlines hadn't yet passed. Planning helped Leo choose five schools.

When Leo returned to school on Monday, he confirmed with the college counselor that he'd be able to get his application fees waived. "I'm not even sure I want to go, so I don't want to pay to apply," he told the counselor. Like nearly every student at Cristo Rey, Leo qualified for a need-based application fee waiver. Over the next two weeks, Leo filled out the applications. Finding the time wasn't easy, since he was working three hours every night at the copy center at Katten, Muchin, the law firm that had employed him through the Corporate Internship Program during his first two years in school. He'd taken the ACT twice, getting scores of 15 and 17. He included the higher of the two scores—many colleges won't accept students with ACT scores below 16—as he carefully filled out the applications. Planning wrote his letters of recommendation.

❋

NEAR THE END OF THE 1998–99 school year, Mike Murray and the team from McKinsey presented their findings to the facilities and finance committee of Cristo Rey's board of trustees. In its third year, Cristo Rey was on pace to lose roughly nine hundred thousand dollars. If the school didn't make changes, it would lose well over one million dollars per year in the coming two years. The consultants pointed out, however, that Cristo Rey was in a unique position to remedy the situation. Because everything about the school was so new, the administration and staff had the flexibility to change just about anything they were doing.

To fix things, the consultants said that Cristo Rey would have to increase revenues and cut costs. Revenue would undoubtedly increase as more students enrolled. Completing the new building was crucial, as it would allow the school to accommodate a higher enrollment. However, increasing enrollment wouldn't solve all its problems. The consultants suggested increasing the cost of the Corporate Internship Program from $19,500 per year (the school had already increased the cost by $1,500 over the first three years) to $25,000. They also enthusiastically supported a proposed change to CIP put forth by one of Cristo Rey's faculty members.

Earlier that year, Foley had shared the school's financial woes with the faculty and had explained to them that McKinsey would be around the school conducting interviews and research. The faculty feared that the financial crunch would result in the destruction of the unique learning environment they had worked so hard to create. When schools need to save money, they often look to increase teacher workload, increase class sizes, or standardize teaching and material. The faculty and administration knew that a one-size-fits-all education would, at best, fail to bring some of Cristo Rey's students up to a level that would prepare them for college. At worst, it might cause these students to disengage completely from the learning process and the school. When that happened, they'd either drop out or be asked to leave. In an effort to help create a sustainable financial model, the faculty devoted some of their spring meetings to brainstorming about ways they could reduce costs without sacrificing quality.

That's when Jeff Susor, the second-year teacher who had taught previously in Micronesia with Jesuit Volunteers International, suggested that Cristo Rey's students work more. "If each student worked one additional day per month," Susor said, "then four students could share a job instead of five and the school could have more jobs and more revenue." At the time, groups of five students held jobs. Each job had a Monday worker, a Tuesday worker, and so on. Susor proposed doing away with that system and making Monday a flex day. On the first Monday of each month, the Tuesday worker would work. On the second Monday, the Wednesday worker would work, and so on through the month. By adopting this system, the school could increase the number of jobs, and revenue, by 20 percent. If Cristo Rey could extend the school year by a week and cut back the time allotted for faculty meetings, the staff could implement the change without losing classroom time. The McKinsey team loved the idea.

The consultants also recommended that Cristo Rey increase its tuition costs. "I don't think the folks at Cristo Rey realized how tight of an economic space they were operating in," Mike Murray says. "The school was a fund-raising machine, and that masked a lot of the problems. There was a lot of talk about balancing the budget. But we studied the economics of the school, and it was pretty clear they were never going to truly balance the budget. The folks at the school were trying to say that revenue from the jobs plus the tuition would cover the operating expenses. But they didn't collect full tuition from every student. Most of the students received financial aid. Using tuition dollars to balance the budget was a myth. There was going to be an operating deficit as long as the school was in business. The question was minimizing it." According to the McKinsey report, if Cristo Rey raised tuition, families who could pay more would pay more. Those who couldn't would continue to receive financial aid. If Cristo Rey could get to a point where its operating deficit consisted solely of the tuition shortfall, the school would likely be able to raise those funds annually.

In addition to ways of boosting revenue, the consultants proposed cost-cutting measures—many of them exactly the types of changes that the faculty feared could fundamentally alter the nature of the school. The consultants recommended the school hire lower-tenured teachers. McKinsey's research showed that 45 percent of Cristo Rey's teachers had fifteen-plus years of experience and a master's degree. Of the many schools they surveyed, only St. Ignatius College Prep and Fairfield Prep, in Fairfield, Connecticut, had more teachers with such experience. Cristo Rey had far more faculty and staff than other private schools that catered to low-income students. To serve 260 students, Cristo Rey had a staff of 43 people. Hales Franciscan, on the South Side of Chicago, served 360 students with a staff of 45. Josephinum Academy, an all-girls school on the near northwest side, served 200 students with only 34 staff members. At the time that McKinsey conducted its study, Cristo Rey's average teacher compensation of $36,400 was only $600 less than the salary of the highest-paid teacher at Josephinum. In addition to hiring younger teachers with less experience, McKinsey suggested that Cristo Rey reduce the annual rate of increase in teacher compensation.

The consultants also recommended that Cristo Rey hire fewer teachers than projected as the school grew toward full enrollment. This would require that the school's current teachers become more efficient. McKinsey's research showed Cristo Rey teachers spending 36 percent of their time teaching, 43 percent preparing for class, 14 percent monitoring students, and 7 percent eating lunch. As a point of comparison, teachers at Josephinum, Hales Franciscan, and St. Ignatius College Prep spent 56 percent of their time teaching, while faculty members at Loyola Academy and Providence–St. Mel, a K–12 school on the west side of Chicago, were in front of the class for 63 percent of their day. Teachers at Cristo Rey were paid $60.10 per teaching hour, as opposed to $38.10 at Josephinum, $31.90 at Providence–St. Mel, and $40.70 at Hales Franciscan.

This recommendation in particular highlighted the differences between the opposing viewpoints on Cristo Rey's board. The academics and educators who had helped create the school knew that creating an effective curriculum took a great deal of time and effort. The board members who had benefited enormously from their traditional educations felt that Cristo Rey's teachers should spend less time talking about how they were going to teach and more time teaching.

McKinsey recommended that the school increase the teaching load from 36 to 55 percent, which would allow the school to cut the total number of teachers by seven and save more than $250,000. The consultants also advised increasing class sizes from twenty-five to thirty. "There are certain fixed costs you encounter when you offer a class," Murray says. "There's the teacher's time, the use of the building, utilities, and all the indirect costs associated with making the class available to students—salary expenses for administrators, and the time required from staff members to prepare schedules and tally attendance and so forth. The more students you can get into a classroom, the more revenue you're generating from your fixed costs."

McKinsey recommended that the school increase the teaching load from 36 to 55 percent, which would allow the school to cut the total number of teachers by seven and save more than $250,000. The consultants also advised increasing class sizes from twenty-five to thirty.

The argument made perfect business sense but flew in the face of much of what Judy Murphy and the founding faculty had sought to create at Cristo Rey. They knew McKinsey's suggestions would not necessarily be implemented by the school's board. Changes, though, seemed inevitable.

✳

LEO HAD HEARD THE kids at school talking about big envelopes versus small envelopes. Apparently one of them meant that you had been accepted to a college and the other one meant you hadn't. He couldn't remember which was which as he held the envelope from Lewis University that had come in that day's mail, and he didn't much care, because he still didn't think he'd go to college.

He opened the envelope carefully, as if he could return it if he didn't like what he found. The first word in the letter was *Congratulations*. "I didn't think I'd get in," he says. "When I got that first letter, it was kind of like 'Oh boy, what am I gonna do now?'" He says he still didn't intend to go to college, but then Planning took him out of class one day and drove him out to Lewis. "What do you think?" Planning asked, after they'd been walking around for a while. "It seems too quiet," Leo said. "Everybody's just out on their own, walking around carrying books."

It wasn't the sight of the campus, the big classrooms, the cafeterias with nice food, or the dorm rooms that eventually changed Leo's mind. In fact, he told Planning he'd rather live at home with his mom or dad so he could keep working at KMZ. What changed Leo's mind was something Planning said. "Leo, you should just try it for a semester. If you don't like it, you can always quit. You don't have to keep doing it. But trying it for a semester won't kill you. You never know—you might like it." Leo still couldn't picture himself on campus. He didn't know if it would be hard or if he could do the work. But Planning was right; he could always quit.

Two days before graduation, Leo and his classmates gathered in the assembly area in the old roller rink to make their final presentations for religion class. Classes had officially ended, so Bridget Rush, the senior-year religion teacher, let the students wear casual clothes. Leo, who'd posted his best GPA in his final semester at Cristo Rey, wore a light blue Nike baseball cap, two chains—one gold and one silver—around his neck, and a dark blue Nike jacket over a thin white T-shirt. He wore a large gold ring—his Cristo Rey class ring—on his right hand. Leo and his classmates had each been asked to develop a presentation addressing the question "What has Cristo Rey meant to you?"

It was an emotional time for Leo. Two weeks earlier, his cousin, Fernando Rojas, had been killed. He was seventeen. Fernando's older brother was a member of the Saints gang. Most of Fernando's extended family was also in the gang. Like Leo, Fernando had avoided becoming fully involved with the gang. But that didn't matter the morning he died. He was walking to school when members of the Saints' rival gang saw him. They either mistook him for his brother or assumed that he, too, was a Saint. They came from behind, holding guns. He probably turned when he heard them coming. And when he saw them, he must have run, because the bullets that killed him hit him in the back. He fell hard to the sidewalk, right next to a fire hydrant. He died there. An elderly woman witnessed the shooting, but no one was ever apprehended.

At the beginning of his presentation, Leo spoke about how he'd never cared about school, how it seemed "dumb to be having classes in a gym." He talked about how midway through his sophomore year, he was on his way to flunking all his classes before he decided to do enough work to pass. Still, he didn't care about school and didn't want to go to college. "Nobody from my family had graduated from college. Nobody had even made it to college. So why even think about it, you know? I just wanted to go to the hood by my house and chill with my friends." Eventually, he "realized college was important, thanks to Mr. Planning." The young Jesuit, Leo said, had taught him a lot and had helped him finish his applications. Then Leo's voice started to waver. He looked down and, hiding his eyes beneath the brim of his baseball cap, said he hadn't wanted to come to Cristo Rey. "But I'm glad I'm here. I'm happy." He told his classmates and the teachers who'd gathered for the presentation—Bridget Rush, Planning, and Frances Thibodeau—that they'd become a family for him. He thanked them all and then said, "Now I realize the true meaning of life."

When he finally lifted his head, everyone could see that he was crying. He wiped his eyes and said, "I'll tell you what my eighth-grade teacher told me once: 'Whenever you want to do something and you think you can't do it, all you need is *ganas*.' Desire, that's all you need." He wiped his eyes again, told his classmates he hoped they could all stay in touch, and sat down as everyone present erupted into enthusiastic applause.

On June 12, 1999, Leo graduated from Cristo Rey Jesuit High School. On the back of the graduation program, the graduating students were listed along with the colleges they planned to attend. Next to Leo's name, the program said Lewis University. Thirty-one of Cristo Rey's forty-four graduates that year would be enrolled in a college or university in the fall. They'd be attending the University of Illinois, Michigan State University, Barat College, DePaul University, Dominican University, and Loyola University Chicago, among others.

On the same day, in Baltimore, Maryland, Steve Planning, SJ, was ordained for priestly ministry before a large crowd of family and friends. "It was wonderful," he says, "but I really missed being at Cristo Rey for the graduation."

Portland's Calling 19

"THE GOAL OF THIS exercise is to develop a belief statement,"
Judy Murphy said to her faculty during the first meeting of the
1999–2000 school year. They had gathered on a steamy August morning in a first-floor classroom outfitted with two underperforming air-
conditioning window units. "Your statement should outline what you
believe about your students and about the act and profession of teaching. The statements should also articulate what we as teachers believe
we deserve, or expect, in return from our students." The entire faculty
was present at the meeting, including seven new teachers. There would
have been more, but Cristo Rey hadn't been able to expand its enrollment, because the new classroom building still wasn't ready.

Three of the new teachers had recently graduated from Georgetown
University and were forming a volunteer teaching community at the
school.* This wasn't entirely welcome news to the balance of the
faculty. Some teachers wondered if it might be part of a larger move

---

*I was one of the three new volunteer teachers from Georgetown. In the prologue,
I pledged to write about the school and not about my experience there. Because
some of my experience is relevant to certain parts of the story, I will relay aspects
of it in footnotes throughout the book. In the spring of 1999, during my senior
year at Georgetown University, I visited Cristo Rey and was treated to a tour by
Fr. John Foley, SJ. At the time, I was researching a writing project and exploring
opportunities for a postgraduate year of service. I was immediately drawn to Cristo
Rey and said to Fr. Foley that it seemed like "a perfect place to volunteer." He said
Cristo Rey had had a volunteer from a different program, but that it had been "too
expensive," so they were dropping it. He made no mention of McKinsey's audit

toward an unpaid staff. The idea seemed inconsistent with Murphy's approach to education, but the teachers knew things were changing. Students were working more, and there was talk that teachers, too, would be asked to work more. A schoolwide belt-tightening was under way, and expenses were being watched much more closely.

The volunteers didn't bother David Dixon, one of Cristo Rey's new paid teachers. Dixon, a former University of Texas swimmer, had just finished an MA in international multicultural curriculum development at University of San Francisco and had taught at public middle schools in the Bay Area before moving with his wife, Lora, to Chicago.

Dixon was amazed by the tenor and content of the faculty meetings during his first week at Cristo Rey. He'd never heard teachers so openly discuss the needs of their students or how they could best respond to those needs through innovative curriculum development. Dixon was amazed to see teachers talking about their struggles to get students to engage deeply with the material. Cristo Rey's teachers were constantly asking, "How can we do this better? How can we inspire our students to learn and to become lifelong learners?" As Murphy was wrapping up the final meeting of the week, Dixon interrupted and asked if he could say a few words. He told the faculty how grateful he was to be at Cristo Rey. At one point, his eyes filled with tears as he recounted his

---

of the school or the cost-cutting efforts that were then under way. Minutes later, it occurred to Foley that Cristo Rey could create its own volunteer program. He asked me if I'd be interested. I said yes and that night called a handful of friends from high school and college who I thought might also want to do it. Two of my classmates at Georgetown, Mike Staff and Andy Stanner, loved the idea. Mike and I had gone to Loyola Academy and Andy had attended St. Ignatius College Prep. All three of us found the idea of working at a new Jesuit school in Chicago very appealing. And Fr. Foley found the three of us very appealing. We'd attended Jesuit high schools and a Jesuit college and were willing to work essentially for free. Fr. Foley asked us to commit to working at the school for two years. We arrived in Chicago in early August 1999 for the first day of faculty meetings.

frustration with an education system that so often seemed to proceed without any regard for its students. Cristo Rey, he said to the faculty members, "is what education should be."

Most of the teachers spent the next two weeks preparing for the start of classes. By the time classes started, however, the curriculum remained undefined. Murphy had also recently received word that some students who had left Cristo Rey and were starting their sophomore year at public schools were being required to redo their freshman year, because the schools didn't recognize the credits from their religion or Active Learners classes at Cristo Rey.

The school year began in the same cramped classrooms that had served the students for the past three years. Somehow, desks for four more teachers were squeezed into the windowless storage room turned faculty office. The volunteers were given a low table—left over from the elementary school—in the corner of the room beneath a sagging bookshelf.

Next door, the new building's exterior was just about complete. Inside, work crews were wiring labs that would hold thirty computers and laying black slate tabletops in state-of-the-art chemistry labs. The teachers' offices would be located in two classrooms on the second floor. Every teacher would have a large desk and a new office chair. Both offices would be equipped with four or five computers, two copy machines, and two printers. The entire building would be wired for high-speed Internet access. Four additional resource rooms, each with fifteen computers, would be spread throughout the school.

The new building was a light at the end of the tunnel for both students and faculty tired of the school's drafty classrooms, rinky-dink computer lab with a few mismatched PCs, dank basement bathrooms, unreliable DSL connection, and treacherously steep basement staircases that inevitably led to traffic jams during passing periods.

Institutions are, by definition, established organizations or foundations, usually dedicated to a particular cause. Cristo Rey sought to live out the Jesuit ideal of *cura personalis*, or, "care for the person."

The new building was also the first physical symbol of a transformation that had begun to take place at Cristo Rey. The school was morphing from a grassroots start-up into a powerful educational institution.

Institutions are, by definition, established organizations or foundations, usually dedicated to a particular cause. Cristo Rey sought to live out the Jesuit ideal of *cura personalis*, a Latin phrase meaning "care for the person." Teachers, administrators, and staff members wanted not just to teach, but also to care for students, to prepare them as people for college and for life. In the early days, the school building felt like a home for a large family. Everyone shared the same two bathrooms and ate together. All the students congregated in the open space in the basement before and after school. On cold winter mornings, many of them would bring along steaming Styrofoam cups of champurrado, purchased from an elderly street vendor who sold tamales and the hot chocolate–like beverage in front of the school. The teachers worked in an adjacent room. Mary Kay Barron, a nurse practitioner, tended to the health needs of the students in much the same way a caring mother would.

"St. Joseph's was a regular high school," Leo Maldonado says, comparing Cristo Rey to his previous high school. "Cristo Rey was more like a family. Everybody knew everybody."

But as enrollment grew, the school began to feel less like a home. It became more difficult for the teachers to connect with all their students in a meaningful way as class sizes increased from fifteen to twenty or twenty-five and occasionally to thirty. The faculty and the administration, who had worked in tandem so beautifully in the early years, began to develop the adversarial relationship evident in most established educational institutions over issues such as compensation, class sizes, and scheduling. In the tension between the faculty and the board, the administration found itself stuck in the middle. Murphy and Foley defended the teachers and the pedagogy to the board. But the board wasn't concerned that the school feel like a home or that the faculty develop a cutting-edge curriculum. They wanted to develop a sustainable model so the school could stay open. In one meeting, board member Steve Baine said, "It's important to remember that we're not a research-and-development institution. We don't have the resources to be developing new ways to teach inner-city children in America. That's not who we are and it's not what we're supposed to be doing."

Both the McKinsey consultants and the board believed that more changes were necessary. The version of Cristo Rey Jesuit High School that would occupy the towering new classroom building at the corner of Wolcott Street and 22nd Place, the one that would have an enrollment of five hundred students, the one that was already talking about another building project—for a new gym, cafeteria, auditorium, library, and classroom space—would have to be dramatically different.

❀

JOEY GARCIA MIGHT AS well have had a bull's-eye on his chest when he showed up at Cristo Rey for the first day of Corporate Internship Program training in his pressed black slacks, olive green button-down shirt, black tie, and large glasses with thick lenses. At eighty pounds, he was probably one of the smallest students—male or female—in the freshman class. He was exactly the type of student that the class bully would choose as his whipping boy. Psychologists and school counselors say that students who are picked on often shut themselves off from the outside world. But Joey was already shut off. The two constants in his life—his mom and his stellar academic performance—were gone. He was lost and lonely. He walked into Cristo Rey that day looking for an anchor, a friend, a home—for something to fill the empty space in his life.

But no one talked to him. It seemed that all the students already knew each other. Joey sat on the edge of his seat at the end of a row in the assembly area. After a while, someone named Mr. Kendall called attendance. All the kids quieted down, which was nice, because then it didn't matter that no one was talking to him. After attendance, Mr. Kendall told everybody to board one of the buses outside. They were going to someplace called Whittman Hart for computer training. Joey climbed onto a bus. He glanced toward the back. All he could see were pairs of students. What if no one would make room for him? There was an empty seat in the front row, and he ducked into it. Soon a teacher sat down next to him. Joey closed his eyes, leaned his head against the window, and fell asleep.

Joey didn't sleep through all of his freshman year. In fact, as soon as classes started he regained his academic form, at least temporarily. In the first quarter, he posted nearly straight As. But he was much more concerned about being accepted at school and having friends, so he decided to run for student council. In the month leading up to the elections, Joey campaigned heavily for himself. Every day he'd rush to the cafeteria so he could be near the front of the food line. He'd eat quickly and then hit the campaign trail. Like many Chicago politicians, Joey believed votes could be bought, or "earned," so he began voluntarily busing cafeteria tables.

"Hi, I'm Joey Garcia. I'm running for the student council. Can I take your tray?"

By the end of the first week, he was cutting deals. He would bus the table where Alex, Tony, Juan, and Oscar sat for three weeks in exchange for their votes. He tried to cut a deal with Veronica and Victoria Garza, the twins who didn't really look alike, though they weren't too interested in having their table bused. But he was able to work out a deal with Urbano, Rafael, and Russ. As the election drew nearer, Joey was willing to do more and more for votes. When other freshmen told him they'd vote for him only if he drank a cup full of chocolate milk, apple juice, rice, crushed crackers, and chili, he agreed. By election day, every first-year student knew Joey. His antics won him the election and the group of friends he'd been looking for.

These were cool kids, the type of friends he'd never had before. By the beginning of the second quarter, Joey was sitting with them in the lunchroom and in classes. They didn't take school very seriously, and, Joey says, they were "always messing around—fooling around, hitting each other, throwing stuff, you know. Just the basic bad stuff. I'm not talking about stealing cars or anything. But they—well, we—were always talking in class. Never paying attention." Joey loved it. For the first time in his life, he was part of the in crowd. "I'd always wanted to be part of that group, making fun instead of getting made fun of."

Joey moved from the front of the classroom to the back. He had a mature sense of humor that often made his teachers laugh. But he quickly became a disciplinary problem, and the quality of his work slipped. Some of Joey's new friends never did their homework. Instead, they'd copy his. "Sometimes they'd copy my homework word for word," he says. "It's hard to believe we never got caught." Their approach to school amazed him and eventually led him to question his own approach. *If they're not doing their homework,* he asked himself, *why should I be doing mine?* By the end of the first semester, he was handing in less than 25 percent of his homework assignments, and his performance on tests and quizzes had dropped dramatically.

Looking back on the experience, he has no doubt in his mind about what happened. "They showed me laziness," he says. "They taught me to be lazy."

❋

In November, just a few weeks before final exams, students at Lewis University were to register for their spring semester classes. For more than a week, Leo's friends had been thumbing through the course book trying to figure out what classes to take during second semester. Just two days before the registration deadline, Leo still hadn't opened the book. "Fr. Planning had convinced me to go for just one semester," he says. "And I was done with one semester." He had taken basic classes and had no idea what he would major in. He hadn't given it any thought, since he didn't expect to be there long enough to have to worry about it. He'd chosen Lewis because they'd offered him the most student aid, and he wanted to make the whole college experiment as inexpensive as possible. At the urging of the school and Fr. Planning, Leo had agreed to live on campus during his first year.

He says that when he showed up on the first day, he wasn't sure he'd make it through the first semester. But it hadn't been that bad. He didn't have class that much, and the classes weren't so boring. The weekends were cool, too. There were parties to go to and girls to meet and intramural sports to play and all kinds of cool stuff to do. Something inside Leo was changing. The doubts that plagued him constantly were melting away. He was doing okay in his classes, better than he'd ever done at Cristo Rey. He was also working harder than he ever had. "Sometime around the end of the first semester," Leo says, "I realized it wasn't that bad. I actually kind of liked it." He decided to register for spring semester classes. To the rest of the world, Leo's decision may have seemed routine. But back at Cristo Rey, Steve Planning knew it was a triumph—a quiet one, but a triumphant nevertheless.

❉

IN DECEMBER 1999, MIKE Heidkamp traveled to Tacna, Peru, with his family and his good friend and fellow Cristo Rey teacher Brent Dexter to marry his fiancée, Charo. Just days after the school's new classroom building opened, in January 2000, Heidkamp's parents held a reception in Chicago for family and friends who hadn't been able to make the trip to Peru. The party was held in Cristo Rey's small gym, and the list of invitees included all of Cristo Rey's faculty and staff as well as every student in the senior class—a group of students who had begun at Cristo Rey as sophomores in the fall of 1997. Of the thirty-nine students who had enrolled then, only twenty-two remained.

Heidkamp taught their senior year social studies/civics class. In the second semester, after intensive training in basic Web design, the students were asked to design and build Web sites for various organizations with which some of their teachers were involved, including a Spanish-language alternative newspaper and a community theater. Each student had to learn as much as he or she could about an organization and then create a site that authentically and effectively represented it. Once the students completed that task, they built Web sites advocating for groups in society that Heidkamp deemed voiceless—refugees, homeless people, or abused children, to name a few. The students also conducted a year-long analysis of the local news media and kept a log of the stories that newspapers and TV stations chose to cover.

Every single one of the seniors showed up for Heidkamp's wedding reception—the boys in ties and jackets, the girls in dresses. Their presence was illustrative of Heidkamp's approach to teaching. He sought to turn the typical teacher-student relationship on its head. He didn't want his students to approach him as an all-knowing, all-powerful presence at the front of the classroom who dispensed knowledge from a seemingly vast reservoir. He wanted relationships with them. He wanted to search for knowledge and understanding alongside them. He wanted to learn from them and challenge them to learn and, most of all, to think.

Belinda Hernandez, one of the twenty-two seniors, says Heidkamp's class helped her take her first tentative steps as a critical thinker. Hernandez, who was the valedictorian of her class at Cristo Rey and has since completed both a bachelor's degree and a master's degree in social work at Loyola University Chicago, now works as the manager of grants and program administration at the Grand Victoria Foundation. "At first I hated Mr. Heidkamp's class because he forced such open participation. He forced you to have a voice. Eventually, I came to love that about it, but it was difficult to get used to. It wasn't easy to understand what he was trying to do at the time. One of the first assignments we had to do was write out a list of one hundred questions related to ourselves. The idea was that we were becoming private investigators and we were investigating our own lives. The process was really eye-opening for me. I think that's when I first started to question everything. Today I'm still asking all the hard questions, and I'm still unable to find the answers."

Hernandez says that many of her classmates thought Heidkamp's class was a waste of time. "Lots of folks complained that we weren't prepared in civics, history, and other core subjects for college. And that's true—we weren't really well prepared. But I've talked to many of the people from class recently, years after we took the class, and their opinions resonate with mine. The class wasn't a waste of time. For me, it was the beginning of a path."

The Heidkamps didn't serve alcohol with the students present at the reception, but that didn't stop anyone from having a good time. For dinner there were trays of carne asada, chicken, beans, quesadillas, and tortillas, and for dessert a tres leches cake. Heidkamp wore a tuxedo and Charo wore her wedding dress. Toasts were made and kind words spoken about the newlyweds. Mariachis played music, and family, friends, staff members, and students danced the night away beneath the flickering fluorescent lights in the low-slung gymnasium that stood in the shadow of Cristo Rey's new building.

No one knew it at the time, but Heidkamp's wedding reception and the opening of the new building marked the end of an era at Cristo Rey. Teachers and students raved about the new classroom building, with its wide hallways, large lockers, and spacious classrooms. The new building came with many new rules as well. Food was no longer allowed in the school. Teachers could drink coffee only out of covered cups. The rules weren't the only changes. The faculty and the students would no longer interact in the same way. The old building had been so small that teachers had seen almost every student just about every day. All the space in the new building meant that teachers would see less of their students, who would no longer gather outside the teacher workspace.

The tight-knit community that had characterized the first three and a half years at the school was expanding. Though no formal prohibitions were ever made, it soon became clear that there wasn't space in the new Cristo Rey for parties like the one the Heidkamps had thrown, which had been, really, a family party. As Cristo Rey became more of an institution, it would become less of a family. The key was finding the right balance.

IN THE SPRING OF 2000, the phone on John Foley's desk rang. Foley, who didn't have an administrative assistant, answered the call himself. "Hi, John. My name is Matt Powell. I'm calling from La Salle High School in Portland. I wanted to talk to you about a new school we're thinking about opening here." Foley reached quickly for a pen and notepad.

Nearly two years before, in the fall of 1998, the De La Salle Christian Brothers, a Catholic religious order founded during the seventeenth century by St. John Baptist de La Salle, had gathered in Chicago for an annual workshop, the theme of which was revitalizing the inner city. The primary ministry of the Christian Brothers, like that of the Jesuits, is education. De La Salle's original idea was to set up tuition-free schools for the children of France's poor and working class. He recruited unmarried young men to help with the effort, and eventually they created a religious order. With the help of seventy thousand lay colleagues, the Lasallian Christian Brothers now educate more than nine hundred thousand students in eighty countries each year.

News about Cristo Rey Jesuit High School had traveled to the American headquarters of the Lasallian Christian Brothers, in Washington, DC. The brothers wanted to learn more, so they invited Foley to speak at their 1998 Chicago meeting. In his remarks, Foley challenged them "to beat the Jesuits by becoming the first group to open another Cristo Rey–model school." Foley had long believed that Cristo Rey could and should be replicated.

La Salle High School, a Christian Brothers high school on the outskirts of Portland, Oregon, was at that time working with the University of Portland to conduct a feasibility study for a new Catholic high school in North Portland, an economically depressed neighborhood that had been without a Catholic secondary school since a fire leveled North Catholic High School in 1970.

In September of 1999, the archbishop of
Portland formally invited the La Salle community
to open a new high school in North Portland.

In December, they held a press conference
to announce the school, which they said would
be virtually tuition free. There was a great deal
of uncertainty about how the school would be
funded. In April 2000, Powell was named project coordinator and
set about trying to determine how to pay for the new school. One
of the Christian Brothers who'd attended the 1998 workshop in
Chicago suggested that Powell get in touch with Foley to see how
they'd done it.

As Cristo Rey became
more of an institution,
it would become less
of a family. The key
was finding the right
balance.

"We're going to open a school in North Portland," Powell
explained, "and we're interested in exploring whether the model
you're using in Chicago might work for us here."

"That's wonderful," Foley said. "We'll do whatever we can to help."

※

CRISTO REY CLOSED ITS fourth year with a small graduation
ceremony in the gym. Twenty-two students accepted their diplomas that day. Twenty-one of them would be pursuing additional
studies the coming fall. Belinda Hernandez would attend Loyola
University Chicago. Other members of the class planned to enroll
at Columbia College Chicago, Barat College, Lewis University,
DePaul University, Dominican University, Mount Mary College,
and Xavier University.

That year, Cristo Rey students generated $1.74 million of revenue
through their work and tuition payments. Seventy-two percent of
the school's income came from the work program. Unfortunately,
Cristo Rey's expenses were $2.6 million, which resulted in a deficit

of $860,000. To a casual observer, it might have seemed that Cristo Rey—even with McKinsey's help—had made little progress. But the school's administrators and board members knew that the financial outlook had improved dramatically.

The new building was open and already paid for. The capital campaign had been an immense success. More important, the additional space meant that Cristo Rey could expand its enrollment and increase revenue. The 22 graduating seniors would be replaced by nearly 140 freshmen. In the wake of McKinsey's report, Cristo Rey's board and administration had agreed to hike the fee for Corporate Internship Program sponsors from $19,500 to $25,000, but the change wouldn't take effect until 2002. In the year they'd just finished, Cristo Rey's students had offset 48 percent of the school's operating expenses with money they'd earned through their work and another 19 percent with their tuition. As enrollment and the CIP fee increased, the students would be able to offset more and more of the expenses. Everyone closely involved with the school knew that it was already working to some degree and would continue to work even better.

Cristo Rey board member Steve Baine says the fact that the Jesuits were thinking about replicating Cristo Rey even before they'd perfected their model is evidence that, from day one, they were thinking like the best venture capitalists. Venture investors look for businesses that are scalable and can be expanded quickly, because rapid growth translates into higher returns.

The Jesuits, though, weren't interested in generating traditional returns with Cristo Rey. "Profits" from the project wouldn't come in quarterly dividends, but rather in the profound impact the school would make on the lives of its students. Both Brad Schaeffer and John Foley knew that many other people around the country were similarly interested in educating the underserved. Because of that, they assumed the new model would grow quickly if it worked.

The circumstances in Chicago had been perfect for opening a school. Chicago is in many ways a Catholic city and has tremendous business resources. Graduates from Loyola Academy, St. Ignatius College Prep, and Loyola University who held influential positions in numerous local businesses had enthusiastically embraced Cristo Rey's work program. Graduates of Chicago's Jesuit schools had also become donors to Cristo Rey. Joseph Cardinal Bernardin, Francis Cardinal George, and the archdiocese had been exceedingly supportive of the school. They'd made the St. Stephen property available to the Jesuits when they were looking for a home for the school, and when the archdiocese decided to sell the land, they sold it to Cristo Rey for a fraction of its true value.

The Jesuits weren't interested in generating traditional returns with Cristo Rey. "Profits" from the project wouldn't come in quarterly dividends, but rather in the profound impact the school would make on the lives of its students.

Because these advantages would not necessarily exist in other cities, it would be no small challenge to create schools elsewhere based on the Cristo Rey model. Foley knew that the Chicago school had much to offer groups such as the one in Portland, but he also knew that the original project in Chicago was far from finished.

A Brilliant Venture... and a Lot of Capital 20

I N THE COURSE OF a couple of hours, the summer of 2000 became a turning point for the Cristo Rey model of education. The team at Cristo Rey might have been tempted to relax—they were, after all, occupying a brand-new building and hadn't taken on any debt to build it. Equally important, they had a much better handle on the financial reality of the school. They now knew that collecting full tuition from every student would generate just enough revenue to offset all the operating expenses.

But Cristo Rey was offering financial aid to more than 75 percent of the student body. As long as the school did that, there would be a deficit. Cutting financial aid wasn't ever considered. Instead, the decision was made to direct all the proceeds from the annual ¡Viva! fund-raiser to scholarship assistance. Any leftover deficit would be made up through other charitable contributions. Instead of raising one million dollars or more each year to keep the doors open, Cristo Rey was faced with raising one hundred thousand to two hundred thousand dollars.

Despite the much-improved financial situation, there remained a great deal of work to do. The faculty had homework for the summer. Still without a curriculum, they'd divided themselves into subject-specific groups (they didn't call these groups "departments," as they'd long resisted the division of the faculty into departments) that would research best practices in curriculum. The subject-specific groups weren't divided along the usual lines. Instead of focusing on the subjects often taught in high schools, Cristo Rey's faculty had chosen to build their curriculum around skills they wanted their students to have when they graduated. One group would work on developing a writing curriculum. Another would work on scientific and research skills. Another would focus on language—both Spanish and English.

Many of the teachers had also begun to express concern about the performance of Cristo Rey's students in college. Faculty members caught up with graduates who came back to visit during the holidays and got updates on many of those who didn't visit. Gustavo Rodríguez was thriving at Xavier and had helped found a student group for Latino students. He was talking about becoming a teacher. Leo Maldonado, much to the surprise of many at Cristo Rey, was excelling in his classes at Lewis. His grades there were higher than they'd ever been in high school. But there was bad news, too. Enrique Garcia*, one of Leo's classmates and one of the most talented students in the class, had dropped out of the University of Illinois. He'd come back to visit Cristo Rey, and when the teachers asked him why he'd left, he said it was "too quiet" in Champaign and that he was homesick. He missed the familiar streets of his neighborhood.

Cristo Rey had succeeded in getting its students into college, but the school was supposed to be preparing its students to *succeed* in college, not just to get in. Many weren't making it. Why? Were the students not prepared for the academic rigors of college-level classes? Or was it something else? Were they unprepared for life in a school where Latinos were a distinct minority? Was it simply homesickness? Many of the teachers felt that answering those questions was critical

---

* Not his real name.

to developing a curriculum that could success-fully prepare Cristo Rey's students for college.

The Corporate Internship Program also had a great deal of work to do during the summer of 2000. During the 1999–2000 school year, it had provided jobs for all of Cristo Rey's 288 students. Only sixty-three of the seventy-two jobs, though, had generated revenue for the school. Cristo Rey hadn't been able to find corporate sponsors for all of Cristo Rey's students, so thirty-six students were working for sponsors who couldn't afford to pay the school—all local nonprofit organizations. Cristo Rey needed every student to have a paying job. The shortfall in paying sponsors translated to a deficit of $175,500. In the coming year, Cristo Rey planned to increase enrollment from 288 to 400, which meant the CIP team needed to find thirty-seven additional paying jobs. Kendall, De La Rosa, and their new assistant directors spent the summer calling on corporate sponsors and holding presentations to try to drum up additional interest in the program.

> Cristo Rey had succeeded in getting its students into college, but the school was supposed to be preparing its students to *succeed* in college, not just to get in.

In the spring of 2000, Jeff Thielman had secured the final gift in Cristo Rey's $14 million capital campaign and, in the process, had proved just about everyone wrong. Over the next month or so, additional gifts Thielman had been pursuing came in and boosted the total amount raised to nearly $15 million. But Thielman—who gives much of the credit for the fund-raising success to Foley—certainly wasn't patting himself on the back. In fact, he and Foley—along with Cristo Rey's board—had already launched the silent phase of a second campaign that would raise money for a new building that would house a gym, a library, a cafeteria, and classrooms. The second building, planned for the property occupied by Cristo Rey's existing gym and cafeteria, had been part of the vision of the board's buildings and grounds committee from the outset. But they didn't think they could raise enough money to construct two buildings at once.

Thielman says he wanted to "raise a couple million" before he stepped down at the end of the calendar year. Despite working seventy to eighty hours a week and living in Chicago, he had maintained a relationship with Christine Power, a Northwestern Mutual Life financial adviser he'd met when he lived in Boston. He proposed over Christmas 1999 and planned to move back to Boston after their wedding at the end of 2000. Foley and Thielman had begun to look for a replacement, but Foley worried that Thielman was irreplaceable.

As the school's director of development and public relations, Thielman had become the primary liaison between Cristo Rey in Chicago and the team planning the new school in Portland, Oregon; he had already invited them to come spend a week at Cristo Rey during the 2000–2001 school year. Additional groups had also called to inquire about replicating Cristo Rey. The archbishop of Los Angeles had asked the Jesuits of the California province to explore the possibility of converting Verbum Dei, a venerable Catholic high school in South Los Angeles, to the Cristo Rey model. Fr. Michael Pfleger, a well-known and occasionally controversial parish priest at St. Sabina, a large, predominantly African American parish on the South Side of Chicago, had begun studying the possibility of opening a Cristo Rey–model school at his parish. There were faint rumblings that a group in Waukegan, Illinois, a blue-collar suburb forty miles north of downtown Chicago, was interested in the model as well.

LOOKING BACK ON HER time in high school, Maritza says one of the most important things she learned was that "you fall and you pick yourself up just to fall again. But you still have to get back up." By the time the summer break between her sophomore and junior years rolled around, Martiza had both fallen and managed to pick herself up. She was glad to see her tumultuous sophomore year draw to a close.

Maritza had enjoyed relatively smooth sailing during her first year and a half at Cristo Rey and had finally gotten used to her chores around the house. She'd learned to speak English and was doing well in school. All that changed when she visited Mexico midway through her sophomore year to spend the holidays with her family. Before the trip, she had learned that her grandmother was sick, but she didn't understand just how sick until she saw her. Her grandmother could barely get out of bed and was no longer able to eat solid food. "She was dying," Maritza says. "I could tell she was dying."

Maritza, though, had a hard time admitting it. "My grand-mother was my mother. She took me in and raised me. She gave me everything she had." After Maritza had moved to Chicago, she and her grandmother had kept in close contact, speaking occasionally on the phone and writing letters. Maritza couldn't bear to see her sick. When it was time for Maritza to return to Chicago for the start of the second semester at Cristo Rey, she left without saying good-bye to her grandmother. "I thought if I pretended she wasn't dying, somehow, maybe, it wouldn't happen."

In the next weeks, Maritza's grandmother called Chicago many times, wanting to say good-bye. Maritza wouldn't take the calls. In mid-February, her grandmother died. Maritza and her mom traveled for nearly twenty-four hours on a series of planes and buses to get to the small village where Maritza's grandparents lived. Maritza and her mother, Socorro, spent a week and a half in Mexico. "I felt like I'd lost everything," Maritza says. In addition to being sad, she was really mad. "I kind of felt God had taken away the only thing I had.

And I was angry because I felt my grandmother had given up on me. I was also very angry with my family, because I felt like I was the only one grieving. Everyone else just went on with their lives."

Maritza and her mom returned to Chicago, and Maritza went straight back to school. Her teachers told her that she could take her time getting back to her homework, but she didn't. She started handing in assignments right away. Yet she knew her life had changed, and her mom's had, too. There had been tension between the two of them even before Maritza's grandmother died. Afterward, it got worse. Socorro's boyfriend, the father of Maritza's brother and sister, had moved out, and Socorro had recently begun dating. Whenever she was gone, Maritza was responsible for her siblings. There were many nights when Maritza missed parties or trips to the movies because her mom was out. Every time it happened, Maritza heard the words of her family members in Mexico: "Don't go up to Chicago. Your mom just wants a babysitter." Maritza felt that she'd been given all the responsibilities, while her mom lived like a carefree teenager, going to parties, having fun, and answering to no one.

The tension between Maritza and her mom reached a boiling point when, a few months later, Maritza didn't come home in time to look after her siblings. Socorro had a date planned and needed Maritza to watch the kids. Socorro's date was outside honking the car horn and Maritza was nowhere to be seen, and Socorro couldn't leave the little kids alone. Eventually, her date left. Socorro was incensed. When Maritza came home a few hours later, a fight erupted. Maritza and Socorro remember the fight differently. Socorro says Maritza hit her. Maritza says her mom hit her.

The next day, Socorro took Maritza to Mujeres Latinas en Acción, a bilingual and bicultural social services agency in Pilsen that offers support to Latina women and their families. The counselors at Mujeres Latinas talked to both Maritza and her mom and eventually checked Maritza into a mental health facility in the western suburbs, where she was diagnosed with depression. "The thing with depression," Maritza says, "is that you're not thinking. You're not doing anything. But when I was there, I realized I had a choice in all this. I realized what I was going through wasn't the end of the world." Her most important realization was that "if I wanted to do something, I had to do it on my own." That resolve would become increasingly important as Maritza began to think about applying to college.

❈

JEFF THIELMAN WAITED ANXIOUSLY, his black Toyota Corolla parked outside the United Airlines terminal at Chicago's O'Hare International Airport. B. J. Cassin and his daughter Cate were flying in from San Jose to see Cristo Rey. Thielman knew that if Cassin liked Cristo Rey, he was capable of making a multimillion-dollar gift. It would be a perfect way to start the silent phase of the campaign for the new building.

The two had first met in June of 1988. Thielman, then in his third year of volunteer service in Peru, had traveled to the United States to raise money for the burgeoning Cristo Rey Center for the Working Child, which he had founded in Tacna. By that time, Thielman had fast-talked the local authorities into donating a substantial parcel of land to the center, and he needed cash to finance the construction of a building. He was on his own, because the center wasn't then officially sanctioned by the Peruvian Jesuits. So Thielman traveled from Peru to Los Altos, California, where he spoke to parishioners at St. Nicholas. Los Altos and Los Altos Hills, quaint communites in

Silicon Valley, were home to many of the businesspeople whose ideas and money were fueling the technological revolution.

B. J. Cassin was one of those people. He'd grown up in Lowell, Massachusetts, the son of a furniture store manager who'd never graduated from high school and a hardworking housewife who was the only one of five children in her family to graduate from high school. His parents stressed the importance of church and education, but Cassin made mostly Cs at Keith Academy, a high school run by the Xaverian Brothers, before enrolling at Holy Cross, a Jesuit college in Worcester, Massachusetts, where he majored in economics. After graduation, he joined the Marines.

In 1960, after five years in Virginia, Japan, and California, Cassin left the Marines and got married. From 1960 to 1969, he worked in various sales and marketing positions at Tidewater Oil, Crown Zellerbach Paper, and Memorex. In 1969, he and four other Memorex employees founded Xidex, a company that produced microfilm, with capital provided by local venture capitalists. They gained 75 percent of the market share before expanding into the manufacture of data storage media. In 1976, Xidex went public. Cassin retired in 1979 but maintained a seat on the board of directors. He then began his own career as a venture capital investor. During the 1980s, he made early investments in a number of new technology companies. His timing couldn't have been better. The remarkable growth of the personal computer industry—fueled in large part by Apple computers and Microsoft's new Windows operating system—created demand for all kinds of new hardware, and even more software. Once a piece of software had been developed, it cost virtually nothing to reproduce. It was a high-margin, high-growth business that made a lot of money for a lot of people, including B. J. Cassin.

On June 5, 1988, Cassin and his wife, Bebe, attended the 8:00 a.m. Mass at St. Nicholas, during which Thielman spoke about the Cristo Rey Center for the Working Child. Thielman spoke quickly, trying to squeeze in as much detail as possible. He told the congregation he had an opportunity to expand the center, thanks to the land the local government had finally given him, and that he needed their help to do it.

Halfway through Thielman's talk, Bebe nudged her husband and said, "You've gotta do something to help this kid." Outside church after Mass, Cassin asked Thielman how much money he needed to raise. "Twenty-five thousand dollars would probably be enough for the building," Thielman said. "But I don't expect to raise all of it during this one visit." He wasn't looking for major gifts. He was counting on various churches to share their collections with him. Thielman hoped to get five hundred dollars from the parishioners at St. Nicholas. Cassin went home and returned minutes later with a five-thousand-dollar check and a business card. He told Thielman to keep in touch. "I didn't know then," Cassin says, "that once I got into Jeff's Rolodex, I'd never get out."

Where there's smoke, Thielman reasoned, there's fire, so that night he called Cassin and asked if he could tell him more about the project. On Monday night, Thielman had dinner with the Cassins. On Tuesday, Thielman went to Cassin's office, located in an attractive business park on Sand Hill Road that housed virtually all of the major venture capital firms in the United States. Cassin introduced Thielman to a handful of venture capitalists. By the time he left, Thielman had collected over twenty-five thousand dollars. Days later, he was on a plane to Peru, where he oversaw the construction of what remains today the main building of the Cristo Rey Center for the Working Child's campus on the outskirts of Tacna.

Back in the States, the computers and computer programs Cassin and the rest of the venture capital community in Silicon Valley had helped fund were becoming more widely used.

One major catalyst was Jim Clark and Marc Andreessen's 1994 release of the Netscape Navigator Web browser. The browser sparked a revolution that had been years in the making. The groundwork had been laid behind closed doors in government labs, university basements, dorm rooms, garages, and fledgling high-tech firms looking for the next big thing. It was carried out by geeks who had discovered methods to communicate instantly with people halfway around the world. The ramifications of such a network of communication were mind-boggling. The geeks, however, didn't know how to include the rest of the world in the network.

But Jim Clark did know. He knew that if people understood the technology that Tim Berners-Lee had developed three years earlier at CERN, they would use it. And if a lot of people used something, there was a lot of commercial potential. So Clark, a Stanford geek turned businessman, hired the guys from the University of Illinois who had cooked up the Mosaic browser and started Netscape Communications. Tens of millions of people downloaded Netscape Navigator, the Web browser they created. Entrepreneurs and established businesses recognized the commercial potential immediately and began building businesses for the Web. Almost overnight, the technological revolution spawned scores of new markets. B. J. Cassin made investments in many of those companies. When the start-ups went public or were bought—which happened with startling regularity during the tech boom—they provided enormous returns.

From 1980 to 2000, many of Cassin's venture investments were enormously successful. He won't say how successful. In fact, he won't say much at all about his work. He's more interested in talking about ways to improve education. For many years, he served as a board member at Saint Mary's College of California, a small liberal arts school run by the De La Salle Christian Brothers, the same religious order that was considering opening a Cristo Rey high school in Portland. For years, Cassin had been providing scholarships to Saint Mary's for high-achieving students from modest economic backgrounds in the Bay Area. Sometimes the students thrived; sometimes they didn't. The failures saddened him. "My parents stressed education," Cassin says. "My mother's sisters went on strike and wouldn't go to work unless my grandparents would let her go to school past the seventh grade because she was a good student and talented. My brother became a teacher. I know what education has done for me personally. I got a tremendous high school education and a great education at Holy Cross."

Cassin wanted to do more. By the late 1990s, he'd become "distressed by the shrinking of Catholic schools, especially in the inner city," and he was looking for new philanthropic endeavors. "I'd been looking for something other than just giving scholarships. That's brute-force philanthropy. It's not sustainable." That's why Cassin had agreed to visit Chicago. He'd been invited by Thielman and Trish O'Brien, a Saint Mary's alum who was volunteering at San Miguel, a small middle school in Chicago run by the Lasallian Christian Brothers. The school served primarily Hispanic immigrants in Chicago's Back of the Yards neighborhood, and much of the staff was made up of volunteer teachers. O'Brien had met Cassin when she was president of Saint Mary's student body and held a nonvoting seat on the board. Like O'Brien, Thielman had kept in touch with Cassin and wanted him to come out to Chicago to see the project he was working on.

In the final week of June 2000, Cassin and his daughter Cate flew to Chicago to visit the two schools. At Cristo Rey, Thielman and Foley gave them a tour of the school and an in-depth explanation of how it worked. Cassin was fascinated and asked Thielman a number of probing questions. "He was interested in how sustainable we believed the school really was," Theilman remembers. "We told him about McKinsey and the changes we'd made."

After the tour, Foley and Thielman took Cassin to dinner at a local Mexican restaurant. Thielman's sense that Cassin liked the school was confirmed when he said, "Well, I like what you guys are doing. What can I do to help?" They were the words Thielman had longed to hear. He'd raised enough money to know those words meant a big gift was on the way, the kind of gift that could become the foundation of a capital campaign.

He was smiling to himself when Foley said, "Well, I think what we probably need the most help with is figuring out a way to help other people who are thinking about opening Cristo Rey schools." Thielman was floored. The plan had been to ask for a lead gift for the capital campaign for the next building. And it was clear they could get it. "Groups in Portland and Los Angeles and around here are asking us for help," Foley continued, "and we're trying to figure out the best way to share what we've learned."

Thielman was the perfect straight man. Though he had no idea what Foley was doing and couldn't believe the lead gift for their campaign was slipping through their fingers, he nodded earnestly.

PART 3

The Mission Realized

———❋———

Summer 2000–Present

Tensegrity (n): A contraction of the words *tension* and *integrity*. Tension is the force created by pulling or stretching an object, and integrity is a state of wholeness or completeness. The combination of the two provides for structures whose shapes are held together by tension and remain flexible and strong.

> *Coined by Buckminster Fuller,*
> *the late inventor, architect, engineer,*
> *mathematician, poet, and cosmologist*

Taking Initiative   21

WHEN B. J. CASSIN considers an investment opportunity, he pays especially close attention to two things. First, is the business profitable, or can it become profitable? Second, how easily can the business be grown? Can it be franchised? Are there obstacles to growth? What would it take to expand the business nationally or even internationally?

He found himself asking those questions of Cristo Rey during his brief visit to Chicago in June of 2000, and he liked the answers. The more he discussed the school with his daughter Cate on their flight back to San Jose, the more he liked it. Cristo Rey's founders knew what was going on and were responding to reality. Cassin liked their approach. Catholic schools in the United States had, for centuries, served the poor. He'd benefited from one of those schools, and it bothered him to see more and more Catholic schools serving only middle- and upper-class students. But that was all they could do, given the shrinking numbers of religious available to staff schools and the inability of poorer populations to pay tuition.

Cristo Rey had found a way around the problem. And the school was profitable—though not in the way typical of most businesses Cassin assessed. He knew that profit meant more than net income and cash flow; it is, by definition, an advantageous gain, a benefit. Cassin thought back to the few minutes he'd spent with Judy Murphy during his visit. Murphy and Jeff Thielman had early

> Just a day after his visit to Cristo Rey, Cassin called John Foley and explained that he was creating a foundation with two million dollars that would help fund the replication of the Cristo Rey school, San Miguel schools, and Nativity schools.

data on the progress of their students, and it was good. There was substantial anecdotal evidence as well. Murphy talked about students with limited English skills expanding their abilities to the point where they could read at grade level and write papers in English. She talked about students who'd never made a grade higher than a C in middle school or in their previous high schools working hard and getting into college. In Cassin's view, that was the main thing—these kids were getting into college, which was definitely an advantageous gain. Cristo Rey also had clear growth potential. Numerous groups were already interested in expanding the model in other cities.

Just a day after his visit to Cristo Rey, Cassin called John Foley and explained that he and his wife, Bebe, were creating a foundation with two million dollars that would help fund the replication of the Cristo Rey school, San Miguel schools, and Nativity schools. A month later, he called again to say they had sold some property and were putting an additional twenty million dollars into the foundation. "Oh my Lord, B. J.," Foley exclaimed, "this is wonderful. My Lord, this is just wonderful."

In the blink of an eye, Cristo Rey Jesuit High School became the Cristo Rey movement.

"Come on, Mom. We're gonna be late," Mayra said, looking at the kitchen clock in the two-bedroom apartment at Nineteenth Street and Ashland Avenue that her family had moved into a couple years earlier. It was orientation day for students and parents at Cristo

Rey, and Mayra—after a week of CIP training stressing the importance of punctuality—didn't want to be late. Cristo Rey was a ten-
minute walk from their apartment, and the orientation was supposed
to start in just twelve minutes.

It's hard to say who was more excited for orientation that fall of
2000, Mayra or her mom, Maria. It had been Mayra's decision to go
to Cristo Rey. She wanted to try the new school, she says, because
"no one in my family who went to Juárez had gotten far in life."
Maria stressed education with all her children and dreamed of sending them to college. She was thrilled about Cristo Rey, which she
figured would help get Mayra into college. Mayra, too, was excited,
but on the morning of orientation her excitement looked more like
anxiety. "Mom, we can't be late. Please. I'm just gonna wait outside
on the sidewalk." Maria was busy tending to her eight younger children. Junior and Henry, the next two oldest, were going to watch the
little kids while Maria was at school, but it was always hard for her
to get out the door.

"Okay, let's go," Maria said moments later as she rushed out the
door and up the concrete steps outside their basement apartment.
She and Mayra headed west to Wolcott and turned left. It was two
minutes before eight and they were still four blocks from school.
Mayra, a few steps ahead of her mom, turned and said, "Can you
hurry? We're going to be late." Walking backward, Mayra looked
closely at her mom and then said, "I can't believe that's what you're
wearing, jeans and a T-shirt. And your shoes don't match the rest
of your clothes. You should take better care of yourself and make
yourself look better."

Maria took Mayra's comments in stride. She nodded and said,
"Okay," and tried to walk faster. Looking back, though, Maria admits
the words stung. "She let me down there. I didn't have the money to

get dressed up. I don't have the money now. I wear what I wear every day." At the orientation, Maria, who had served for ten years on both the Parent-Teacher Association and the Local School Council at the elementary school her kids attended, listened intently. By the time she left, she was even more convinced that Cristo Rey was a dream come true. She'd initially worried about the tuition—even though the school was designed to be affordable, Maria knew there was no way she could pay twenty-two hundred dollars a year. But the school had given Mayra an application for financial aid. The application asked Maria to list the family's annual income. Her husband didn't provide anything for the family. He could fix VCRs and TVs, but Maria says she never saw a dime of the money he made—most of it went toward buying booze. By the time Mayra started high school, her dad had also begun dabbling in cocaine. Mayra knew because she'd seen him and some of his friends snorting it on the porch behind their apartment. "He tried not to do it in front of us," Mayra says, "but we were kids—curious, you know." Maria totaled up the food stamps and welfare checks she received and the money she made from selling her handmade piñatas. It came to just over ten thousand dollars.

She received word in the summer of 2000 that Mayra would receive full financial aid. The school was a godsend. And the orientation only strengthened her opinion about Cristo Rey. The school wanted its graduates to go to college; that was Maria's goal, too, especially for Mayra.

Maria had stressed the importance of education for all her children. By volunteering on the Local School Council—a job that gave her an opportunity to be in the school most days—she was able to keep track of all the kids. She constantly pushed them to do their homework. She knew that their cramped apartment wasn't the ideal place for homework. People were always coming and going. There was usually a pot of beans or rice on the stove and someone eating at the small kitchen table. Despite the many distractions at home, all the ball games Mayra played, and all the time she spent at the park, she had somehow stayed focused on school. Every night she put on her headphones and did her homework. Maria knew the younger kids looked up to Mayra. If Mayra did well at Cristo Rey and got into college, it would make it easier for the others to go. If they could see Mayra doing it, they'd be able to see themselves doing it.

Maria was excited about Cristo Rey after the orientation, but it didn't soothe the hurt from Mayra's comments earlier in the day. That night, Maria sat her daughter down at the kitchen table. "This is me," Maria said, touching her chest. She was wearing the same T-shirt she'd had on that morning. "This is who I am, and I wanna feel good about myself. And I don't ever want you to change and to start seeing people for what they have. This is life. It's the way life is. Not everybody has the good things. But you make of life what you can and you live with it the way God wants you to." Mayra didn't say anything. Maria couldn't tell if she was even listening.

✳

CRISTO REY WAS CHANGING rapidly, and this was especially clear at the start of the 2000–2001 school year. Just over 150 freshmen had enrolled in the school, by far Cristo Rey's largest-ever incoming class. They replaced the 21 seniors who had graduated the year before. Enrollment at the school had increased to almost 400 students.

They started the school year in the new building. When Mayra and her classmates walked into Cristo Rey's state-of-the-art new classroom building for the first time, there was little doubt in any of their minds that Cristo Rey was a "real" school—meaning it physically resembled the public and private schools their friends attended. Four years ago, Leo, Gustavo, and their classmates had felt that Cristo Rey, with its small student body, narrow hallways, and "little kid" bathrooms, was more like a house than a legitimate school. But when Mayra's class arrived, they entered a facility that truly looked like an educational institution.

Another shift, invisible to the students, had taken place, and it was a painful one for both the faculty and the administration. It was set into motion when one of Cristo Rey's teachers—an extremely talented Mexican American woman who taught both Spanish and English—became pregnant at the end of the 1999–2000 school year. The woman was engaged to the baby's father at the time, and the school's administrators told her she could not return the following year unless she got married.

They cited a number of reasons for this mandate. First, Cristo Rey is a Catholic school that embraces and promotes the teachings of the Catholic Church, which forbids sexual intercourse outside of marriage. The administrators felt they could not have a teacher on staff openly reject the church's teachings. In addition, three of Cristo Rey's female students had become pregnant since the school opened its doors. Cristo Rey allowed the students to stay in school and went out of its way to help them. The pregnancies, though, were troubling, and the school's administrators had been discussing a variety of measures to address the issue. Having one of the most popular teachers in the school pregnant and unmarried would not help. Whether they admitted it or not, the students at Cristo Rey, like students at any high school, looked up to their teachers, which meant that every teacher, intentionally or not, was setting an example.

The pregnant teacher was a great asset to the school. She'd been raised in the United States by Mexican parents and was able to understand the tension that existed between the traditional Mexican values of many of Cristo Rey's parents and the values of the teenage pop culture embraced by the students. She understood, too, the delicate situation her students faced as children of immigrants growing up in a foreign culture. More than anyone else at the school, she could understand how the students battled to be like other teenagers but were reminded constantly that they were different from the majority population. She was fluent in Spanish, and she was one of only two Mexican American teachers at Cristo Rey.

The teacher refused to rush her wedding and was not allowed to return to Cristo Rey. During the first faculty meeting of the 2000–2001 school year, the teachers, outraged by the administration's decision, sidestepped the planned agenda and initiated a discussion about their colleague's dismissal. "What happens," one faculty member asked, "if a male teacher fathers a child out of wedlock? Will he be dismissed?" The consensus seemed to be that he would not be dismissed unless the administration became aware of the fact that he'd had a child. "Then we have a double standard," one of the faculty members said. "Female teachers are held to a higher standard because they become visibly pregnant." The discussion became more and more heated, and the administrators became more and more defensive. Cristo Rey's employee handbook, which included a clause about living in accord with the teachings of the Catholic Church, was cited repeatedly. Questions were raised about sexual orientation. If a teacher was gay, would he or she be dismissed? No clear answers were given.

The first meeting of Cristo Rey's fifth school year stood in sharp contrast to the final meeting of the previous year, when members of the faculty and administration had gathered to tell stories celebrating teaching and all that had been accomplished that year. Though the tension was, for the most part, invisible to students, the relationship between Cristo Rey's faculty and administration had been fractured,

Though the tension was, for the most part, invisible to students, the relationship between Cristo Rey's faculty and administration had been fractured, quite possibly permanently.

quite possibly permanently. The tension wasn't just a result of the teacher's dismissal. The faculty had gone a year without a pay raise, and they'd been asked to teach more classes.

Teaching more classes might not seem unreasonable, especially given the findings of the McKinsey study—that Cristo Rey teachers were in the classroom far less than their colleagues in peer schools. Teaching more and preparing less, though, was a philosophical break from the commitment by the faculty during the school's early years to custom build a curriculum for the school's students. There was also another important practical matter: Cristo Rey still hadn't settled on a formal curriculum. That meant that each year teachers were essentially building their classes from the ground up, which is a great deal of work. Because of the complex schedule that resulted from Cristo Rey's Corporate Internship Program, when teachers were asked to teach more, they were usually asked to teach another class and not just another section of a class they were already teaching. On the surface, an additional forty minutes of instruction time didn't seem so bad. But it was usually coupled with the responsibility of developing an additional curriculum.

In many ways, the changes at Cristo Rey made sense. The school was becoming an institution, and at nearly every educational institution there exists significant tension between faculties and administrations. From the start, though, Cristo Rey had hoped to be different.

Points and the Spread

22

MAYRA'S BASKETBALL PRACTICES IN junior high usually started with layup lines and ball-handling drills. The first day of high school tryouts, held in early November, was completely different. There were only twelve girls that day—six more were at work. After stretches, the coach split them into two teams of six and gave one team black pullover jerseys. Mayra had heard that the girls' team had won only one game the previous year, but she wasn't taking tryouts lightly. She sized up the other team quickly as the coach lined them up for tip-off. After starting the scrimmage, he sat listlessly on the sidelines with a notebook in his lap and a whistle in his hands.*

The ball traveled the length of the court twice. No baskets were scored. Two of the four possessions ended with passes sailing out-of-bounds. On another, one of the girls dribbled off her foot. After the fourth turnover, Mayra had seen enough. She ran toward the

---

*I was the girls' coach that year—and I wasn't exactly excited to be there. Mike, Andy, and I had coached the team during our first year at the school, and it had been a disaster. We won just one game (the last of the season, played against another school's freshman team) and lost twelve, most of them decisively. The bad memories of the season were fresh in my mind when Dan Bowden, Cristo Rey's athletic director, asked me if I was interested in coaching the girls' basketball team again. "No," I said, emphatically. Weeks later, Bowden said, "I think you've got to do it. I was told we don't have enough money in the budget to hire a coach. So I think it's your job whether you want it or not."

girl inbounding the ball and clapped her hands twice. After taking the pass, she walked the ball up the court, surveying the defense. It was unfamiliar territory for her. She'd never been the point guard in grade school; someone else always brought up the ball. In the games she played with her uncle at Barrett Park, Mayra always guarded guys—sometimes boys from the neighborhood and sometimes men twice her age—and she had come to think of herself more as a defensive player. Many of the guys were fast and strong. She'd learned to move her feet and use her body to keep them from an easy trip to the basket. Now, however, Mayra was playing offense. She wanted to pass the ball, but the girls on her team were just standing still. No one was open, or trying to get open.

When Mayra was five feet from the three-point stripe, her defender rushed out to meet her. Mayra accelerated, and the defender turned to run in an effort to keep up. Just as Mayra moved past the right end of the free throw line, she crossed over her dribble, and the defender sailed past her. Left wide open, Mayra knocked down a jump shot with seeming ease. She sprinted to the other end of the court and set up to play defense, all the while telling herself it was a good start.*

---

*Mayra's jumper in the first five minutes of the first day of tryouts helped change my attitude. So did a conversation with Julie Minikel-Lacocque, Cristo Rey's girls' soccer coach. There was a spirit on the sidelines of the soccer field that had been lacking completely from the basketball team. So when Bowden told me I'd been sentenced to coach again, I scheduled a meeting with Julie to ask her what I could do to get similar results. Julie, who had played college soccer, helped me understand that few people took Cristo Rey's female athletes seriously—not other students, not their parents, and not most of the teachers. I hadn't taken them seriously during my first year. Julie talked about female athletes being more open to instruction than males and being goal oriented. I clearly needed to change my approach.

❋

MAYRA AND HER 152 freshmen classmates had boosted Cristo Rey's enrollment to 394 students. For the first time, the school was covering more than half its operating expenses with revenues generated through CIP. Cristo Rey's reputation in the neighborhood had improved dramatically, and teachers no longer had to recruit students off the street. In fact, more students were applying to Cristo Rey than the school could accept, and with each passing year the caliber of incoming students—as measured by standardized test scores and grades—improved.

The credit for Cristo Rey's turnaround goes to a number of different groups: the board of trustees, who called for change; the faculty and administration, who worked hard to implement the changes suggested by McKinsey; and the students, who took on an additional day of work each month to help increase revenue. Perhaps no one person, though, was more responsible for the turnaround than Rosemary Croghan. Croghan was the only board member who believed that the perspectives of both the educators and businesspeople on the board were entirely valid. She knew that growing the school and providing student-centered education wasn't an either/or proposition; Cristo Rey had to do both. It had to serve students in new and unique ways and had to be careful about its finances. Because she understood and respected both perspectives, she was able to get both sides to discuss compromises and to understand each other. In doing so, she just may have saved Cristo Rey.

Cristo Rey's stabilization and success, coupled with news coverage of the announcement of the Cassins' foundation, sparked interest around the country in replicating the model. At the time, no one, including B. J. Cassin, knew just what the foundation would look like or how it would work. Just before the 2000–2001 school year

The credit for Cristo Rey's turnaround goes to the board of trustees, who called for change; the faculty and administration, who worked hard to implement the changes; and the students, who took on an additional day of work each month to help increase revenue.

started, Cassin hired Thielman, who was getting married and moving back to Boston, to be the executive director of the Cassin Educational Initiative Foundation. Thielman had become Cristo Rey's point person on the replication effort, speaking regularly with the group in Portland and fielding calls from groups all over the country requesting more information.

During the fall of 2000, Thielman and Cassin set about developing the mechanics of the foundation. Ultimately, they decided on a three-pronged plan. Any group seeking to open a school would have to conduct a feasibility study, not unlike the one Jim Gartland had done in Chicago. The foundation would fund the studies with grants of up to seventy thousand dollars.

The risk that the foundation would fund a study that wouldn't ultimately be approved as a school was one Cassin was "glad to take," if it helped weed out schools that ultimately shouldn't open.

The foundation's second initiative would be making larger grants to help offset the start-up expenses of the new schools. The third component of the foundation's work involved establishing a national network of Cristo Rey–model schools.

In late September, Thielman flew to Los Angeles, where the California province Jesuits had begun a formal process to discern whether or not to convert Verbum Dei to the Cristo Rey model. In late September, St. Sabina, Fr. Michael Pfleger's South Side parish, launched a feasibility study. In October 2000, Thielman hosted Matt Powell from Portland at Cristo Rey. He spent a week at the school studying how the Corporate Internship Program worked. A month later, after the Cassin Foundation made a gift enabling Powell to hire a Corporate Internship Program director, the board of trustees in Portland officially adopted the Cristo Rey model for their new school.

In October, John Foley led a group of American educators on a journey to Peru to study the Fe y Alegría educational movement. Foley was joined on the trip by Rich Clark, a Loyola Academy graduate who'd become principal of St. Ignatius High School in Cleveland, Ohio; Fr. Jim Stoeger, SJ, a graduate of St. Xavier High School in Cincinnati, a former principal of Brebeuf Jesuit Preparatory School in Indianapolis, and then the provincial assistant for secondary education in Chicago; and Fr. Larry Reuter, SJ, a former president of Loyola Academy who was then the vice president for mission and ministry at Loyola University Chicago. In the seven years since Jim Gartland had taught in a Fe y Alegría school in Peru, the movement had doubled in size. It was operating more than 1,000 schools and employing 35,000 people, in addition to running 67 radio stations, 900 extension education centers, and more than 700 alternative education centers. That year, Fe y Alegría schools would educate more than one million students.

The team from Cristo Rey was interested in that growth. How had a tiny grassroots movement started in a Venezuelan home by a lone Jesuit grown so quickly and effectively? At the time, Cristo Rey's leadership was uncertain about how it could grow the school into a network while maintaining the effectiveness of the school and the integrity of the mission. The travelers found that much of Fe y Alegría's growth resulted from the Jesuits' willingness to hand over administration of the schools to lay collaborators. However, in an effort to create and maintain standards for the schools, the Jesuits had developed a governing body and a supporting organization for them. While Jesuits, with their diminishing numbers, were able to staff only a tiny fraction of the schools, they were able to provide resources, standards, and training to all of them through the central office. The visit proved fruitful on a number of levels. It provided Foley, Stoeger, and Reuter with a framework for developing a national network of Cristo Rey–model schools and inspired Rich Clark to attempt to open a Cristo Rey–model school in Cleveland.

In December, Thielman received a call from Bill Ford, a New York educator and the nephew of Ita Ford, the Maryknoll nun who, along with three other missionaries, was murdered at the hands of Salvadoran guerilla forces on December 2, 1980. Ford was interested in opening a school in New York.

Days later, Thielman hastily packed his belongings and returned to Boston. His good-byes were brief. He knew he'd travel back to Chicago regularly. In January 2001, Thielman received a call from Todd Austin, a young educator who said the Diocese of Austin was interested in bringing a Cristo Rey school to Texas. In February, Thielman contacted a team of Christian Brothers in Tucson, Arizona, who were preparing a feasibility study for a new school there and offered to be a resource if they were interested in considering the Cristo Rey model.

The Cristo Rey movement was in full swing.

❄

MAYRA MADE THE BASKETBALL team.

She was surprised when the team spent half the second practice sitting on the gym floor and sharing with one another their goals for the season. The coaches* had given each of them a homework

---

*Mike, by that time, had joined the coaching staff. Andy didn't coach the basketball team as he'd already put in a full (and successful) season as coach of the girls' volleyball team.

assignment after the first practice: they had to write out their goals, both as individuals and as a team. During the second practice, the players and coaches combined their lists to create twelve team goals, which were written on a large piece of poster board and posted in the oversized closet the team used as a locker room. The goal at the top of the list was to win ten games.

The season didn't start well, with Cristo Rey dropping all three games in the Foreman High School Thanksgiving Tournament. After the tournament, Cristo Rey suffered a humiliating 74–16 loss to North Lawndale College Prep. All but one of North Lawndale's five starters were at least three inches taller than Alma Alvarado, a junior who at five foot three was by far Cristo Rey's tallest player. Winning ten of their twelve remaining games looked unlikely.

Four hours before the girls' fifth game, the opponent, Chicago International Charter School, called to forfeit. It was the girls' first win. The next game was against Noble Street Charter High School, a new school on the near northwest side of Chicago. The student population at Noble Street was similar to Cristo Rey's, though it was a bit more diverse. After losing blowouts to predominantly African American teams, the Cristo Rey girls seemed happy to see another team made up mostly of Latinas. Cristo Rey won 43–22. Mayra had to work that day but made it back to school in time to watch the fourth quarter from the bench. She couldn't wait to get back out there after the win. The next game was at Holy Trinity, a Catholic school on the near northwest side. It wasn't a perennial basketball power in the city of Chicago, but it had had a program for decades, and the team had a handful of talented players and was very well coached.

The win against Noble Street had helped the Cristo Rey team refocus on its goals. They were 2–4, and for the first time they'd accomplished two of their goals in a game. They had scored ten points

Girls' sports aren't a big part of Latino culture, and many of the Cristo Rey parents would've rather seen their daughters working after-school jobs. The girls struggled to take themselves seriously as athletes. After winning three games, they started walking a little taller.

in each quarter and had held their opponents to fewer than eight points in each quarter.

They went into the Holy Trinity game with the same goals, but things didn't go too well. Cristo Rey trailed 18–11 at the half. After halftime, though, they looked like an entirely different team. Mayra started the scoring by hitting a jumper from the right elbow. Then Alma took over, scoring six straight points. Mayra Garibay, a bruising junior guard, scored six more in the third quarter. When the dust settled, Cristo Rey had earned a 39–30 victory.

Next was a 37–31 win against Noble Street. Alma led all scorers with seventeen, and Mayra had her best game of the year, scoring twelve points. The girls had evened their record at 4–4 with their four-game winning streak. The winning streak was exhilarating for both players and coaches. Cristo Rey's female athletes got little, if any, respect from male students. Girls' sports aren't a big part of Latino culture, and many of the Cristo Rey parents would've rather seen their daughters working after-school jobs than playing games. The girls struggled to take themselves seriously as athletes. After winning three games, though, they started walking a little taller. At the beginning of the season, few of them believed they were really capable of winning games. But they'd set goals and shown up for morning practices, running their suicides and practicing their layups over and over. It had paid off. They were winning. More important, something inside of them seemed to be changing. They began to believe a bit more in themselves and to take themselves seriously.

Cristo Rey's final game of the season was against Chicago International Charter School. After wins against St. Greg's, Notre

Dame, Chicago International, and Noble Street and another forfeit win, Cristo Rey entered the game with a 9–6 record and some serious swagger. All that stood between the girls and their goal of winning ten games was a team they'd already beaten. Cristo Rey opened up a 13–6 first-quarter lead, but the scoring slowed in the second quarter. Chicago International fought back into the game and went into halftime trailing 19–15. Cristo Rey played well after halftime and had a seven point lead going into the final quarter.

Unfortunately, the Cristo Rey girls relaxed. All season they'd made up for their lack of offensive prowess by playing tenacious person-to-person defense. But in the fourth quarter against Chicago International, they let up. With just a minute left, International pulled ahead 32–31. Cristo Rey, who had scored only two points in the quarter, failed to score on its next possession. Everyone but Mayra retreated quickly to the defensive end. Mayra lingered at the half-court line. International's point guard waited for the inbounds pass near the free-throw line. Everyone in the gym knew International would bring the ball up slowly, trying to run down the clock. As soon as International's center passed the ball in, Mayra made her break. She timed it perfectly, arriving just as International's point guard turned carelessly toward the other basket. Mayra knifed toward the ball. Somehow, International's guard spun away, avoiding a turnover, and pushed the ball up the left side of the court. By the time Mayra made it back to the defensive end of the floor, the point guard had passed the ball to the shooting guard, who was being hounded by Mayra Garibay at the top of the key. The International guard was twisting to get away from her and trying to get rid of the ball. She made a sloppy bounce pass toward the point guard.

This time Mayra made the steal. She pushed the ball up the floor and finished with a careful layup to put Cristo Rey up 33–32 with just forty seconds to play. But Cristo Rey's defense didn't hold up. One of International's forwards banked in a short jumper to put them back up by one with fifteen seconds to go. Mayra brought up the ball and eventually found Mayra Garibay on the right baseline. She floated a soft jumper as time expired. The ball rattled into the basket and then, inexplicably, bounced back out. The loss left the team one win shy of its goal. Cristo Rey finished the season 9–7. The night of the final game ended in tears and frustration. The girls' many accomplishments were overshadowed by a single loss.

They'd been so close.

Pedagogy of Humanity 23

Mayra didn't take Active Learners until the second semester of her freshman year. By the time she enrolled, the class, then in its sixth semester, was a well-oiled machine. Mike Heidkamp was no longer teaching it. Carolyn Alessio, a first-year English teacher who'd come to Cristo Rey after writing for the *Chicago Tribune*, Lisa Chiss, a second-year English teacher, David Dixon, a third-year English teacher, and Liz Hauck, one of the new Jesuit alumni volunteers, were each teaching one section. Heidkamp was pursuing an M. Ed at DePaul University and was teaching only two sections of a senior-level civics class at Cristo Rey.

He was using the somewhat flexible civics content to try and prepare Cristo Rey's seniors for life in college. "At Cristo Rey," he says, "minority students were in a very clear majority. The school was almost totally homogeneous and not representative of the outside world or of the colleges and universities our students would attend. A lot of the civics class was geared toward preparing our students for the reality of being in a totally heterogeneous environment and for some of the forces they'd encounter there."

The focus of the civics class, Heidkamp explains, "was on ideas of deconstruction and reconstruction. Students should be able to look at the world, take it apart, and examine what works and what doesn't work," he says. "Then they should be able to take those pieces and reconstruct them into something newer and better. Critical thinking without the ability to re-create isn't all that helpful." The civics class began with a psychology unit. In order to thrive in completely new environments in college, Heidkamp believed his students would need an understanding not only of who they were as individuals, but also of how people often understood—or failed to understand—one another.

The curriculum he planned didn't get beyond the psychology unit, which included a Myers-Briggs Type Indicator assessment, personal journals, a variety of online personality tests, extensive readings, and discussions on psychology. As a final project for the unit, students were asked to build their own personality test. "What kind of test would you create if you were trying to understand someone else's personality?" Heidkamp asked them. "What information do you need? And what kinds of questions do you have to ask in order to get the information?"

Along with the final assignment, one of the seniors, Lucy Díaz de León, handed Heidkamp a neatly written two-page letter in which she expressed her dissatisfaction with the content of the class. She pointed out that in less than a year, she and her classmates would be in college. While the personality stuff was certainly fun, she believed they needed more rigorous preparation. They needed to know historical events and dates, famous presidents, and wars.

Though Heidkamp disagreed with her, he was thrilled to receive the letter. "It was a great moment," he says. "As a teacher, it's what I've always wanted. I've wanted my students to say to me, 'Hey, justify what you're doing. Prove to me that it's important.'" Heidkamp told the class about the letter and eventually polled the students about what they wanted to get out of the class. Most agreed with Lucy. They believed they needed to learn history. They felt they'd be expected to know it when they got to college and felt they hadn't really studied it thus far in high school.

Heidkamp switched gears. He brought other faculty members into the class and asked his students to interview them. The goal was for the students to discover what things they must learn before enrolling at a college or university. Heidkamp also asked his students to send e-mails to history professors at colleges around the United States—including Ivy League schools such as Yale and Harvard—to ask the experts what they needed to learn. Much to the students' chagrin, the professors almost unanimously said they needed, above all, to learn how to think critically, write well, and speak well.

> By the time the students had fashioned arguments for their historical events, they'd already learned far more than they ever could have from a lecture—and they were teaching each other.

The students, though, still wanted to focus on history, so Heidkamp divided the class into groups and gave each of them a couple of battered history textbooks from his collection. Each group was required to compile a list of historical events they thought were important to learn. Then they had to develop three historical units based on their list of events. Next, the students were required to present summaries of their three proposed units to the class. The reports included written reports and websites with links to additional information. After each group had presented, the students voted for the units they felt were most important to learn. Heidkamp then gave lectures on the three units that received the most votes.

By the time the students had fashioned arguments for their historical events, they'd already learned far more than they ever could have from a lecture—and they were teaching each other. Instead of being bombarded by historical information and regurgitating it on an exam, they were using it to create arguments. Every week or so, Heidkamp delivered lectures—to the extent that he ever lectured—

on the world wars, the Revolutionary War, the American Civil War, the Mexican-American War, the Holocaust, and the civil rights movement in the United States. With Lucy's help, Heidkamp had developed a class that challenged his students to think critically and creatively and gave them the history lessons they wanted.

❋

HEIDKAMP'S SECOND-SEMESTER LECTURES ON the civil rights movement dovetailed neatly with much of the work he was doing in his classes at DePaul, and this eventually led to another shift in the civics course's content. One of Heidkamp's professors had assigned readings from *Pedagogy of the Oppressed*, the landmark book by Brazilian educator and social activist Paulo Freire. "Dehumanization," Freire says in the first chapter, "although a concrete historical fact, is *not* a given destiny but the result of an unjust order that engenders violence in the oppressors, which in turn dehumanizes the oppressed." The purpose of the book, Freire says, is to develop a pedagogy that will help the oppressed "in the incessant struggle to regain their humanity."

Pedagogy of the Oppressed grew out of Freire's 1962 experience of teaching some three hundred impoverished farm workers how to read over the course of just forty-five days. Teaching them to read wasn't nearly enough for Freire, who felt he must also teach his students to question the social structures that tolerated their poverty while allowing others to enjoy wealth and abundance. Freire claims that critical thinking and analysis are learned behaviors, skills that can be taught and practiced. Without these skills, most of the farm workers would be condemned to poverty. A few brave and enterprising souls might beat the odds and make it on their own. But without the ability to critically analyze the situation from which they'd come and the economic and social structures that might have contributed to it, these lucky few would be unprepared to change those realities and would instead simply adopt the customs and practices of their new peers. The situation facing the rest of the farm workers would not change.

Freire's main complaint about the divide between rich and poor centered on the question of humanity and what he perceived to be the dehumanization of the poor. Poverty, while hardly desirable, was certainly tolerable. But Freire believed those who lived in poverty were rarely, if ever, afforded the same rights and dignity as other, more privileged human beings. *Pedagogy of the Oppressed* is a good summary of his efforts to address this problem and has become one of the foundational works of critical pedagogy, a teaching approach designed to cultivate in students a critical consciousness—the ability to question dominant powers and dominant perspectives.

Heidkamp's time in Peru, his relationship with his wife, Charo, and his experiences at Cristo Rey had helped him develop a critical consciousness and had changed the way he approached education. For him, teaching had become much more than an enjoyable job that provided him with autonomy and the freedom to feed his intellectual curiosity. It was an avenue through which he could in some small way change the world and make it a better place for people like Charo and the students at Cristo Rey—people who, because of the color of their skin or their station in life, were sometimes treated as less than fully human.

Heidkamp knew that the school's founders had made a conscious choice to educate students who had grown up in poverty, had been underserved by the educational system, and had few options. The school they had created was succeeding. Each year Cristo Rey gave a small percentage of the high school–aged students in Pilsen the tools they needed to gain acceptance to colleges and universities.

Those students would eventually enter the workforce, many of them in high-paying white-collar jobs. Some might go to graduate school and take even higher-paying jobs.

But was that enough? Preparing students to enter the workforce and be successful was a noble goal and would certainly help some students break the vicious cycle of poverty. But if those students didn't feel compelled to come back to their neighborhood and address the realities that caused the poverty in the first place, what had Cristo Rey really accomplished? Could the school prepare its students to take an active role in effecting change in their community, their city, their country? Could Cristo Rey prepare its graduates to understand the realities of the economic and social structures their parents had encountered and that they, too, would eventually encounter? Could it prepare them to challenge conventional wisdom and ask the difficult questions? If not, then the situation facing Latino immigrants in Pilsen—and much of the rest of the United States—would never actually change.

Like Freire, Heidkamp knew his students could bring about change only if they were taught to think critically about the world in which they lived, to ask the hard questions. At DePaul, Heidkamp had been studying how markers of difference—race, gender, age, class, and sexual orientation—tended to affect the quality of education a student received. In addition to the work his students were doing on their historical subjects, Heidkamp challenged them over the latter half of the second semester to grapple with how race affected them and others. All the students were minorities and felt comfortable with the discussion. That changed when they moved to gender. Tensions arose between male and female students as a variety of viewpoints entered the discussion. Heidkamp repeatedly pushed the students to listen and think before reacting. Often, entire class periods were spent in small and large group discussions. There were often far more questions than answers. But the students were learning to ask questions, hard questions that a lot of other people were afraid to ask. That was the important thing. It was a skill that would serve them well in college and in life.

✳

INSIDE THE MEXICAN FINE Arts Center Museum, Maritza could smell and feel spring. When she looked up from her algebra II textbook, she saw kids running down Nineteenth Street in shorts and T-shirts on their way to Harrison Park. The Cristo Rey boys' baseball team was in the park practicing, and as she gazed out at the trees and shingled rooftops sparkling in the Saturday sunshine, she thought about taking a break and walking over to the park to watch the practice.

During her sophomore year, Maritza had worked at the Mexican Fine Arts Center Museum—the largest Latino cultural organization in the country and the only Latino museum accredited by the American Association of Museums—through Cristo Rey's Corporate Internship Program. She'd initially been assigned to the gift shop but soon proved she was capable of much more, and the museum hired her over the summer. During Maritza's junior year, she was assigned to the investment bank R. W. Baird, so the museum hired her on weekends and on school breaks. When not involved in a project, Maritza, who was by that time fully bilingual, worked the museum's reception desk.

On that sunny Saturday afternoon in the spring of 2001, Maritza was taking advantage of an unusually slow day at the museum to do homework. It had become harder and harder for her to get work done at home because her mom was spending more and more time out partying. She'd often come home at two in the morning; it seemed so irresponsible to Maritza, not to mention unfair. When her mom was out, Maritza was expected to pick up the slack.

Maritza decided to skip the trip to the park and returned to her math problems—one of which had her completely stumped. Thirty minutes later, she was stuck on the same problem when Linda Tortolero, the daughter of the museum's executive director, breezed through the lobby. Linda had just graduated from college. Maritza figured she was probably good at math and asked her for some help.

Linda worked through the problem with Maritza and then asked her if she'd started to think about colleges. Maritza said she was definitely going to college and planned to go out of state. Over the next few weeks, Linda helped her put together a list of colleges to research, all of them out of state but still a reasonable drive from Chicago. During those conversations, Maritza bombarded Linda with questions. Linda had gone to a school called Brown. It was a good school on the East Coast, and she'd chosen it in part because of its diversity and the flexibility of its curriculum. It sounded like a great place, and Maritza asked Linda if she should put it on her list of schools to research. "Brown's hard to get into," Linda said, "and it's really far away. Focus on these for now." By the time she was done researching schools a month later, Maritza had added Brown to her list.

✱

AT A FACULTY MEETING in the spring of 2001, admissions director Rosy Santiago said the school had accepted by far its most talented and qualified incoming class. Their grades were better than those of their predecessors, and their standardized test scores were much higher. Cristo Rey had received far more applications than it had spaces, more proof that the school was doing well. It seemed like good news, but for many of Cristo Rey's teachers it was a red flag. Julie Minikel-Lacocque, who left Cristo Rey at the end of the 2000–2001 school year to pursue a master's in ESL and Spanish education, says she probably would have left Cristo Rey even if she hadn't been going back to school, because "the way a lot of us saw it, the school was no longer fulfilling its mission. They were accepting very different students than the ones in the first years."

Minikel-Lacocque had been teaching at Cristo Rey since its second year. Like the other longtime teachers, she had worked closely with those first students who probably would not have been in school at all were it not for Cristo Rey. That group required a great deal of personal attention, and many of the teachers developed close mentoring relationships with their students. The more qualified students who were being accepted to Cristo Rey needed less personal attention. Many of them wanted to learn; they didn't need to be convinced to learn. This fact worried Cristo Rey's teachers. They felt the school was in grave danger of losing sight of its mission. In their view, these were not the students Cristo Rey was founded to serve.

John Foley sees it differently. "Our first students were wonderful. They weren't exactly the students we expected to have. We thought we were going to have people beating down our doors. Instead, partly because of the agreements we made with the archdiocese, we ended up trying to convince people to come to Cristo Rey. The students we got that year weren't necessarily the students we set out to serve." Foley notes that Cristo Rey was created to serve primarily students in the neighborhood who couldn't get into Whitney Young or St. Ignatius College Prep or other nearby college prep schools. "The first few years, though, we basically ended up serving students who were, for one reason or another, not in school or totally dissatisfied with their schools." Cristo Rey's mission, Foley says emphatically, was not to serve these students, though he's quick to point out that the school owes a tremendous debt of gratitude to those students who took a chance on the school in its early years.

The fact remained that the school was changing. The building was bigger, and each incoming class was bigger than the previous one. Class sizes were sometimes creeping up past twenty-five. The hallways were crowded, and the cafeteria was a zoo. Teachers' schedules were much fuller, leaving less time to spend with individual students. And the face of the faculty was changing. In spring 2001, Judy Murphy surprised the entire school community when she announced she'd step down as principal at the end of the year. She was the first of Cristo Rey's founding administrators to leave the school. Fr. Steve Planning, the charismatic Maryland Jesuit who had convinced Leo Maldonado to take a crack at college, had received word that he'd been assigned by his provincial to a struggling parish in Camden, New Jersey. The first three Jesuit Alumni Volunteers were wrapping up their second year of service and preparing to leave. So, too, were a handful of teachers, many of them to go back to grad school. Many of the remaining faculty worried the school might lose its direction after the departure of Murphy, a great advocate for the school's student-centered education and innovative curriculum.

One teacher was happy with the direction in which the school was headed. Jim Wall was an anomaly at Cristo Rey—an old-school educator in a decidedly new school. He eschewed group work and arranged the desks in his classrooms in perfectly straight rows. On the first day of his English class, he laid down the law with his students. He dismissed the idea that Cristo Rey's students needed to be given special treatment because of their life circumstances. They could do the work, even if it meant working harder than their peers at other college prep schools. Wall drilled them in the basics of writing—how to build sentences with nouns and verbs, how to build paragraphs with sentences, how to build arguments with paragraphs, and how to build essays with arguments. He held students to high standards and wasn't at all afraid to fail them when they didn't meet expectations. When Wall discovered that some of Cristo Rey's early students were either incapable of or unwilling to do college prep work, he helped Rosy Santiago develop a new application process that involved the entire school community and the applicant's family and would, they hoped, do a better job of identifying those students who truly wanted to be at Cristo Rey and were, as a result, willing to do the work. While many of Cristo Rey's teachers were wary of the Corporate Internship Program, Wall embraced it and believed it was a tremendous learning opportunity that wasn't being appropriately integrated into the curriculum. During his fifth year at Cristo Rey, he spent half his time developing ideas for integrating the work experience into the curriculum. He also continued to oversee the production of *Pasión*, Cristo Rey's literary/arts magazine, and *Corazón*, the school's yearbook, both of which he'd created.

Days before Cristo Rey offered contract renewals to teachers, Murphy called Wall into her office and told him that he wouldn't be coming back to Cristo Rey. For Wall, the news came as a complete and entirely unwelcome surprise. Wall, though, is still quick to praise Murphy for the work she did at the school. "She did a yeoman's job, there's no doubt about it." It's no secret, though, that he and Murphy had completely different philosophies about education. "I had reservations about a lot of what we did at Cristo Rey," Wall says. "If it was new and different, we tried it. We were pulling these untested and unproven glitzy ideas out of education magazines and trying them all."

Wall had made his feelings known, often questioning the merits of nontraditional education. While much of the faculty advocated teaching primarily Latino literature to Cristo Rey's students, Wall gave the students a steady diet of Shakespeare and English classics. His independence might have ultimately cost him his job. Wall suspects that Murphy worried that he might, in her absence, try to undo all the work that had been done by the faculty during the school's first five years. Despite the school's growing enrollment and the changes the school had made at the recommendation of the McKinsey consultants, Murphy left Cristo Rey having succeeded at creating a new and better school uniquely focused on preparing its students for college and life.

Wall left Cristo Rey with a hole in his heart. He was able to sit through only a few minutes of the 2001 graduation and was in his car on his way home as the teachers made their way slowly to the back of St. Adalbert's Church, a huge Catholic church located a few blocks northeast of Cristo Rey (the school's small gym couldn't accommodate the crowd), and applauded as the seniors marched down the aisle. Fifty-two students graduated that day. Forty-nine of them had been accepted to college and planned to enroll that fall.

Cristo Rey finished the year with a $973,000 deficit. Much of it stemmed from the fact that the Corporate Internship Program was still charging only twenty thousand dollars per job. In the coming year, CIP would increase the fee to twenty-five thousand dollars, and the school would increase enrollment by 20 percent. No one was happy about the deficit—despite the fact that they'd again been able to cover it with fund-raising—but no one on the board or in the administration viewed it as catastrophic. If they were able to find enough paying jobs in the coming year, they would be able to cut the deficit by more than 50 percent.

Cristo Rey was still a work in progress. But it was working.

Portland and Providence 24

THE SUMMER OF 2001 was a crazy one in Portland, Oregon. The craziness had really begun months earlier, in January, when Matt Powell, who had been named president of Portland's new high school, De La Salle North Catholic, set about preparing for the school's opening in the fall of 2001. He found himself up against the same prospect that Cristo Rey's founders had faced exactly five years earlier. Powell and Mike Jacobson, the recently hired Corporate Internship Program director, had nine months to prepare a building, find students, find corporate sponsors, develop a curriculum, hire teachers, hire staff members, and develop policies and procedures for the school. They were working alone, though Powell's wife, Jamie, often pitched in.

By the beginning of summer, there was no question the school would open. There was some question, however, about how many students would attend. As was the case at Cristo Rey, De La Salle North Catholic wasn't overwhelmed with applications. When the founding faculty first met in July of 2001, the school was still looking for students. Opening with too few students meant that De La Salle, like Cristo Rey, would likely struggle to make ends meet in at least its first year of operations.

❋

JOEY GARCIA HADN'T EXACTLY taken Cristo Rey by storm during his first two years there. From the day he arrived at Cristo Rey, he wanted little more than to make friends. Since his mother's death, there had been a hole in his life, and he wanted desperately to fill it. Looking back, Joey says he wasted the better part of his first two years at Cristo Rey doing whatever he thought other people wanted him to do in an effort to earn their friendship. Not surprisingly, his grades suffered.

His disciplinary record was also spotty. He screwed around a lot in class, was frequently given demerits, and served many after-school detentions. Midway through his freshman year, a foray into online pornography at his CIP job at Loyola University Chicago got him fired—and nearly kicked out of school. It all started with the video games he'd been playing at his Aunt Susie's house. At the beginning of his freshman year, when he was focused on school, he hadn't had time for the games. But as the year wore on, he played more and did less homework. Still, he wasn't as good a player as his cousins. He'd heard them talking about cheat codes, which allowed players to skip ahead to the more advanced portions of a game, and he thought the codes might help him get better. His cousins told him about a Web site called Cheat Code Central, where he could find many of these codes.

During a quiet morning at work during the second semester of his freshman year, Joey opened up Yahoo.com and tried to search "cheat code central" but inadvertently typed "cheat *coed* central." Yahoo quickly generated a page of search results. Joey scanned the list looking for the names of some of the video games he played, but the links he saw had nothing to do with video games. He couldn't resist the temptation to check out the sites that talked about "hot coeds" and "cheating on your wife," and with a single click Joey entered the universe of online pornography. The page featured nude women who were apparently just sitting around waiting to have affairs with visitors to the Web site. Joey panicked. He knew the people at Loyola could monitor the Web sites employees were visiting. He closed the page quickly. The next week, no one said anything. He ran another search and visited a few more pages. He couldn't believe how much there was. Two weeks later, Joey was called out of class to Carlos De La Rosa's office. De La Rosa knew about the Web sites Joey had been visiting—and so did the people at Loyola. Joey was horrified. He worried that people at school would find out and think he was a pervert. But it was worse than that. De La Rosa told him he'd been fired from his job and could be expelled from school. "If you can't keep a job," De La Rosa explained, "you can't stay at Cristo Rey." In order to remain at school, Joey was required to sign a contract stating he wouldn't visit any more illicit Web sites and would behave in a professional manner at all times at work. He readily signed it. He worked at school for a couple of months until he was assigned to General Growth Properties, a real estate investment trust.

Despite his disciplinary missteps, Joey did demonstrate unfailing dedication to a variety of student groups. As manager of the basketball team, he never missed a game and attended most practices. The boys' coach, a local businessman, paid Joey for his work operating the scoreboard and maintaining the official scorebook at games. Joey often volunteered to do the same thing for many of the girls' games. He was the consummate professional. When the referees arrived, Joey always introduced himself, showed them to the locker room, and offered them a bottle of Gatorade. He was just as dedicated to the student council—he had, after all, won his seat by bussing cafeteria tables. He never missed a meeting. At the student dances he helped organize, he worked the coat room or sold sodas out of the small kitchen adjacent to Cristo Rey's gym. His student council colleagues usually ditched their work,

Going into his junior year, Joey vowed things would be different. He wasn't going to fall behind in school or goof off so much in class. He was going to do homework and study for tests and get good grades. He knew he could do it.

convincing teachers and chaperones to cover for them so they could go dance. Joey, though, kept working. He never asked for a break and stayed with the teachers after every dance to sweep the floor and take out the trash.

All these activities left little time for schoolwork, and Joey's grades continued to suffer. He made the volleyball team but didn't get to play in any games because he was academically ineligible for the entire season. He made mostly Cs, with an occasional B or D. In some classes he started strong but then gave up. In others he blew off everything at the start of the quarter and then worked furiously to complete enough assignments to pass the class. By the conclusion of his sophomore year, in June 2001, Joey had compiled a 2.55 grade point average. After earning a 2.6 and a 3.0 respectively in his first two semesters, he'd dropped to 2.4 and 2.2 in his sophomore year.

Going into his junior year, Joey vowed things would be different. He wasn't going to fall behind in school or goof off so much in class. He was going to do homework and study for tests and get good grades. He knew he could do it.

By THE START OF its sixth year, Cristo Rey had begun to hit its stride. The question was no longer if the school would survive, but how it would thrive. Development director Josh Hale, like his predecessor, Jeff Thielman, worked at a breakneck pace to solicit large lead gifts for Rey of Hope II, the capital campaign that would fund Cristo Rey's new gym, library, cafeteria, and classroom building. The groundbreaking was slated for the end of the school year. In the fall of 2001, thanks to a freshman class of 152 students, the school's total enrollment climbed to 497. The faculty had scaled up to accommodate the additional students, and the Jesuit Alumni Volunteer Program had accepted four new volunteers, bringing the total number of recent college grads volunteering at the school to seven.

The returning sophomores had distinguished themselves during their first year at the school. They were a different breed of students from most of their predecessors. They came from the same neighborhoods and the same economic situations, but they were serious about school—and often very bright. Verónica Cortez, who excelled on the volleyball court, had come into the school with off-the-charts math scores. As a sophomore, she was more mathematically advanced than many of the seniors. Then there was Sergio Garcia. He didn't always bring home perfect grades, but his teachers knew he was extremely bright. His command of the English language was remarkable. He did all of the reading for his freshman English class and, much to the surprise of his teacher, Carolyn Alessio, often incorporated unfamiliar words such as *rapscallion* into his classroom comments. Alessio had encouraged him to look up words he didn't recognize, and he had heeded her advice. His vocabulary grew daily, and he shared it with students at the local library, where he was a volunteer tutor. The rising sophomores were by far Cristo Rey's most well-rounded class, and the incoming freshmen looked to have a similar composition.

There was, though, still a great deal of work to be done. To the board's dismay, the faculty still hadn't finalized a curriculum. Patricia Garrity, a longtime teacher and archdiocesan leader, had been hired during the 2000–2001 school year to serve as the curriculum director and was named principal after Judy Murphy announced her retirement. Garrity, who spoke fluent Spanish, hoped to have a more formal curriculum assembled by the end of the year.

In the meantime, Mike Heidkamp, who continued to teach half-time while completing his studies at DePaul University, and David Dixon were teaching a senior-level social studies/civics class designed to address some of the thorny issues of discrimination and racism that had dominated the latter half of Heidkamp's civics class the year before. The two teachers shared the belief that many of the difficulties facing the world—poverty, unemployment, crime, and lack of education—resulted from institutions and people who wielded great power treating other groups of people as less than human. Heidkamp and Dixon had designed a class to address these issues, as well as prepare Cristo Rey's students for the complexity of life as minorities on large college campuses.

"Part of education," Heidkamp says, "is about teaching people to assimilate and develop a 'common culture.' But what does it mean if you're starting from the outside and moving in? What do you have to check at various stages? If you're already starting at the center, and that common culture is your culture, then you don't have to check many things at the door. David and I were asking ourselves how we could prepare our students to enter environments where they'd likely be asked to deny parts of themselves."

For Heidkamp, the class was about much more than college preparation. "Think about it in terms of democracy and pluralism. The whole idea is that we're not all the same and that it's okay to not be the same. I find that many times it's those who are on the outside, that are on the margins, that most understand that we're still not there, that we don't have a true democracy. The people on the margins know where the problems are. They can see them very clearly. Their voices, which are often muffled, and their perspectives hold the key for us to be a politically vibrant society and a true democracy."

By the end of the summer, Heidkamp and Dixon had carefully outlined the material they planned to teach, though they didn't have a name for the class. "It might have been called history or critical thought," Heidkamp says. "Or deconstruction and creation. Or issues of creativity. Basically, it was a social studies class." It was a class that would pose difficult questions and allow its students to ask difficult questions—some of which would eventually create conflict between the two teachers and Cristo Rey's administrators.

When training for the Corporate Internship Program at De La Salle North Catholic in Portland began in August 2001, seventy-six students had enrolled at the school.

❋

WHEN TRAINING FOR THE Corporate Internship Program at De La Salle North Catholic in Portland began in August 2001, seventy-six students had enrolled at the school. Just as Cristo Rey had done, De La Salle North Catholic had accepted virtually everyone who had applied. Matt Powell remembers two of the most at-risk students: Sam and Billy Holiday, cousins from North Portland. Through the interview process, the staff at DLSNC discovered that Billy was being raised by his grandmother. From first grade to seventh grade, he had lived in seven different foster homes. Billy says he spent the first years of his life in a "drug house." It wasn't a healthy place for a child, but it was home and he missed it terribly. Each time he was assigned to a new home, Billy says, he'd lie in bed and pray that he could go back home with his family. His dream came true when he moved in with his grandma during seventh grade. He planned to go to Grant High School, but his Aunt Edna, Sam's mom, heard about De La Salle North Catholic and made him and Sam apply.

Sam and Billy were both present when the first day of training started with a presentation about the school's dress code. It was clear that most of the students already understood the dress code; they had shown up in shirts, ties, blouses, and neatly pressed slacks. Sam and Billy, though, were wearing jeans and T-shirts. Both of them had their hair pulled into tight cornrows, another violation of the dress code. "Neither of them looked happy during the dress code presentation," Powell recalls. The next morning, when CIP training resumed at eight o'clock, neither Billy nor Sam was there. They still hadn't arrived by nine. During the brief lulls in the training program, the teachers talked among themselves about whether they might be trying to change too much too quickly in the lives of their students. Powell recalls wondering if they'd been too tough on the cousins.

Then, a few minutes after ten, the doors to the school opened, and Billy and Sam came in together wearing shirts and ties, and without cornrows. They went straight to Powell. "Sorry," Billy said. "The barbershop didn't open till nine."

De La Salle North Catholic held its first classes on September 4, 2001. The freshman class numbered seventy-one students, and Billy and Sam were still enrolled. That Thursday, the school held a ceremony marking its opening. Fr. John Foley and Jeff Thielman attended with B. J. and Bebe Cassin. A press conference was held, and B. J. Cassin offered remarks for the reporters assembled. When they addressed questions to De La Salle North Catholic's students, Billy Holiday stepped up to the mic and answered them.

❋

CRISTO REY'S INCOMING FRESHMEN lived up to their billing. Through the first quarter, they demonstrated a surprising commitment to school—and to their homework—that exceeded that of the previous year's freshman class, which had been widely viewed as Cristo Rey's best. One of the new freshmen, Frank Rojas, was struggling to sever his affiliation with the Two-Six gang.

As a student with acknowledged gang ties, Frank was an anomaly at Cristo Rey. "Frankie came to us a few months into his freshman year and admitted being part of a gang," says Fr. Sean O'Sullivan, SJ, who had recently joined the Cristo Rey staff as its director of counseling. "He told us about it because he wanted help getting out. He was afraid, though, of what the gang would do if he left. He'd have to be beaten out, and he was so small he might not survive. If he left without the beating, he was afraid the gang would take it out on his sister."

Frank was allowed to stay at Cristo Rey on two conditions. First, he could never bring any sign of gang life—clothes, haircuts, gang signs, tagging on notebooks or bathroom walls—into the school. Second, he had to take steps—with the help of the school and a gang intervention specialist from the local YMCA—to get out of the gang. If he failed to follow through on either, he'd be dismissed from school. He gladly accepted the terms and thrived at Cristo Rey, where he was well liked, especially by the girls. It was clear to Frank's teachers that he was bright and had enormous potential.

In April of his freshman year, Frank showed up at school with three small lines carved into his right eyebrow—a well-known sign of gang membership. By the end of the week, he'd been dismissed from school.

Many members of the faculty and administration understood that Cristo Rey's students lived in a perennially gray area. When they left school every afternoon, the students couldn't pretend that gangs didn't exist. They had to get home safely. They had to forge alliances with the other kids in the neighborhood. They could not always avoid having friends in gangs, and some of them had more formal ties without becoming full-fledged members themselves.

Cristo Rey, though, had drawn a line in the sand. Gang affiliation and involvement would not be tolerated. Any sign of it inside the walls of the school would lead to expulsion. The goal was to keep Cristo Rey a safe place for learning. Some of Cristo Rey's graduates debate the efficacy of the policy. Some say there were gang members in their classes and that everyone knew who they were and which gangs they were "tight with." But since opening its doors in 1996, Cristo Rey, which doesn't have metal detectors, has never seen a gang-related fight or shooting and has never confiscated a weapon.

Maritza and Providence 25

EVER SINCE HER BRIEF stay in a mental-health facility after a fight with her mom, Maritza had been even more devoted to school. She reminded herself often of the realization she'd come to during her week there: *If you want to do something, you're going to have to do it on your own.* She reminded herself often, too, of her grandmother's dream that she be an independent woman. The key to that, she knew, was getting a good education.

During her senior year, Maritza came to school an hour early every day. Three days a week she met with Rosa Sánchez or Sr. Frances Thibodeau, who had agreed to give her and three junior girls French lessons. On the days she didn't meet with her French tutors, Maritza usually went to the calculus help sessions offered by her math teacher, Germán Indacochea. In addition to playing volleyball, Maritza served as editor of *Lateeno Magazine*, a literary and arts magazine published by Cristo Rey students. David Dixon, who moderated the magazine, said it would likely have folded without Maritza's dedication. When she didn't have other commitments after school, she often went to see Rudy Kraus, her physics teacher, for extra help with the class, which perplexed her. She volunteered at the Little Brothers of the Poor Thanksgiving dinner and at Misericordia, a home for the developmentally disabled in Chicago. During the autumn of her junior and senior years, she traveled with a group of Cristo Rey teachers and students to an annual protest of the School of the Americas at Fort Benning, Georgia.

Each night she spent between two and four hours on her homework in the small apartment she shared with her mom, her sister, and her brother. "I needed quiet," she says. "If no one was around, I'd work at the dining room table. Otherwise, I'd go into my bedroom and kick my sister out." Often she was doing work that hadn't been assigned to her classmates. Both David Dixon and Francisco Piña, Maritza's English and Spanish teachers, regularly gave her extra assignments in writing or reading—sometimes entire books. Usually they'd pull Maritza aside after class and give her the material. Initially, Maritza had protested. Piña told her she was a writer gifted with a unique perspective and the innate ability to express it, but she needed to practice. Dixon gave all his students the opportunity to rewrite essays for higher grades. Though Maritza's were often the best in class, she never missed a chance to do a rewrite.

"I knew there was a reason they were giving me the extra work," she says. "They thought I could do it." This is as close as she'll come to an admission of talent. Part of it is humility. Part of it, though, is doubt. As a new student in the United States, she had been plagued by doubt and fear that she didn't know English as well as everyone else. The doubt had stayed with her. Maritza's belief that she was ultimately responsible for her success or failure motivated her, but it also increased the anxiety associated with the doubts. What if she couldn't do it? What if she didn't get good grades? What if she didn't get into college? What if she couldn't find a job, or hold down a job?

The extra assignments during her senior year helped. "My teachers at Cristo Rey had confidence in me when I didn't." Their confidence buoyed her through the college application process. She worked closely with some of the school's English teachers to craft a personal statement that would serve as the primary essay for most of her applications. Just after Thanksgiving, she dropped off completed applications for DePaul University, Southern Illinois University, University of Notre Dame, Marquette University, Carleton College, and Brown University at the office of Jaime Contreras, the college counselor. Maritza hadn't told anyone else where she was applying. Even Linda Tortolero, her mentor at the Mexican Fine Arts Center Museum who had helped her develop an initial list of schools, didn't know.

As soon as the applications were sent, in early December, Maritza panicked. She worried that she had applied to schools that were too hard to get into. Contreras assured her that she had applied to a great mix of schools and would get into a good number of them. But she didn't believe him. She worried incessantly that she wouldn't be accepted anywhere.

✹

JOEY'S PLANS FOR HIS junior year didn't materialize, as evidenced by his first-semester report card:

English	C-
Spanish 3	B
Spanish as a Second Language	B-
Math	C+
Chemistry	B-
Religion	B-
U.S. History	C
CIP	B

These grades added up to a GPA of 2.4, exactly the same average he'd had in the first semester of his sophomore year. It was much lower than he wanted, yet he knew it was probably higher than he deserved. His grades had been far worse at the close of the first quarter, but Sr. Frances Thibodeau, his religion and English teacher, and Stephan Graham, his chemistry teacher, urged him to get caught up and made it very clear that if he chose not to, he'd fail their classes. When Joey arrived at Cristo Rey, he had no doubt that he'd eventually go to college. "I didn't know where I'd go. I figured one of the big colleges like University of Illinois or Notre Dame or Duke. I knew about them because I saw their football and basketball games on TV."

By the midpoint of his junior year, however, he was beginning to wonder if he really was cut out for college. He wanted to do well but couldn't bring himself to do the work. Instead, he went to student council meetings, hung out on the church steps outside school, tutored at the local library, or managed the basketball team. Each night when he got home to his grandma's apartment or his aunt's house—he alternated between the two for much of high school—he'd leave his schoolbag by the door and watch TV or play video games. He was then, and remains today, an avid sports fan who could talk baseball, basketball, or football with anyone. He knew music, too; when he wasn't watching TV, he was listening to the radio. Joey wanted to be doing his work. He knew he should be doing his work, but everything else seemed to get in the way.

THE POSTER BOARD TAPED to the wall of the utility closet turned locker room of the Cristo Rey girls' basketball team at the start of the 2001–2 season* listed the following goals:

---

*My two-year term at Cristo Rey ended in June 2001, but I continued to coach the girls' team during the 2001–2, 2002–3, and 2003–4 seasons.

Finish the season with a winning record

Score forty points per game

Hold opponents to twenty-eight points per game

Score ten points per quarter

Hold opponents to seven points per quarter

Be on time for practice EVERY DAY

Get better every day

Remain academically eligible as individuals and as a team
all season

Grow and improve as people, students, and basketball
players

Beat Juárez

Beat Our Lady of Tepeyac

Score fifty points in at least one game

Win our first state play-off game

Just as they'd done the year before, the girls had begun the season by creating a list of individual goals and then combining them into a list of team goals. The only difference was that the goals stated at the outset of the 2001–2 season were far more ambitious than those from the previous season. After their success of the previous year, the girls weren't content to aim for a handful of wins. They wanted to accomplish something no boys' or girls' Cristo Rey basketball team had ever done—finish a season with a winning record.

Beating Juárez, the sprawling public school located just four blocks east of Cristo Rey, was another new goal for the season. So was beating Our Lady of Tepeyac, a private all-girls Catholic high school located about fifteen blocks west of Cristo Rey. The season marked a renewal of the rivalry between Cristo Rey and Our Lady of Tepeyac, which had become so intense that administrators from both schools had agreed the teams would not play each other for two years.

The girls' goals may have seemed a bit too ambitious, but they came into the new season expecting big things. The roster included six seniors, four of whom had been regular starters during the previous year. For the first time, the girls' program was able to field both JV and varsity teams. Seven of the varsity players had attended a week-long basketball camp at Lake Forest College during the summer. The four-day camp, which involved ten hours of basketball each day, had resulted in tremendous individual and team improvement. The question in their minds was no longer whether they could win a game. The question was whether they could win the majority of their games.

Cristo Rey opened its season for the third consecutive year at the Foreman High School Thanksgiving Tournament, where they'd never won a game. Their improvement in ball handling and shooting over the previous year was immediately evident as they won their first two games.

Cristo Rey's opponent in the final game of the tournament, Schurz, had also won its first two games. The tournament championship and a two-foot-high trophy were on the line in the third game. At halftime, Cristo Rey was down eight points—a huge margin in games that often saw teams score fewer than eight points in a quarter. But Cristo Rey's offense scored twenty-two points in the second half. With just nine seconds left, Cristo Rey had erased the entire eight-point deficit and held a three-point lead. In the final seconds of the game, Schurz's five-foot-ten center ended up with the ball four steps inside the half-court line. She panicked, turned, and heaved a pro-length three-pointer that nearly cracked the backboard before falling through the basket and tying the game. Schurz won the game in overtime by three points. When the final buzzer sounded, their players stormed the court, jubilant. The Cristo Rey girls didn't move. They stood where they were, hands on hips or knees, exhausted and in disbelief. They'd never before been so close to being champions.

Despite demonstrating so much promise, the team failed to achieve most of its most coveted goals. After opening up a 12–4 first-quarter lead in their only game against Juárez, the girls folded and ended up losing 57–27. They lost their game against Our Lady of Tepeyac and also lost their play-off game to University High by a demoralizing score of 74–21. They ended the season 8–14.

As disappointing as the season had been, things would only get harder for Mayra and the Cristo Rey girls' basketball team. In addition to losing six seniors in the coming year, they would also lose their gym.

❀

PART OF MARITZA THOUGHT it was silly to apply to a place like Brown. There was a reason Linda Tortolero, the museum director's daughter, hadn't encouraged her to apply there. Maritza probably didn't belong there. And she probably wouldn't get in. Maritza had "safety" schools on her list, but none of them felt safe. She knew by now that there were no guarantees in life.

That's why the first acceptance letter came as such a relief. It was from DePaul. Additional acceptance letters came from Carleton College, Southern Illinois University, and Marquette University. By the end of March, she'd heard from everyone but Brown, and the only school so far that had not accepted her was Notre Dame. Much to Maritza's surprise, her teachers started asking her on an almost daily basis if she'd heard from Brown. She'd only told three people at school where she was applying. She didn't like it that everyone knew, and she didn't understand why everyone cared so much.

> Maritza didn't find out Brown was an Ivy League school until days after the thick envelope arrived at her apartment containing the news that she'd been accepted.

Maritza didn't know Brown was an Ivy League school and didn't know she was the first Cristo Rey student to apply to one of the Ivies. She'd never been to Brown's campus and hadn't even seen a brochure from the school. She knew only that she wanted the same college experience Linda Tortolero had so enjoyed. Cristo Rey's teachers were pulling for her. Getting a student into one of the Ivies was a rite of passage. It would mean Cristo Rey had prepared at least one student for what many consider the pinnacle of American higher education.

Maritza didn't find out Brown was an Ivy League school until days after the thick envelope arrived at her apartment containing the news that she'd been accepted. She told only Contreras. But that week, many of Cristo Rey's teachers sought her out to congratulate her. She didn't understand all the fuss. It wasn't until the end of that week that she found out why everyone was so excited. Jim Gartland, Maritza's religion teacher, pulled her aside to tell her that a student from St. Ignatius College Prep had also been accepted to Brown. Then he said, "You're the first Ivy Leaguer. It's a really amazing accomplishment."

"What do you mean, 'Ivy Leaguer'?" Maritza asked.

"You got into Brown," Gartland said. "You're the first one."

"What? Brown's an Ivy League school? No one told me this."

Minutes later she was in Contreras's office. "Why didn't you tell me Brown is an Ivy League school?"

"I thought you knew," he said, laughing. Maritza's acceptance to Brown, he says, was one of the highlights of his work at Cristo Rey. Maritza's mom wasn't as impressed. When Maritza told her she'd been accepted at Brown University and that she thought she'd go, her mom shrugged. "It's far away," Maritza said, "on the East Coast."

"I don't know how you'll pay for it," her mom said. Fortunately, Brown had offered Maritza a generous financial aid package, most of it scholarship money she would not have to repay. She had also earned an HACER scholarship through the Ronald McDonald House, along with a scholarship from the Hispanic Scholarship Fund.

❋

IN HIGH SCHOOLS AROUND the country, second-semester seniors are often the least ambitious students in the building. Having already been accepted to college, few of them have incentive to push themselves academically. Mike Heidkamp and David Dixon, though, weren't about to let the seniors in their class take the rest of the semester off. They still had too much critically important material to cover.

Maritza shared her teachers' sentiments about the importance of the class. It was divided into sections: racism, sexism, classism, discrimination based on sexual orientation, and ageism. Even though taking it meant she wasn't getting exposure to political science or U.S. history or the history of European civilizations, she says, "it was a really good class. I learned to see things differently in civics. I don't know how to explain it. Things happen around the neighborhood and you see them and say, 'Yeah, yeah, whatever, it's normal.' Then you realize it isn't normal. It only happens in certain parts of the world. It doesn't happen everywhere."

Heidkamp and Dixon wanted their students to be challenged to see the world—and their own worlds—in new ways. During one discussion in class, sparked by a column in the *Chicago Tribune* in which John Kass argued that one of the biggest obstacles to unity in this country is our refusal to simply call ourselves Americans, a student, Nick Morales, shared the following story:

My dad is outside washing his truck and I'm sitting on the steps, and our neighbor comes out. The neighbor is one of those guys who has Mexican flags everywhere— on his house, on his truck. And my dad says to him, "You're an American now; get rid of those Mexican flags and put up some American flags. You gotta understand that we're living in America, not Mexico. You need to be proud of the fact that we're American." And that's fine. But when my dad drives his truck into a gas station and he gets out to pump gas, the people there look at him and they don't see an American. They see a Mexican.

"It's an incredibly complex issue," Heidkamp says. "There are questions of race and racism. But there's something more basic than that. There's a question of how we choose to define ourselves, how we name ourselves. Nick saw his dad struggle with that. He identified himself one way. The world identified him differently. Those are issues our students will encounter in college, and we wanted them to grapple with them before they headed off to school."

Dixon and Heidkamp wanted their students to be able to look at their world—country, city, neighborhood, and school—critically. But it didn't do any good to simply hurl criticism at the establishment— though the teachers did give a homework assignment that required students to write letters in response to Kass's column. Students had to be able to create solutions to the problems they encountered. During the second semester, Heidkamp and Dixon assigned a project in which students were required to become agents for change. "They had to do something—offer a workshop, teach a class, or mount a campaign—to address an important issue," Heidkamp says. "At the end of the year, they'd have to present their work to the class." The assignment began with questions. Throughout the year, Heidkamp and Dixon had pushed their students to question everything. One of those questions touched off a chain of events that eventually led to the departure of the two teachers.

"If the Corporate Internship Program is such a good thing," asked Mayra Garibay, a sometimes brash senior, "then why don't they have it at St. Ignatius or Loyola Academy?"

"The question," Heidkamp says, "wasn't about the merits or demerits of the Corporate Internship Program. It was a question about the economic reality of the students' lives. That was something we'd talked about a lot in class. The Corporate Internship Program allowed them to be at Cristo Rey. That was good, but students at St. Ignatius didn't do it. Why not? What was different about the lives of Cristo Rey students? Those were good questions to be asking."

When John Foley and Preston Kendall got wind of the discussion, they didn't agree. CIP was the school's lifeblood, and they were understandably protective of it. They didn't like the idea of Cristo Rey's students questioning the work program, and they were wary of the material Dixon and Heidkamp chose to teach. Some of their concern stemmed from a phone call Kendall had received from an angry corporate sponsor. One of the company's Cristo Rey interns had been interviewing employees at the firm about racism in the workplace. The firm was, at the time, engaged in a discrimination lawsuit, and the conversation alarmed the sponsor. It also worried Kendall, who felt the civics teachers should have cleared the project with him.

The situation escalated toward the end of the semester when Foley received an e-mail from a United States congressman (no one can remember who it was, and the e-mail has long since been lost) about the contents of Heidkamp and Dixon's course. One of Cristo Rey's Jesuit Alumni Volunteers had invited a friend who worked for the National Organization for Women to observe Heidkamp and Dixon's class while she was visiting Chicago. Somehow, the e-mail invitation was forwarded to a Capitol Hill distribution list. A day later, the congressman wrote to Foley, "Since when are Jesuit high schools supporting abortion?" Not long after the e-mail arrived, Foley summoned Dixon and Heidkamp to the conference room adjacent to Foley's office. Kendall and Garrity were there with the volunteer who'd sent the e-mail.

Since Cristo Rey's founding, there had been some tension between the externally focused work program and the internally focused academic departments. They needed each other but functioned almost completely separately. At best, there was minimal cooperation. At worst, there was a mutual suspicion, a feeling that one side was somehow undermining the other. From the faculty's perspective, Cristo Rey's most important work took place in the classroom, and the Corporate Internship Program was simply a way to pay for it. The faculty didn't claim to understand business and didn't really care to. For the educational work they were doing, it didn't matter.

Kendall, on the flip side, was a businessman who sought to use his experience and expertise to serve others. He knew that if the Corporate Internship Program failed, Cristo Rey would close its doors. This reality presented more pressure, he says, "than I ever faced in the business world." Kendall guarded the reputation of the internship program carefully. When a member of the media, a community leader, a student, or a faculty member did anything to undermine the program, Kendall responded swiftly and firmly. There was too much at stake not to.

Kendall believed that Heidkamp and Dixon were subverting the Corporate Internship Program through their civics class. Heidkamp and Dixon believed that certain sectors of corporate America and elements of the Corporate Internship Program reinforced powerful cultural perceptions that Cristo Rey students and their parents were less important, less successful, and ultimately less human than their white counterparts.

> Kendall believed that Heidkamp and Dixon were subverting the Corporate Internship Program through their civics class.

Heidkamp and Dixon were handed a copy of the e-mail and asked to explain it. The meeting, during which the e-mail was discussed only briefly, was explosive. Foley and Kendall, both of whom were upset, questioned the validity of the material Heidkamp and Dixon had chosen to teach the seniors. Heidkamp and Dixon, neither of whom knew anything of the e-mail, tried to explain that they had nothing to do with it and vigorously defended the content of their class, insisting that it offered invaluable preparation and training for college and life.

On the day in early April when contract renewals were delivered to Cristo Rey's faculty members, both Dixon's and Heidkamp's mailboxes were left empty. Days earlier, Dixon had learned that his wife, Lora, a longtime Department of Commerce employee, had been appointed a commercial attaché for the U.S. Foreign Service and would be tasked with promoting U.S. commercial and trade interests in Argentina. While it stung a bit not to receive a contract, Dixon knew that he and his wife would likely be moving within a year or two anyway.

Heidkamp, on the other hand, met three times with Kendall in an effort to move past the mistrust. Garrity moderated the meetings and at the conclusion of the third one offered Heidkamp a contract. Heidkamp, though, was still upset by the response to the e-mail. "There was a troubling lack of communication and trust," he says. "We weren't doing anything even remotely related to [condoning] abortion, but the e-mail sort of confirmed what some people thought about our class. There was a hypersensitivity to outsiders' perceptions, and the belief was that the e-mail was true and we were wrong. I think that's what sometimes happens when there isn't open and fluid dialogue between people. We end up developing and relying on preconceived notions." Heidkamp ultimately turned down the contract and took a job at the University of Notre Dame, though he says leaving Cristo Rey pained him.

＊

IN EARLY JUNE, CRISTO Rey closed the books on its sixth year. Maritza and eighty-three of her classmates graduated on June 7. Seventy-two of them had, by that time, enrolled in four-year colleges, while nine more had enrolled in two-year colleges. Only two students had decided not to continue studying. Cristo Rey's operating deficit at the end of the year was just $590,000, by far the lowest since the school had opened. Revenues from the Corporate Internship Program had covered 66 percent of the school's operating expenses.

Laying Foundations 26

O N AUGUST 19, 2002, Verbum Dei High School became the third school in the Cristo Rey Network when it converted to the Cristo Rey model. B. J. Cassin, John Foley, and Jeff Thielman traveled to Los Angeles for the school's reopening. Verbum Dei was originally founded in 1962 to serve young men in the Watts neighborhood of South Los Angeles. Three years later, long-standing resentment over the police department's treatment of African Americans erupted into prolonged riots after the arrest of a black man on drunk-driving charges. Many of the middle-class residents of South Los Angeles moved out, and the area slipped into a severe economic recession.

Verbum Dei remained through the decades of economic struggle, the riots, and the crack cocaine epidemic of the 1980s. Unfortunately, it fell on hard times during the 1990s, when the student body, made up primarily of low-income African American and Latino students, couldn't keep pace with the steep increases in costs. The school was in danger of closing when Roger Cardinal Mahony invited the California province Jesuits to consider taking it over and possibly reorganizing it under the Cristo Rey model. The Cassin Foundation funded a feasibility study and provided seed money to make the transition.

Later in August 2002, San Juan Diego Catholic High School opened in Austin, Texas. Sponsored by Bishop Gregory M. Aymond

> As executive director of the Cassin Foundation, Thielman continued in overdrive, helping new schools conduct feasibility studies and then prepare to open their doors.

and the Diocese of Austin,* San Juan Diego became the fourth school in the Cristo Rey Network. Feasibility studies—each funded by the Cassin Foundation—were also under way for schools in Cambridge, Massachusetts; Cleveland, Ohio; Denver, Colorado; New Bern, North Carolina; Lawrence, Massachusetts; New York City; Tucson, Arizona; and Waukegan, Illinois.

As executive director of the Cassin Foundation, Thielman continued in overdrive, helping new schools conduct feasibility studies and then prepare to open their doors. He hired a designer to create a CD full of useful documents he'd collected from different schools and sent it to new schools and groups conducting feasibility studies. Eventually, he put all the resources on a Web site he helped design. Thielman, who had moved back to Boston after his wedding and kept a small office at Boston College, worked alone, although he received help from Bobbi Dolan, B. J. Cassin's über-assistant, who worked out of Cassin's Sand Hill Road office in Silicon Valley.

❋

AMID THE LOUD MUSIC and laughing in the dark blue Hyundai Accent, Maritza worried silently about the end of the road trip to Rhode Island and the beginning of her life as a college student. She and Yecenia Barajas, one of her closest friends from the neigh-

---

*San Juan Diego left the Cristo Rey Network in 2005. To participate in the network, member schools commit to serving low-income students. San Juan Diego was only the second Catholic high school in Austin and attracted students from a variety of economic backgrounds, so it eventually opted to accept a broader population, though that meant leaving the network.

borhood, were driving east on Interstate 90, past the seemingly endless open spaces in Indiana and Ohio. The car was packed to the gills. Maritza's friends and coworkers at the Mexican Fine Arts Center Museum had thrown her a good-bye party and given her everything she needed for college. The staff at R. W. Baird had also given her money, though they stipulated that it could not, under any circumstances, be used for books. The drive was great fun. Maritza and Yecenia laughed as they recalled the times they'd spent together—trips to the movies, concerts, and summer days at Six Flags Great America. But Maritza couldn't shake the fear that she'd never be able to succeed at Brown.

Deep down, she knew she wasn't ready. She didn't know enough. She didn't belong at an Ivy League school. She'd probably be home in a semester. Everyone at Cristo Rey had made such a big deal about her getting into Brown, but it wouldn't mean anything if she failed out.

The drive continued through Pennsylvania, New York, and Connecticut before concluding at a cluster of brick buildings on a hilltop in Providence. They drove past some ornamental gates while trying to find the dorm that would be Maritza's home for the next year. Later Maritza would learn that those gates, the Van Wickle Gates, were opened only twice a year, once during convocation, when new students entered the school, and once during graduation, when students left the school. Though she didn't see it that day, there was a quote from Cicero on the gates that seemed to describe her perfectly and likely would have given her great comfort:

> These studies fortify one's youth, delight one's old age; amid success they are an ornament, in failure they are a refuge and a comfort.

Maritza's studies had fortified her and had been a refuge and a comfort in hard times. But as she and Yecenia drove past the gates, Maritza was nervous about her future studies. The anxiety made it hard to breathe. This was a college—an Ivy League college. All she could think was *What the hell am I doing here?*

They found the dorm and carried all her stuff upstairs. Yecenia helped her unpack and get settled. By mid-afternoon, Yecenia was back on the road. That night, Maritza walked around campus and the nearby parts of Providence by herself. She walked past a couple of small restaurants. Inside, behind windows dotted with condensation from overworked air conditioners, were bright lights and smiling faces laughing over plates of warm food. Many of the kids in those restaurants were her future classmates. They were there with their parents, their new roommates, and their roommates' parents. They were celebrating the beginning of college, the start of a new adventure. Yecenia was long gone, probably somewhere in New York. In another ten or twelve hours, she'd be back in Chicago.

In another six months, Maritza figured, she'd be back home as well.

✸

WHILE CRISTO REY–MODEL SCHOOLS around the United States were experiencing some of the same struggles that Cristo Rey had faced years earlier, the original school in Chicago set about fine-tuning many of its programs. At the start of the 2002–3 school year, the leadership team—John Foley, Cristo Rey's president; Pat Garrity, the principal; Josh Hale, the director of development; Preston Kendall, the Corporate Internship Program director; and Chris Nanni, the associate principal—rolled out a number of changes designed to improve and strengthen the school.

Kendall introduced a nine-step program that he and Carlos De La Rosa had developed to help Cristo Rey students who'd been fired from their jobs prepare to return to the workplace. In the past, students who were fired from their CIP jobs were usually dismissed from school. The severity of the policy had resulted in many talented students who'd made one or two mistakes getting kicked out of school. It didn't serve the students or the school particularly well. The students were generating most of the revenue that kept teachers in the classroom and the lights turned on. As the school grew, more and more students would encounter difficulties at work. Cristo Rey quite literally could not afford to expel all of them.

Kendall explains that the program "wasn't designed to be a free pass for everyone." Particularly egregious missteps—like a Cristo Rey freshman's decision to write herself a two-thousand-dollar check from her employer, a prestigious Chicago law firm—still resulted in expulsion. But some students just didn't take directions well or made a bad decision and mouthed off to a supervisor. Some simply didn't understand what they were supposed to do at work and were afraid to ask for help. Kendall and De La Rosa were convinced that many of these kids could thrive if they were given some extra attention—and if they understood that their work was important for their futures and for the school's well-being.

The new program required fired students to write letters to their former employers, the school's work program, and their parents. In the letters, they had to explain how their behavior led to their dismissal from work. "We hoped," Kendall says, "they would also apologize, though we didn't require it." Next, the students had to read *The Seven Habits of Highly Effective Teens* and write a report detailing how those habits could have helped them succeed at work. "It's the Ignatian Pedagogical Paradigm again," Kendall says. "We were trying to get the students to reflect on their experience, to make it their own, and then take action by developing a plan for what they would do differently in the future. They had to move forward into action." Students who completed each of the steps were reassigned to vacant CIP jobs. The vast majority, Kendall says, "ended up having success in their jobs." Those very few who chose not to complete the program were expelled.

By fall of 2002, much of the tension between the school's academic team and its CIP team had abated. Only three of the school's founding teachers remained, and many of the faculty's most strident CIP opponents had left. But the school and the work program still remained separate. In an effort to unite the two groups, Cristo Rey's leadership team sent four of the school's new faculty hires to work. Jason Dillon, Emily Kazefy, Felipe Morel, and Bernhard Walke were hired as teachers during the summer of 2002, but when school started in the fall, they taught only 75 percent of the usual load and spent the rest of their time at work, with their students. For the first eight weeks, they worked regular CIP jobs at Katten, Muchin & Rosenman, a law firm that had been one of Cristo Rey's most dedicated corporate sponsors from day one. The teachers worked the same jobs their students worked and reported on the experience at faculty meetings. After eight weeks, they switched gears and shadowed Cristo Rey students at a number of different companies.

Dillon says the most valuable part of the experience was developing "an understanding and appreciation of the work the students were doing. It was an eye-opening experience. I saw students who struggled in the classroom but were all-stars in the workplace. I remember one student's face gleaming with pride as he took me on his rounds through several floors of an office building, collecting and documenting faxes that needed to be sent out." Dillon also noticed a surprising connection between students and their supervisors. "I believe these relationships heighten the students' maturation process. They empathize with their adult coworkers and learn very realistic expectations about the workplace, as well as the dedication that their own parents commit to their work lives in order to support their children."

"It was an eye-opening experience. I saw students who struggled in the classroom but were all-stars in the workplace."

The biggest change at Cristo Rey in the fall of 2002, though, wasn't Kendall's nine-step program or the new teachers' work assignments. It was the gaping hole on the south side of Twenty-second Place, where Cristo Rey's gymnasium and cafeteria had stood until the middle of the summer, when they were leveled to make room for a new gym, cafeteria, and library. Students were told that construction would take a year. The new building, slated to open just a year later, would have a brand-new gym, locker rooms, and an exercise/weight room. The building would also house an improved and expanded cafeteria and the school's first library—at the time, the school relied on a few shelves of donated books.

The new building—which would be connected to the existing classroom building by an enclosed second-floor walkway—would also include a handful of new classrooms, though none of the students knew this. The board's building and grounds committee had pushed for the additional classrooms amid continued debate about the optimal size for the school. Cristo Rey's administrators still believed five hundred was the right number, but many board members wanted to expand to six hundred or seven hundred students. If Cristo Rey's fixed costs could be spread over an additional one hundred to two hundred students, they said, the school would become much more stable financially. Even if the administration didn't want to expand now, incorporating additional classrooms into the new building would give them the option to boost enrollment at a later date.

As classes got under way, students buzzed excitedly about the new building. Mayra Hernandez, though, was worried. During the first week of school in the fall of 2002, she sought out the athletic director to ask where the sports teams would play while the gym was under construction. It was a good question. The volleyball team would practice at the gym at Harrison Park and would play all of its games on the road, but no one knew where the basketball teams would play. Gym space in Pilsen was hard to come by during the basketball season.

✻

IN THE FIRST QUARTER of the 2002–3 school year, Cristo Rey's leadership team also instituted a new program designed to address the seeming lack of motivation in the lowest quartile of students, a group whose effort and performance substantially lagged behind that of many of their peers. The apparent lack of motivation concerned both the faculty and the administration. What would happen when these students started taking college classes? At Cristo Rey, teachers were breathing down their necks and constantly cajoling them to do their work. In college, these students would be expected to be self-starters; no one would take the time to convince them to do the work.

So the leadership team announced that students deemed academically ineligible—the standard for ineligibility was two or more Ds or one or more Fs—could not participate in extracurricular activities until the conclusion of the next grading period in which their grades met the standards for eligibility. In the past, academic eligibility restrictions had been applied only to student-athletes, and had been evaluated weekly. The new policy would evaluate eligibility much less frequently and would be applied to all students and activities. The aim of the revised policy was, first and foremost, to give students more time to spend on their homework and, second, to use extracurricular activities to motivate them to bring up their grades.

The new policy had disastrous consequences for Joey. Despite the promise he made to himself at the outset of his junior year, his grades had continued to fall—his GPA in the second semester was 2.2, his lowest since entering Cristo Rey.

Joey says his low grades were the result of a lack of effort. In math, chemistry, and art, in which he received an A and two Bs, he credits his teachers for inspiring him to do well. "I hated chemistry," Joey recalls. "I got straight Fs in chemistry. Then I remember Mr. Graham—I don't know why, maybe he just knew I could do better—but he grabbed me after class one day after the first quarter, and he said, 'Why are you failing?' And he made me a deal. He was the first one that started it. He said, 'You do all the homework, every single homework assignment, and you pass my tests, then you'll pass the class. I'll forget about the first quarter. You miss one homework assignment, and I forget the deal.' After that I started doing the homework, and I started liking it."

The second semester of Joey's junior year, though, was full of distractions, the biggest of which was his successful campaign to become vice president of Cristo Rey's student council. Joey coveted the job and campaigned hard in the months leading up to the election. His victory was a triumphant moment. From his first days at Cristo Rey, he'd wanted to be a part of the student council. He'd wanted to be a part of anything, really. He'd ascended from a lonely freshman to the second-most powerful student in the school. But the election distracted him, and he finished the semester with two Ds, which made him academically ineligible. He'd been on the list before, when it meant nothing more than attending a couple of mandatory study halls during the week. He didn't mind that; in fact, he really liked Br. Dave Henderson, the Jesuit who ran them.

But in the fall of 2002, Joey learned that those two Ds would disqualify him from participation in extracurricular activities, including student council. "They impeached me. Because of my stupid grades, they didn't let me serve as the vice president. I felt like Richard Nixon. I tried to tell them, 'I am not a crook,' but it didn't matter." He laughs as he tells the story, but there's a trace of regret on his face, and he readily admits that his "impeachment" devastated him. The ineligibility policy motivated some of Joey's classmates, but it had the opposite effect on him. His grades in the first semester of his senior year were awful, his worst as a Cristo Rey student. In what was possibly the most important semester in the eyes of colleges and universities, Joey posted a 1.7 GPA. He was still ineligible for extracurricular activities so he spent his afternoons goofing off with his friends. School had become even less of a priority for him.

A lot of students were working on their college applications, but not Joey. With his grades, he knew no college would want him. He'd always wanted to go to college, and in quiet moments he sometimes wondered what had happened, how he'd gone from being a great student to such a bad student. But he tried not to think about it too much.

❊

ON THE MONDAY AFTER Thanksgiving, the phone on Fr. Sean O'Sullivan's desk rang just as the school day began. It was Frank Rojas's father. Frank, the gang member who had been dismissed from Cristo Rey after showing up at school with lines carved into his eyebrows, had enrolled at Kelly High School. Over Thanksgiving weekend, he and a handful of his fellow gang members—he still hadn't severed his ties with the Two-Sixes—had gone to a party. On their way home, while driving through Latin Kings territory, they stopped and started smashing in the windows of parked cars. They were drunk and were making a lot of noise. When people started to come out of their houses, Frank and his friends tried to take off. A Latin King, though, fired a shot into their car as it pulled away. The bullet entered Frank's head through his right eye. His friends pulled him down into the backseat and rushed him to Mount Sinai Hospital.

Minutes before Frank's dad called O'Sullivan, the doctors had told the family that Frank had only hours to live. O'Sullivan was pulling on his jacket even before he was off the phone. He drove quickly to the hospital. Frank was in a coma. The doctors had removed a section of his skull to alleviate the swelling in his brain. It would be a miracle, they said, if he made it through the day. O'Sullivan and Frank's parents stood beside his bed and prayed together. Frank defied the odds and made it through the night. The next day, O'Sullivan visited again, with Bridget Collachio, one of Cristo Rey's Jesuit Alumni Volunteers; and Patty Vasquez, Cristo Rey's dean. The doctors still didn't think Frank would make it. But he proved them wrong and made it through another night. He made it through the next night, too. And the next.

Frank eventually regained consciousness. The first time he noticed O'Sullivan in the room, he asked how things were at Cristo Rey and how his freshman teachers were doing, naming them one by one. Collachio, O'Sullivan, and Vasquez continued to visit him frequently during his recuperation at a rehabilitation hospital.

✵

WITH JUST TWO MINUTES to play in the first quarter, Elizabeth Martinez, a senior guard for Cristo Rey's varsity team, knocked in a baseline jump shot to tie Juárez. It was the first game of the year, and for Mayra, it was the biggest game of the year. She wanted desperately to win. Most of her friends from junior high went to Juárez, and her brother was a freshman there. Her best friend was Juárez's point guard. It wasn't the personal connections, though, that made her want to win. It was the fact that kids at Juárez laughed at Cristo Rey. They said Cristo Rey was small and Cristo Rey's students were nerds who took school too seriously. Juárez students made fun of Cristo Rey's little gym, its grade school building, and the fact that the students, in addition to paying extra, had to go to work.

Mayra didn't think Cristo Rey's varsity team was ready for a game, much less a game against Juárez, the toughest team on their schedule. So few people had come out for Cristo Rey's team that the coaches hadn't even made cuts. Midway through the first week of practice, Jessica Maldonado, one of the best juniors on the team, quit because her mom was making her get a job. When first-quarter report cards came out, four of the girls on the team became ineligible. Cristo Rey's varsity team went from twelve players to seven. Attendance at practice had been bad, in part because they were practicing at Cooper Elementary Dual-Language Academy—four blocks north and three blocks east of Cristo Rey—while the gym was under construction. The changes to the eligibility policy instituted that year by Cristo Rey's leadership team prohibited ineligible students from attending practice—in the past, they had been allowed to remain a part of the team but had been forbidden from playing in games. The coaches combined the JV and varsity teams for practice but still rarely had enough players for a complete scrimmage.

Despite all the problems to date, Cristo Rey and Juárez were tied at eight with just two minutes left in the first quarter. This was unfamiliar territory; in all of Cristo Rey's previous games against Juárez, they had been blatantly overmatched. Mayra, who'd scored half of her team's points, glanced at the scoreboard. *We're in this*, she told herself. *We can win this.* On the sidelines, her coaches were saying the same thing.

When the quarter concluded, the score was 14–8 in favor of Juárez. The final score was 43–15. Cristo Rey lost its next two games before beating Perspectives Charter School. The highlight of the season was a 28–27 comeback win over Chicago Waldorf School. Mayra hit the game-winning jumper with just fifteen seconds to play. Cristo Rey, though, wouldn't win again. They finished the season with two wins and seventeen losses.

But there was reason to hope. By the time the season ended, the frame of Cristo Rey's new gym was in place, and it appeared it would be ready for the coming season.

Not Just a Mission   *27*

M ORE EVIDENCE OF CRISTO Rey's progress came in spring of 2003 when the junior class received its Preliminary SAT/ National Merit Scholarship Qualifying Test (PSAT/NMSQT) scores. Administered every spring by the College Board and the National Merit Scholarship Corporation, the PSAT/NMSQT provides practice for the SAT and determines recipients of National Merit scholarships.

Mayra's class posted by far the highest PSAT scores seen up to that point at Cristo Rey. The best score belonged to Sergio Garcia, the junior class's resident rapscallion. Sergio wouldn't mind being called a rapscallion. He knew the word had multiple definitions: a rascal or scamp, a deceitful and unreliable scoundrel—or one who is playfully mischievous. Sergio wasn't either of the first two, but he would have welcomed the third definition. His sophisticated sense of humor—honed from hours in front of the television and conversations with anyone he could talk to—regularly prompted loud outbursts of laughter from his teachers. His easygoing demeanor endeared him to both the best and the worst students, to the beloved popular kids and the often ignored "losers." Sergio liked everyone. And everyone liked him.

In the wee hours of the morning on Sunday, March 23, a month or so after his PSAT scores arrived in the mail, Sergio was coming home from a party in the neighborhood when someone fired

In the wee hours of the morning on Sunday, March 23, a month or so after his PSAT scores arrived in the mail, Sergio was coming home from a party in the neighborhood when someone fired a gun into the car he and his friends were in. The bullet hit Sergio. The driver rushed him to Mount Sinai Hospital, where he died less than an hour later. A brief obituary in the *Chicago Tribune* reported that Sergio was an "inquisitive and critical thinker" and "an unforgettable presence in class."

The story didn't mention the rumors circulating that Sergio, who wasn't in a gang, maintained close relationships with many gang members. Nor did the obituary include the fact that a letter from the admissions office of Georgetown University had arrived for Sergio days after his death. The school was impressed by his performance on the PSAT and invited him to apply.

No one was ever apprehended in Sergio's murder. He was just another casualty in the gang warfare that to this day plagues Pilsen/Little Village. "His death showed me how little I knew about violence and loss, and the fractured lives of many of our students," says Carolyn Alessio, Sergio's English teacher. His life and death are indicative of the incredibly difficult decisions young men in the neighborhood must make on an almost daily basis. Cristo Rey's handbook says it does not accept students who are members of gangs or affiliated with gangs. But what, exactly, is affiliation? There's a huge gray area, and in order for Cristo Rey's male students to be able to walk to the bus stop each day, they have to be friendly with their peers who control the corners in the neighborhood. They have to live in the gray area.

ON MAY 21, 2003, headlines in eighty-three newspapers around the United States—including the *Boston Globe*, the *Chicago Tribune*, the *Chicago Sun-Times*, the *Cleveland Plain Dealer*, the *Los Angeles Times*, the *New York Times*, the *Seattle Post-Intelligencer*, the *New York Post*, and the *Washington Post*—trumpeted a major development for the Cristo Rey Network:

Gates grant will help expand model high school program

The multibillion-dollar Bill & Melinda Gates Foundation, started by the Microsoft founder and his wife to bring innovations in health and learning to the global community, was supporting the Cristo Rey movement with a grant of $9.9 million. During Jeff Thielman's years as Cristo Rey's director of development and his time as executive director of the Cassin Foundation, he had watched the remarkable growth of the Gates Foundation with great interest. He had long thought that the Cristo Rey model fit well with the Gates Foundation's focus on ensuring that all people have access to great education. Despite that, he never expected what he describes as a "once-in-a-lifetime phone call" from Tom Vander Ark, executive director of the Gates Education Initiative, in December 2002.

A Denver native, Vander Ark had led a consulting practice for Cap Gemini and had headed one of Washington State's larger school districts before coming on board at the Gates Foundation. The Gates Education Initiative sought to increase high school graduation rates and had made numerous investments in small alternative-model high schools. When Vander Ark first read about the Cristo Rey model in a fall 2002 story about the approval of plans for a new Cristo Rey school in Denver, he suspected it was a perfect fit for what the foundation was trying to accomplish. He called Thielman to say that the Gates Foundation was interested in partnering with the Cristo Rey Network.

Before their partnership could be formalized, though, the Cristo Rey team had a lot of work to do. The Gates Foundation was a well-oiled charitable machine accustomed to granting hundreds of millions of dollars each year. They did everything by the book. The Cristo Rey Network, on the other hand, had flown by the seat of its pants since B. J. and Bebe Cassin's gift led to its informal inception. When Vander Ark called Thielman, the network hadn't been formally organized or incorporated. Thielman, who was running Cassin's foundation, had become the de facto head of the Cristo Rey Network, which consisted of little more than a snazzy Web site Thielman says "was designed to try to make us look bigger and more established than we really were" and an annual conference Thielman had instituted to enable those involved in the creation and administration of Cristo Rey–model schools to share resources and best practices. If the partnership worked, the Gates Foundation would eventually make a gift to the Cristo Rey Network. The network, though, wasn't set up to receive or manage gifts. It didn't have a staff, an office, a bank account, a mission statement, or a plan for how to use the money.

"Most foundations have large multimillion- or multibillion-dollar endowments," Thielman says. "They make grants with the interest spun off by the endowments. B. J.'s foundation was different. He said, 'Here's this money. Go spend it opening schools for poor kids who don't have good schools.' There was never a plan for us to spend only 5 percent a year." That meant the Cassin Foundation would run out of money quickly, which meant the Cristo Rey Network would eventually have to start raising money. To do that, it would have to be organized as a nonprofit corporation. That was part of the network's five-year plan—until Vander Ark called. A week later, Thielman was filing incorporation documents, forming a board, opening bank accounts, and developing a system through which the network could accept and disburse funds.

As discussions with the Gates Foundation progressed, another important question emerged. The Gates people wanted to know what measures the Cristo Rey Network had taken to ensure the future success and integrity of the schools. Fortunately, since the summer of 2002, Thielman and Preston Kendall had been working to codify the policies and procedures of the different schools into a set of standards that could be used both as a guide for new schools and as an evaluative tool for existing schools. The mission, principles, operating procedures, and spirit of Cristo Rey Jesuit High School had been passed on to new schools through personal relationships and by example—all groups conducting a feasibility study were required to visit Cristo Rey. There was some fear, though, that as the pace of the replication efforts picked up, the quality of the schools might diminish. Thielman, Cassin, Kendall, and John Foley all felt that some standardization was needed to ensure that the core principles of Cristo Rey remained at the center of all the new schools.

The standardization effort had been prompted in part by the approval of a feasibility study in New Bern, North Carolina, in the summer of 2002. The committee conducting the study in New Bern had tried years earlier to open a Catholic school but had found that local families couldn't afford the required tuition. They wanted to start a Cristo Rey–model school to serve both low- and middle-income students. All the other Cristo Rey schools, however, served exclusively low-income students. Up to that point, the only formal requirements to be a Cristo Rey school were that the school be Catholic and use a Corporate Internship Program to offset most of its operating expenses. But was there more to being a Cristo Rey school?

Many, including Thielman, Kendall, Foley, and Cassin, began asking that question after the New Bern study was approved.

Thielman and Kendall, working closely with Fr. Jim Stoeger, the Chicago Province's assistant for secondary education, completed the first draft of the Cristo Rey Network's mission effectiveness standards and guidelines for assessment in January 2003, just in time to present them at a meeting of the presidents of Cristo Rey Network schools. A copy of the document—a brief summary of which follows—was sent to the Gates Foundation.

A Cristo Rey Network school:

1. Is explicitly Catholic in mission and enjoys church approval on a diocesan and local level, with sponsorship by a religious congregation if required by the diocese.

2. Serves the economically disadvantaged, is open to students of various faiths and cultures, and is culturally sensitive and community based.

3. Is family centered and plays an active role in the local community.

4. Is accredited by a recognized regional accrediting association and has a college preparatory curriculum designed for a high level of student engagement in their learning.

5. Requires participation by all students in a work program that follows the Corporate Internship Program (CIP) developed at Cristo Rey Jesuit High School in Chicago.

6. Has an effective administrative structure—normally including positions such as a separate president, principal, CIP director, and development director—and a board structure that includes religious, education, community, business, and civic leaders; complies with all applicable state and federal laws, including immigration, labor, and not-for-profit tax laws.

7. Is financially sound: at full enrollment—normally three hundred to five hundred students after five years—the school's revenue from tuition and work study covers more than 90 percent of operating expenses; in addition, the school maintains an aggressive development/advancement program to ensure financial stability.

8. Seeks to understand and improve how its students learn and grow.

9. Is an active participant in the collaboration, support, and development of the Cristo Rey Network.

In March of 2003, two months after the Cristo Rey Network finalized its mission effectiveness standards, the Gates Foundation formalized a $9.9 million grant to the network. The Cassins, by that time, had already pledged $9 million of the Cassin Foundation's $22 million to the Cristo Rey replication effort. The Gates seal of approval lent immediate credibility to the Cristo Rey movement. The $18.9 million from the Cassin and Gates foundations would be used to open a total of sixteen Cristo Rey Network schools, including those that were already open or planning to open.

The team in New Bern was nearly halfway through its study when the Gates Foundation pledged its support to the Cristo Rey Network. The announcement further energized the New Bern business community, which had already expressed great excitement for the project. It appeared that the Cristo Rey work program would give the people of New Bern the Catholic school they'd wanted for years. But there was one problem. The mission effectiveness standards submitted to the Gates Foundation stated explicitly that Cristo Rey Network schools would serve "the economically disadvantaged."

New Bern was still planning on a student body that would be only 80 percent "economically disadvantaged." The other 20 percent would be from families who could afford other private schools, were they available. Ultimately, that 20 percent kept the New Bern feasibility study from earning approval. The board of the Cristo Rey Network concluded that the school's student makeup was not consistent with the mission of the Cristo Rey Network.

✺

MARITZA WAS IN TEARS as she picked up the phone and dialed. She wanted to come home. She was midway through her second semester at Brown and still felt that she was in over her head. She hadn't talked about it to anyone at school. Not her friends or the counselor. She hadn't told her mom, because she knew her mom would tell her to come home, and deep down Maritza knew that going home wasn't the answer. The homesickness, though, was tearing her apart. She was tired of feeling like she didn't belong.

She was calling Oscar Sánchez. She had met him at the museum during her sophomore year, and they had become fast friends. He was a student at the University of Illinois and called her every couple of weeks. Right away he could tell Maritza was upset. "I want to come home," she said.

"If you come back to Chicago, I'll drag you back there by your hair," Oscar told her. "Brown is your home now. It's where you belong." He gave her no sympathy and didn't suggest that coming home was even a remote possibility. It was exactly what she needed.

Toward the end of the year, Maritza shared her struggles with some of her friends at school. Much to her surprise, they all felt the same way—like they didn't belong and weren't smart enough to be there. Halfway through her sophomore year, Maritza says, she finally accepted that she deserved to be at Brown, just like all the other students. "I never felt like I fit in, though. I just began to accept that I came from a different place. I had different life experiences and thought about my education in a different way."

❊

AT FIRST, JOEY WAS happy he wasn't applying to college. His friends stressed out about the process constantly. It was their senior year, when they were supposed to be having fun, and they were worried about homework and grades. Whatever time they didn't spend on homework they spent filling out applications, which often required them to write extra essays. It all seemed stupid to Joey. Even though Joey had once planned and expected to go to college, the extra work—especially the essays—didn't really seem worth it to him.

But midway through the spring, when some of his friends —Oscar Galvez, Juan Santoyo, Tony Corona, and Ciro Castro—started getting letters back from different colleges, Joey had a change of heart. Oscar got into DePaul. Tony got into Lewis—he wanted to do a program in aeronautical engineering. Jaime Contreras, the college counselor, had been bugging Joey for months about his applications, to the point that Joey avoided the second floor of the old building, where Contreras's office was located. But when his buddies started to get letters back from colleges, Joey found himself hoping that Contreras would make him apply.

In late March, Joey finally submitted applications to four colleges. He didn't know it at the time, but Contreras sent a personal letter of recommendation to the admissions directors at each school, in which he attempted to explain Joey's academic underperformance and tardiness in applying. Within three weeks, Joey received acceptance letters from Northeastern Illinois University and Morton College. But his acceptance at both was "conditional." In order to be admitted, he had to attend a bridge program. The next day he took the letters to Contreras.

"What does this mean?" Joey asked.

"Well, it means different things at different schools. But there's usually a class or two before school starts. Or, sometimes, you spend the first semester taking basic courses. And there's usually a component that runs through the first two years where they will offer extra assistance or tutoring or assignments to make sure you're learning everything you need to know."

"So it's extra work?"

"Not necessarily," Contreras said. "You can still graduate in four years if you take an extra class here and there. I wouldn't think of it as extra work as much as an opportunity." But Joey knew exactly what he thought of it. It was a slap in the face. He didn't need extra help, or tutors, or extra classes. His standardized test scores had been low, but he knew he could do college-level work. He could've gotten straight As in high school if he'd wanted to—he'd gotten an A in chemistry after making his deal with Mr. Graham. The best student in the senior class, a girl who always got straight As, was in Joey's chemistry class, and he'd beaten her on the tests. That's the kind of student he was. He didn't need a bridge program, and, frankly, he didn't want to do the extra work. That, he knew, was his problem: laziness. He could do the work but just didn't want to.

Despite his reservations, and at the urging of Contreras, Joey completed the Free Application for Federal Student Aid. But in the back of his mind, Joey already knew he wasn't going to enroll if he had to do a bridge program.

Two months later, Joey and his sixty-nine classmates graduated at St. Adalbert's—the new gym was still under construction. During the graduation ceremony, Fr. John Foley spoke about how much Cristo Rey had changed during the four years the graduates had spent there. They'd started their classes together in the cramped quarters of St. Stephen's school building, which, by the time they graduated, was simply called "the old building." During their four years at Cristo Rey, enrollment at the school had increased by nearly seventy-five percent. Standardized test scores of both incoming and outgoing students had improved dramatically. The school was nearing completion of a third building.

Foley could also have talked about the fact that during the 2002–3 school year, Cristo Rey students had, through their work, covered 65 percent of the school's operating expenses. He could have mentioned that the ¡Viva! fund-raiser had set another record when it raised more than $205,000 for scholarships at Cristo Rey. He could have stressed that Cristo Rey—with its manageable deficit of $592,000—was officially on solid financial ground. Instead, he talked about the high school students in Austin, Portland, and Los Angeles who were following the lead of their peers in Chicago and funding their own education. He talked about how all of them shared the same dream of attending college and finding a better life.

The back of the graduation program listed the colleges and universities Cristo Rey students would attend in the fall. Everyone had been accepted somewhere. Grisel Murillo was following Maritza to Brown. Other students were headed to Xavier University, Saint Louis University, the University of Tampa, Creighton University, and Southern Illinois University, among many others. Next to Joey's name was Western Illinois University. But Joey knew it wasn't true.

Even though he had an unconditional acceptance to Western, and even though his teachers had urged him to enroll at Northeastern or Morton to take advantage of the bridge program, he'd decided he wasn't going to college. "I kind of decided that school life was too much for me. Why start something when you know you're going to quit?" He told his teachers he was going to get a job and study for the ACT so he could get into DePaul University, one of the schools that hadn't accepted him. Weeks after graduation, Joey took a job assembling and delivering lockers, chairs, tables, and shelving systems for a local manufacturer.

A Historic Win 28

WHEN LEO MALDONADO BEGAN his studies at Lewis University, he didn't expect to make it through the first semester. He had agreed to give it a try only because Fr. Steve Planning had bugged him about it so much. But Leo made it through the first semester, getting Cs in each of his four classes. He also discovered Sigma Lambda Beta, Lewis's de facto Latino fraternity. In order to pledge during the summer before his sophomore year, Leo would need a cumulative GPA of 2.5. His first-semester GPA was 2.0. Despite the fact that he'd never in his life had more Bs than Cs on a report card, Leo rallied and made all Bs in his second semester to lift his GPA to the required level. He was accepted to the fraternity and declared a major in marketing.

By the time classes started for his sophomore year, Leo's approach to education had completely changed. He was doing homework and considered most of his classes "pretty cool." Without even realizing it, he'd become a college student—and a pretty good one at that. Three years later, in the autumn of 2003, he began his final semester at Lewis. Because his acceptance to Lewis had been contingent on completion of a bridge program, Leo needed an additional semester of classes to complete his degree.

One thousand miles west, in Denver, Planning was busy launching Arrupe Jesuit High School, the fifth school in the Cristo Rey Network and the third operated by the Jesuits. After leaving Cristo

By the time classes started for his sophomore year, Leo's approach to education had completely changed. He was doing homework and considered most of his classes "pretty cool." Without even realizing it, he'd become a college student.

Rey, Planning had spent a year serving at an inner-city parish in Camden, New Jersey, but he missed the excitement of a high school, particularly a Jesuit high school like Cristo Rey that seemed so fundamentally Jesuit in that it very clearly responded to a great need. When Planning heard that one of his classmates from theology studies, Fr. Thomas G. Cwik, SJ, was running a feasibility study for a Cristo Rey–model school in Denver, he called and asked to be considered for any administrative positions at the school. Days later, despite his provincial's repeated admonishments to focus on the work in Camden, Planning was on a plane to Denver. "When you can see the will of God so clearly," he says, smiling wryly, "sometimes you've got to point it out to your superiors."

Planning interviewed for the position of principal with Dick Campbell, an adviser on the feasibility study. Midway through the interview, Planning said, "It sounds to me like you guys need a president, not a principal. You don't need a schedule of classes yet; you need a building, and jobs, and money."

"Can you do that?" Campbell asked.

"I think so," Planning said.

Planning's provincial allowed him to take the job, and a few months later he moved to Denver to prepare for the school's opening in the fall of 2003. He worked on locating a building and hiring a faculty and staff. He engaged in prolonged negotiations with the Archdiocese of Denver. As had been the case in other cities, individuals from the business community—many of them graduates of the local Jesuit high school and university—promoted the school tirelessly in an effort to recruit corporate sponsors. Arrupe was slow to attract students, just as its predecessor in Chicago had been, but still managed to open its doors late in August of 2003. Local media covered the school's opening, which was attended by Fr. John Foley, B. J. Cassin, and Jeff Thielman of the Cristo Rey Network.

By then, groups in Oakland, Detroit, Sacramento, Minneapolis, Indianapolis, Birmingham, and Washington, DC, were considering launching feasibility studies.

❋

WHILE 86 PERCENT OF Joey's graduating class began their college or junior college classes in the fall of 2003, Joey was just beginning his second job, as a security guard at a Jewel food store in Chicago. Br. Dave Henderson, SJ, Cristo Rey's much-loved facilities director, knew a manager at a local security firm and had been able to get Joey, all ninety-seven pounds of him, a job as a guard. Joey monitored the parking lot at Jewel, making sure no one broke into or vandalized customers' cars.

The paychecks were nice but the job was pretty boring—most of the time. After his first run-in with a shoplifter fleeing the store, though, Joey started to think that a boring job wasn't the worst thing in the world. When Joey saw the shoplifter, who outweighed him by at least one hundred pounds, running out of the store, his first thought was to get something to block the doors. "I looked for a shopping cart, but there wasn't one nearby. And I'm just thinking to myself, man, I hope he trips and falls before he gets to me." He didn't fall. "I knew very well I had no chance of taking him down," Joey says. "I was just hoping I could slow him down." As the shoplifter ran through the doors, Joey stepped in front of him, and got flattened. He managed, though, to trip up the thief, who was apprehended by the in-store security guards. "He went to jail," Joey says. "Me, I just learned that I'm not a very good blocker."

At the time, Joey was living in an apartment he called "the bachelor pad" with three of his friends from Cristo Rey, all of whom were taking classes at local colleges and universities. The apartment was two blocks from Cristo Rey, and when he wasn't working, Joey often wandered over to school to visit with his former teachers. He missed the place. It had become like a home to him, and he knew the people there cared about him. That fall, Cristo Rey's athletic director offered Joey a part-time job as manager of the boys' and girls' basketball teams. The new gym was loaded with bells and whistles and required a lot of upkeep, and the coaches of both teams wanted to be able to focus on coaching. The manager would maintain the gym and keep score at games. Joey jumped at the chance.

CRISTO REY NEARLY REACHED its full enrollment in the fall of 2003, when it opened its doors to 497 students. Unfortunately, there weren't jobs for all of them. The Corporate Internship Program had struggled to keep pace with the increase in the student body and had also seen higher-than-usual sponsor attrition as a result of the dot-com crash, the 2001 recession, and the September 11 attacks. That fall, Dan Considine, a successful entrepreneur who'd recently sold his own business, was hired as the school's business manager and chief financial officer, which allowed Preston Kendall to focus entirely on the Corporate Internship Program.

Considine spent his first few days on the job studying Cristo Rey's books. "It was really clear that this was a top-line business. Generating as much revenue as possible was and is absolutely critical to the school's success," Considine says. But Cristo Rey had only 98 paying jobs at the time and needed 115. "Finding jobs had to be a top priority. If we didn't get enough, the school would regress into a precarious financial position." Considine suggested to Paul Purcell, the school's new board chair, that the board create a jobs committee. Two weeks later, Cristo Rey's administration and the board's new committee went into overdrive looking for new jobs.

"Tony owns his own business. When he makes the decision to hire a student or to hire a second student, he's basically giving up his own money."

When Anthony McGuire, whose engineering firm had been one of the first corporate sponsors, heard about the job deficit, he offered to hire another student. "I want to make this school work," McGuire told Carlos De La Rosa. "I can't do two jobs forever, but I'll take an extra student for this year."

"Tony's decision was really remarkable," De La Rosa says. "Tony owns his own business. We didn't have too many people like that who were CIP sponsors. When he makes the decision to hire a student or to hire a second student, he's basically giving up his own money. It's not a sliver of the HR budget; it's money he would otherwise be taking home at the end of the year. Cristo Rey works because our students work. But it works, too, because our corporate sponsors care about those students."

Loyola University Medical Center, a sprawling hospital and outpatient-care facility in Maywood, Illinois, greatly reduced the job deficit when it hired a total of forty students to fill ten jobs. Archipelago, the wildly successful electronic stock exchange, also became a corporate sponsor. By early November, Cristo Rey had boosted its total paying jobs to 113. Existing corporate sponsors had encouraged friends to hire students, and board members on the newly formed jobs committee had put the squeeze on their friends and colleagues. Cristo Rey also deserves a lot of the credit, for refining the student training program and officially implementing the nine-step employability program for struggling student workers. The fact that the Cristo Rey community was able to virtually erase the job deficit in little more than a month, Kendall says, "is a tribute to the kids. They're the ones that go into the office every day. They're the ones doing the work. If people are excited about the program, it's simply because the students have them excited."

Of the extraordinary growth and success of the job program, Foley says, "I can literally say it never occurred to me that it wasn't going to work. I don't know if that's believing in fate or just being totally out of it. But . . . we just couldn't afford to let it not work. That's the way I feel about it now. But it's still precarious."

The 2003 job shortfall made it abundantly clear that Cristo Rey couldn't afford to get fat, dumb, and happy. Job deficits translated into financial deficits. As the Corporate Internship Program became more and more efficient, the school relied more heavily upon it. Cristo Rey needed jobs to survive.

✸

MAYRA COULDN'T WAIT FOR the start of basketball season. Her senior year was going to be different—the team was going to have a winning season. They were going to beat Juárez, Our Lady of Tepeyac, and Roycemore, three teams they'd never before beaten. She could feel it. During the summer between her junior and senior years, she'd attended the National Point Guard Camp on a scholarship provided by a Cristo Rey donor. "The camp really stressed preparation," she says. "They want you to be prepared for practice and for games so you can practice smart and play smart." On most evenings after her job as a camp counselor ended, she'd go to Harrison Park to practice by herself. Sometimes she played in games with her Uncle Sergio. Occasionally she'd go into the alley behind her house to dribble and practice her spin moves.

Cristo Rey's gym still wasn't ready when tryouts began, so they were held at the José Clemente Orozco Community Academy, on Eighteenth Street. Tryouts were divided into two sessions, one for new players and one for returning players. Mayra showed up in time to watch the new players, one of whom was a freshman named Clara Rebolledo. Each time Clara, who was three inches taller than any other freshman, got the ball in layup lines, she took a strong dribble, a long step, and then launched off her left leg and laid the ball softly off the backboard and in. Mayra was soon standing next to the coach. "We need that girl, the tall one, on varsity," she said. After fifteen minutes of tryouts, the coach agreed. Clara, who'd been moved by her eighth-grade coaches onto the boy's team, made the varsity team, and proved to be a great addition.

The new gym opened in time for Cristo Rey's first game of the season, against Noble Street Charter High School. The gym was magnificent. It had bleachers on both sides, large glass backboards, and a Cristo Rey logo emblazoned in two spots on the floor. Unfortunately, Cristo Rey did not start the new season well, losing four of their first five games. This wasn't the start the players or the coaches had hoped for. But the coaches felt this was the best team Cristo Rey had ever fielded, even though they didn't have the wins to prove it.

After a win over the Young Women's Leadership Charter School and losses to North Lawndale College Prep and Our Lady of Tepeyac, the girls were 2–6. Mayra was frustrated. She was almost halfway through her senior season, a season she'd been looking forward to for ten months, and they'd won only two games. On top of that, she was scoring less than she ever had. The coaches talked all the time about

Mayra's defense. They used her as an example for the team, but she wanted to score. She wanted to help the team win.

Cristo Rey went on to lose six of its next seven games. Their one win came against Roycemore, a small private college-prep school on Chicago's North Shore. It was Cristo Rey's first win against Roycemore in nine tries, but it was little consolation. After fifteen games, the Cristo Rey girls were 3–12.

They were used to losing seasons, but this season seemed different. In years past, they'd lost most games by twenty to fifty points, and sometimes even seventy. This year, though, they weren't getting blown out. They were competitive in almost every game they played.

The sixteenth game of the season was against Juárez. In years past, Cristo Rey had played Juárez twice a season. This year, though, because of Cristo Rey's conference schedule, the two teams would meet only once—in Cristo Rey's new gym. Mayra knew it was her last chance to beat them. Unfortunately, two of the senior starters, Jessica Maldonado and Samantha Agüero, were absent from school the day of the game. That meant Nancy Liera, a senior who hadn't played since freshman year, would be in the starting lineup along with Linda Ramos, a sophomore guard.

Linda played great in the first quarter and helped Cristo Rey outscore Juárez 15–3, much to the surprise of everyone in the gym. The Cristo Rey girls were running fast breaks, getting open layups, playing solid defense, and making their jump shots. Mayra didn't score in the quarter but had two steals and anchored a stellar defensive effort.

The second quarter didn't go nearly as well. Juárez outscored Cristo Rey 13–8. By halftime, the score was 23–16. Juárez came out of the halftime break strong and outscored Cristo Rey 12–7 in the third quarter, cutting Cristo Rey's lead to just two points. The pace of scoring slowed markedly in the fourth quarter as both teams focused on defense. With just over forty seconds to play, Juárez's center pulled down an offensive rebound and laid it in off the glass to tie the game. Clara inbounded the ball to Mayra, who turned around and was met by two Juárez defenders. She dribbled the ball between her legs, snapped her head to the right, and then accelerated to the left. The head fake got one of the two defenders off balance, and Mayra took off past her. The defender raced to catch up and at the half-court line reached for a steal. She caught Mayra's arm and the referee whistled her for a foul.

They were used to losing seasons, but this season seemed different. In years past, they'd lost most games by twenty to fifty points. This year they were competitive in almost every game they played.

It was Juárez's seventh foul of the half, and it meant Mayra was headed to the free-throw line for a one-and-one situation. If she made the first free throw, she'd get a chance at a second one. If she missed the first, the two teams would fight for the rebound. The clock said there were twenty-six seconds left in the game. Mayra knew she had to make the free throws. If she didn't, Juárez would likely get the ball back and would have a chance to win. For a split second doubts crept into her mind. She hadn't been shooting well, and she hadn't been scoring like she used to. As she walked toward the free-throw line, she fought off the doubts. *We can beat Juárez*, she told herself. *We can beat Juárez.* She took a deep breath as the ref tossed her the ball.

The first shot didn't go where she'd aimed. It was headed for the left side of the rim, not the back. It caught the rim and bounced to the right toward the middle of the backboard. It kissed the glass, fell onto the back of the rim, bounced into the air and then went in. Cristo Rey's bench exploded into cheers. Joey, who was manning the scoreboard, pumped his fist. Mayra didn't flinch and didn't look to the bench. She adjusted her feet and waited for the ref to give her the ball for her second shot. When she got it, she went through the same routine and then drained her free throw. Nothing but net.

Cristo Rey 36, Juárez 34. Juárez pushed the ball up the floor. Ten seconds or so into their possession, Nancy Liera stepped in front of a pass and knocked it away. Clara snagged the loose ball and fired it to Linda. Juárez fouled Linda in order to stop the clock. Linda went to the free-throw line and made both of her free throws.

Cristo Rey won the game 38–34.

Afterward, the coaches told the girls it was a historic win. No Cristo Rey team, they said, had ever beaten a Juárez team, in anything. It may have been only their fourth win, but it proved to every girl on the team something they'd all suspected. They'd gotten better. A lot better.

The Juárez game was in mid-January. Many college applications were due that week. Mayra, though, hadn't even looked at her applications. She didn't have time. She was focused on basketball and school. On top of that, things at home were crazy. Her little brother Henry, who suffered from life-threatening end-stage renal disease, had been sick. When Mayra's mom took him to the doctor or the hospital, Mayra was responsible for watching the eight remaining siblings, including Michael, who was a year and a half old. When she was in charge, it was impossible to get schoolwork done. So she'd stay up late, after all the kids had gone to sleep, to do it. Her college applications sat untouched in a big envelope that the college counselor had given her.

A Woman for Others 29

A T THE START OF the second semester of the 2003–4 school year, juniors and seniors at Cristo Rey enrolled in a host of new electives. Some took creative writing, poetry, or journalism, while others elected to take additional math or Spanish classes. It was the first year Cristo Rey was able to offer a full slate of electives to upperclassmen. Freshman students weren't given as many choices. They were required to take art, English, algebra I, religion, biology, Spanish I (which could be replaced with English as a Second Language), physical education, and keyboarding and basic computer applications. Active Learners, the class that had long been the face of the school's innovative curricular approach, was no longer offered. The Chicago Public School system's unwillingness to give credit for Active Learners to students who transferred out of Cristo Rey hastened its demise. So, too, did the fact that some colleges were skeptical of the course's merits, given that it delivered so little content.

On the surface, it may seem that much of the innovation and creativity that had defined Cristo Rey's early years had been stripped away as enrollment grew and more teachers were hired. Pat Garrity, Cristo Rey's principal, doesn't think so. "The work the founding teachers and administrators did lives on in everything we're doing here today. Cristo Rey is a fundamentally student-centered institution. We are student centered in far more than just the curriculum. Focus on the student drives every one of our decisions. In the end,

As both the enrollment and the faculty grew, there was a shift away from the more experimental courses such as Active Learners and civics, to more traditional subjects, such as U.S. history and classic literature.

this school exists only because of the kids, and the decisions we make as teachers and administrators reflect that."

Garrity's words are a tribute to the work done by Cristo Rey's early faculty members and by Judy Murphy, who insisted that Cristo Rey be different and responsive to the needs of its students. As both the enrollment and the faculty grew, though, there was a shift away from the more experimental courses such as Active Learners and civics, to more traditional subjects, such as U.S. history and classic literature. Much of the desire for the shift, Garrity says, came from the students. When Cristo Rey graduates who'd gone on to college returned to the school over their Thanksgiving and Christmas breaks, teachers asked them if they felt adequately prepared for college. Much to the teachers' surprise, many of the students said they didn't. They felt they hadn't studied the historical events or read the books they needed to in order to participate in discussions about history and literature.

It's quite possible that the Cristo Rey graduates couldn't yet perceive or understand how their innovative high school curriculum had prepared them for college. But the fact that a number of graduates—many of whom had been the cream of the crop at Cristo Rey—were saying they wished they'd studied more traditional subjects seemed critically important to Garrity. Their feedback helped shape the official curriculum that was formulated during Garrity's first two years as principal. The curriculum Cristo Rey settled on, Garrity reiterates, "is fundamentally student centered. For ten years we've been designing curriculum with the needs of our students in mind. That's what we're continuing to do."

IT WAS EARLY FEBRUARY when Fr. Sean O'Sullivan, Cristo Rey's director of counseling, learned that Mayra hadn't yet applied to college. It was, luckily, perfect timing. O'Sullivan knew that a donor to the Jesuits in Cincinnati, Ohio, had made three full scholarships to Xavier University available to graduates of Cristo Rey. Only one Cristo Rey student, however, had applied to Xavier by the deadline for regular admission. The Jesuits connected to Cristo Rey had recently been asked to encourage more students to apply in order to take advantage of the scholarships.

O'Sullivan knew Mayra well and knew her family could not pay for her to go to college; she was an ideal recipient for the scholarship. Mayra's basketball coaches, meanwhile, made phone calls and sent e-mails to local Division III colleges to introduce Mayra, who'd expressed a desire to continue playing basketball. Lori Kerans, head coach at Millikin University, a small school in central Illinois, liked what she heard and invited Mayra to apply.

For two weeks at the end of February, Mayra met regularly with O'Sullivan, college counselor Araceli Goméz, and her basketball coaches to work on applications. Her team of advisers helped her prioritize applications based on their deadlines. Then they helped Mayra put the finishing touches on her personal statement, which she'd begun in her senior English class. They stayed with her after school so she'd have a quiet place to fill out the college applications as well as the Free Application for Federal Student Aid.

By early March, Mayra had submitted applications to Dickinson College, in Carlisle, Pennsylvania; Millikin University, in Decatur, Illinois; and Xavier University, in Cincinnati, Ohio. Despite two wins over Our Lady of Tepeyac in the final weeks of the basketball season, and near misses against long-time foe North Lawndale

College Prep and Chicago Public School giant Manley, and despite being named co-MVP of Cristo Rey's varsity team for the second time, the chances of Mayra playing college basketball seemed slim. Her one shot was at Millikin. If she was accepted, she'd have to make the team as a walk-on.

❋

THE CRISTO REY NETWORK experienced dramatic growth and change in the year after receiving the $9.9 million grant from the Bill & Melinda Gates Foundation. Schools had been approved in Ohio, New York, Massachusetts, Arizona, and Illinois and were scheduled to open in the autumn of 2004. On January 5, 2004, Preston Kendall began work as the Cristo Rey Network's vice president for work study and administration. Carlos De La Rosa took over as director of Cristo Rey Jesuit High School's Corporate Internship Program. Kendall's arrival was a sea change for the Cristo Rey Network. He was the first full-time employee for the rapidly growing network, which had initially been run out of Jeff Thielman's briefcase. Kendall wouldn't be the only employee for long, though. He would soon be joined by Fr. John Foley, who planned to step down as Cristo Rey's president at the conclusion of the 2003–4 school year and become the Cristo Rey Network's first president after a brief sabbatical.

The Cristo Rey Network set up shop in the six-flat building across the street from the original school. It wasn't an accident that the network was located in Chicago and that its first three employees—Thielman, Kendall, and Foley—were veterans of the original school. The network's goal was simple: to help other groups start and run Catholic high schools that served low-income students by giving them an opportunity to fund their own education through a Corporate Internship Program.

The network became steadfastly committed to the mission effectiveness standards it had created to define itself. If a group failed to fully embrace any of the nine standards, its feasibility study was rejected. "We got better and better at identifying groups capable of conducting successful feasibility studies," Thielman says, "which was important because as news of the Cassin and Gates grants spread, we had many, many groups coming forward wanting to do studies." By the end of the 2003–4 school year, the network had approved schools in Baltimore, Indianapolis, Kansas City, Minneapolis, Omaha, and Washington, DC.

By the end of the 2003–4 school year, the network had approved schools in Baltimore, Indianapolis, Kansas City, Minneapolis, Omaha, and Washington, DC.

✼

BY THE TIME MAYRA donned her maroon cap and gown in June 2004, she had been accepted to Dickinson, Millikin, and Xavier. Two months earlier, after learning she'd gotten into Xavier, her top choice, Mayra received bad news. Two other Cristo Rey students had also been accepted, and they had been selected to receive the two remaining scholarships.

It wasn't the end of the world. Mayra had a number of good options. Dickinson was a great school, and it had made a generous financial aid package available to her. She was scared, though, by how far away it was from Chicago. Millikin was also a good option. She visited the campus, which she liked, and had a great meeting with the school's director for diversity. Mayra said she felt at home there and was ready to accept their equally generous aid package when Josh Hale, Cristo Rey's development director, found an anonymous donor willing to provide her with a full scholarship to Xavier

University. It was a dream come true. The scholarship would cover her tuition, room and board, and books. She planned to get a job to help pay for trips home to Chicago.

The 2004 Cristo Rey graduation ceremony, held in the new gym, was the first one on school premises since the twenty-two students of the class of 2000 had graduated in the old gym. The graduates marched in to *Pomp and Circumstance*. Cristo Rey's freshman, sophomore, and junior classes packed the bleachers. Seats on the floor filled up with the families and friends of the graduates, more students, Cristo Rey alums, community leaders, corporate sponsors, and donors.

Some of the early graduation ceremonies at Cristo Rey had been a bit chaotic, but by the time the class of 2004 graduated, the ceremony was pretty well perfected. The first order of business was the passing of the torch from the graduating leaders of the school's student council to the rising seniors. Then came the valedictory address. Valedictorian Verónica Cortez, who had excelled both in the classroom and on the volleyball court, was headed to Brown University in the fall. In her address, she spoke of how much she'd changed during her four years at Cristo Rey. She talked about her fear of failure when beginning school as a freshman, her apprehension on the first day of work in the Corporate Internship Program, and her feeling that she didn't fit in. She talked, too, about all she had learned during her four years in the workplace and in the classroom.

She recalled that "Mr. Heidkamp wanted us to understand we need to fight for what we believe in and that we should use our cultural heroes as examples." She quoted Socrates, saying "the unexamined life is not worth living." On behalf of her class, Verónica thanked the teachers "for caring, for pushing us beyond our limits, and for letting us know that we can do it. Thank you for teaching us to think outside the box and for really getting to know each and every one of us." Though Heidkamp hadn't been at the school for two years, he was the only teacher mentioned by name. Verónica concluded her speech with the following announcement: "Ladies and gentlemen, I present to you the class of 2004. They are the youth that will break down all the stereotypes and make their names known."

Then the students received their diplomas. Most of the graduates walked across the stage slowly. Some glanced out into the gym. Many of them were the first in their families to finish high school and attend college. In the gym, their parents, grandparents, aunts, and uncles watched with pride. Some of the parents wore dress clothes. Others wore blue jeans and work shirts and held their cowboy hats in their hands.

When diplomas had been distributed, the faculty presented senior awards. Over the school's first eight years, these awards had taken many forms. In 2002, the administration created a series of awards designed to reflect Cristo Rey's Graduate at Graduation statement, which said graduates should be open to growth, religious, intellectually competent, loving, committed to justice, and work experienced. The Men and Women for Others Award was the highest honor given to a Cristo Rey student and was awarded to two seniors, a male and a female, at graduation each year. The recipients exemplified all the attributes Cristo Rey hoped to see in its graduates.

The Men and Women for Others Awards were the last two given out at the ceremony. The thought that she might win one of them hadn't entered Mayra's mind. When the faculty called Mayra's name, she wasn't really paying attention. She was thinking about Cincinnati—she'd never been there and found herself spending a lot of time wondering what it would be like. Then her name was called, and the audience started clapping. She made her way up to the front of the stage to accept her award.

Mayra wasn't sure why she had been chosen. Nothing about her life seemed that remarkable. She played sports—volleyball and basketball all four years, softball during her freshman year, and soccer in her sophomore, junior, and senior years—because she loved them. She never skipped practices or games, even when she had better things to do, because she knew commitment to a team was serious. She took care of her brothers and sisters because she loved them and that's what she was supposed to do. She worked hard and did her homework because she wanted to go to college so she could have a better life and set a good example for her siblings. She wasn't the top student in her class, although she was a regular on the honor roll. During her four years at Cristo Rey, she never goofed off in class and was always respectful of her teachers and classmates. For the most part, she went about her business quietly.

Mayra's mother, Maria Hernandez, was in the audience as her daughter accepted her award. She was proud of Mayra for everything—the award, her dedication to sports, her hard work at school—but nothing could overshadow what her daughter had said to her a year ago at the conclusion of a Cristo Rey student retreat. Cristo Rey, like most Catholic schools around the United States and around the world, had instituted a campus ministry program that offered a variety of spiritual retreats, during which students spent one to three days away from school reflecting on different aspects of faith and spirituality. At the closing ceremony of the Cristo Rey retreat, to which parents were invited, the retreatants were given an opportunity to address the crowd to explain what the retreat had meant to them.

During her brief remarks, Mayra told her mom she loved her, and then she apologized. Though Mayra didn't say it explicitly, Maria knew she was apologizing for her comments on the first day of school nearly three years earlier. "It hit me to the heart when she apologized," Maria says. "I knew she wasn't that way, caring about the way people look or what they have, but it felt good to hear her say it."

❄

THE CLASS OF 2004 graduation was a symbolic moment. It was Cristo Rey's seventh graduation and came at the end of the school's eighth year of operations. The class of 2004 was the school's largest graduating class and the first to graduate in the new gym. The school's physical plant—after eight years and nearly twenty-seven million dollars—was finally complete. Its curriculum, while still fundamentally dynamic, had been finalized. The school had reined in its spending, and its massive budget deficits had become a thing of the past. In order to finance the construction of its new gym, cafeteria, and auditorium building, the school had borrowed millions of dollars. The fund-raising campaign, however, had been so successful that the school hadn't had to use it. Dan Considine, the CFO, was investing the money and generating substantial income for the school. Additional gifts were being placed into the school's growing endowment. Cristo Rey's enrollment had stabilized, and there was talk at the board level of expanding it further. The Jesuit Alumni Volunteer Program was thriving and regularly attracted talented graduates, mostly from Jesuit colleges and universities around the United States. The ¡Viva! fund-raiser was immensely successful each year, and the school's fund-raising efforts continued to be fruitful.

Cristo Rey was clearly working. Each of the 101 students sitting onstage had worked all four years in order to pay for his or her education. They'd worked at some of the most prominent advertising agencies, banks, insurance and media companies, and law firms in

Chicago. They'd also worked in small nonprofit organizations, museums, and neighborhood health clinics. After graduation, 99 percent of them would attend college, many of them on full scholarships.

But the students couldn't have done it alone, and many of the people who had poured their hearts and souls into creating a new school for them were seated around the gym, watching with pride as the maroon line made its way off the stage and toward the back of the gym. Fr. John Foley, who would step down as Cristo Rey's president after the graduation, sat onstage with principal Pat Garrity and Cristo Rey's new board chair, Paul Purcell, CEO of the Milwaukee-based investment bank R. W. Baird. Fr. Jim Gartland, who had authored the feasibility study that led to Cristo Rey and had been chosen by the board of trustees to become the school's next president, sat near the front of the gym. Germán Indacochea, Mary Morrison, and Sr. Frances Thibodeau, the only remaining founding faculty members, sat in different corners of the gym with their students. Mike Heidkamp, who had taught the graduating seniors when they were freshmen, stood in the back of the gym. Fifteen of the sixteen Jesuit Alumni Volunteers who had served at the school sat together in the bleachers. Rosa Sánchez, who'd been teaching at Cristo Rey since its second year, sat with her students. John Croghan and his wife, Rosemary, who had served as Cristo Rey's board chair for seven years, sat not far from Bob Hulseman, who along with the Croghans had made incredibly generous contributions that helped buoy Cristo Rey through difficult financial times. Anthony McGuire, the Regis High graduate whose engineering firm had been one of the first five corporate sponsors to sign on, sat near the front of the gym with his wife, Lynn. Many Jesuits from the Chicago Province were there. Scores of corporate sponsors—some of them CEOs and some administrative assistants who supervised Cristo Rey students—also attended.

None of these groups had gotten exactly what they wanted as the school was shaped and its policies formed. The school didn't look like what the Jesuits had initially planned. Nor did it look like what the progressive educators had envisioned as a dream school in the inner city. Nor was it the model of efficiency that the businesspeople on the board believed it could be. It was a jumbled mess of compromises.

None of these groups had gotten exactly what they wanted as the school was shaped and its policies formed. And that, as much as anything, is why it worked.

And that, as much as anything, is why it worked. Cristo Rey benefited enormously from the multitude of perspectives that contributed to its creation. The school never would have been created if the Jesuits had not turned to the business community for help. It surely would not have survived financially if the educators had been left to their own devices. And without the almost maniacal commitment by Cristo Rey's faculty to create high-quality, customized college preparatory classes, Cristo Rey's students would not have kept coming to school, and it would have failed despite the best business plan.

The different perspectives weren't always assimilated cleanly or immediately. Jim Wall, whose contract wasn't renewed at the end of the 2000–2001 school year, found it too painful to sit through all of the final graduation he attended. He has since spent hours in conversation with other former Cristo Rey teachers who wish they could have left the school on different or better terms.

The partings were painful because each and every teacher had contributed to the very creation of the place. They had built a school. Their perspectives, beliefs, and experiences were all relevant. Few educators are ever given such an opportunity. When they didn't get to leave the school they had helped create on their own terms, it was painful. It was as if they'd left a part of themselves behind. In reality, they had. The Jesuits, teachers, administrators, donors, and corporate sponsors have all given pieces of themselves to make Cristo Rey succeed. So, too, have the students. The result is a mosaic, a vast compilation of all those pieces. It is still a work in progress. But it is working.

Conclusions 30

A S THIS BOOK GOES to press, the following Cristo Rey–model schools are educating some 4,500 students around the United States:

Arrupe Jesuit High School, Denver, CO
Christ the King Preparatory School, Newark, NJ
Cristo Rey High School, Sacramento, CA
Cristo Rey Jesuit High School, Baltimore, MD
Cristo Rey Jesuit High School, Chicago, IL
Cristo Rey Jesuit High School, Minneapolis, MN
Cristo Rey Kansas City High School, MO
Cristo Rey New York High School, NY
De La Salle North Catholic High School, Portland, OR
Don Bosco Cristo Rey High School, Washington, DC
Holy Family Cristo Rey High School, Birmingham, AL
North Cambridge Catholic High School, MA
Notre Dame High School, Lawrence, MA
Providence Cristo Rey High School, Indianapolis, IN
San Miguel High School, Tucson, AZ
St. Martin de Porres High School, Cleveland, OH
St. Martin de Porres High School, Waukegan, IL
St. Peter Claver High School, Omaha, NE
Verbum Dei High School, Los Angeles, CA

Additional schools have been approved in Brooklyn, Chicago, San Diego, Cincinnati, and Detroit, and feasibility studies are under way in Houston and San Francisco. Deloitte Consulting is currently working with the Cristo Rey Network to develop best practices for accounting procedures and to explore strategies to minimize the exposure of Corporate Internship Programs at network schools to employer taxes.

❋

Cristo Rey Jesuit High School today has 110 corporate sponsors. Included in that list are some of the city's most prominent law firms, investment houses, cultural institutions, consulting companies, and banks. Seven companies who sponsored Cristo Rey students in 1996 remain sponsors today. They are: Aon Corporation; Katten Muchin Rosenman, LLP; Loyola Press; National Museum of Mexican Art; McGuire Engineers; O'Keefe Lyons & Hynes, LLC; and Tribune Company.

"We're currently employing thirty-two Cristo Rey students through the Corporate Internship Program," says Edward B. Shealy, director of human resources at Katten Muchin, "and every year people say, 'I hope we get more Cristo Rey students'." The Cristo Rey students at Katten work in the firm's accounting, office supplies, office services, marketing, conflicts of interest, billing and collections, and records management departments. Each of them, Shealy says, meets or exceeds expectations. "All of the managers and supervisors are very happy with the work product we get from the students. The people here very much look forward to and appreciate the youthful and industrious spirit the students bring to our office." As further evidence that Katten Muchin is pleased with the work its student workers do, Shealy points out that the firm has hired three Cristo Rey graduates to work full-time at the firm.

Moria Waddy, Chicago Director of Human Resources for Sidley Austin, LLP, also recently hired a Cristo Rey graduate, Margarita Tellez, to join the team she manages. "The work ethic of the Cristo Rey students is incredible," Waddy says. "I often find it's better than some of our employees. They're on time. They want to do a good job, and they want to learn." Everyone at Sidley, Waddy says, enjoys working with the students. "It's almost like seeing a child grow up. When they're freshmen they're crawling, but by the end of their sophomore years, they're usually running. It's like they're totally different people. We enjoy watching them grow. We want each of them to improve in their jobs." Waddy, in many ways, treats her student workers as if they were her children. Hearing her talk about them, it's clear she wants for each of them the same thing any parent wants for her children. "We want them to have success, and we do what we can to prepare them to be successful."

❊

In the fall of 2005, the Chicago Province Jesuits launched Chicago Jesuit Academy (CJA), a Nativity middle school on the west side of Chicago. The school was the brainchild of Matthew Lynch, a then twenty-eight-year-old St. Ignatius College Prep and Georgetown alum with an MBA from Washington University in St. Louis. CJA is unique among Jesuit schools in the province in that no Jesuits work there. Fr. Michael Class, SJ, who was the Chicago provincial's executive assistant, or socius, when the school opened, says Cristo Rey's success helped pave the way for CJA. "Cristo Rey changed the way a lot of people in the province think. People aren't nearly as afraid of risk." Taking a risk on CJA seems to be paying dividends so far. In the school's first year, standardized test scores indicated that CJA's students—all fifth graders—boosted their reading ability by

2.16 grade levels and their mathematical ability by 2.56 grade levels. Thanks in part to these accomplishments, *Chicago* magazine named CJA one of the top twenty-five private elementary schools in greater Chicago in October 2006.

❈

In September of 2007, the Chicago Province Jesuits officially announced the opening of a second Cristy Rey-model high school in the city of Chicago. Christ the King Jesuit College Preparatory School will open its doors in fall of 2008 in Austin, a predominantly African-American community on the West Side of Chicago.

❈

In the fall of 2006, Cristo Rey Jesuit High School celebrated its tenth anniversary. For the past three years, it has been operating at full enrollment, though the administration and the board of trustees are considering expanding enrollment to 600 in an effort, as Cristo Rey's president, Fr. Jim Gartland, often says, "to do the greatest good for the greatest number." A final decision about increasing enrollment won't be made carelessly, though, says Peter Beale-DelVecchio, Cristo Rey's current director of development, who recently helped complete a five-year strategic plan for the school. "We simply won't expand enrollment unless we can continue to offer high-quality college prep education and meet our benchmarks for student retention." The five-year plan also includes numerous measures designed to increase the four-year student retention rate from 65 percent to 80 percent. The average retention rate at Cristo Rey Network schools is just under 60 percent, and it is currently the focus of countless improvement efforts at the school and network levels. Preston Kendall has developed detailed financial projections that suggest labor costs for faculty and staff will increase more quickly than the fees Corporate Internship Programs can charge, which will eventually create new financial challenges for both the original school and those modeled after it. Though a plan isn't yet in place to address the new challenges, they won't catch anyone by surprise.

The Team

B. J. Cassin continues his work as a venture investor. He also currently serves as chair of both the Cristo Rey Network board and the Nativity / Miguel Network board. On June 1, 2005, the Cassin Foundation announced it was no longer accepting grant applications. In less than five years, the foundation had given away, or committed to give away, all of its funds. The foundation helped fund feasibility studies for fourteen of the first sixteen Cristo Rey–model schools and provided start-up funding for fifteen of them—all but the original Cristo Rey. The gift from Mr. and Mrs. Cassin, and the subsequent creation of the Cristo Rey Network, paved the way for the initial grant from the Bill & Melinda Gates Foundation. In 2006, Bill Gates announced he would step back from his responsibilities at Microsoft to focus on his philanthropic efforts. Weeks later, billionaire investor Warren Buffett announced he would give $31 billion of his more than $40 billion fortune to the Gates Foundation. In November 2006, the Gates Foundation made an additional six-million-dollar grant to the Cristo Rey Network to fund additional Cristo Rey Network feasibility studies and schools.

Rosemary Croghan returned to Cristo Rey's board after a brief break. She also serves on the boards of Loyola Academy, Loyola University Chicago, and the Cristo Rey Network. She and her husband, John, continue to lend their support to a variety of civic and religious organizations in greater Chicago. The Croghans' generosity serves as an example for board members at Cristo Rey and other Cristo Rey Network schools.

Carlos De La Rosa continues to serve as the director of the Corporate Internship Program at Cristo Rey.

David Dixon and his wife, Lora, now live in Guadalajara, Mexico, where Lora continues her work as a commercial attaché for the U.S. Foreign Service and David writes and raises their son, Gavin.

Fr. John Foley, SJ, stepped down as president of the Cristo Rey Network in October of 2007, when he became the Network's chief executive officer. Robert Birdsell, a former management consultant and teacher in Jesuit high schools, took over as president and is now responsible for the day-to-day operations of the Network's central office. Foley remains the Network's chief visionary and strategist. On October 9, 2007, Georgetown University president John J. DeGioia conferred an honorary Doctor of Humane Letters on Foley in honor of his work with the Cristo Rey Schools. On October 1, 2007, Fr. Foley was one of five people honored with a St. Elizabeth Ann Seton Award from the National Catholic Educational Association. The awards are given annually to those who have made outstanding contributions to Catholic education.

Pat Garrity continues to serve as Cristo Rey's principal.

Fr. Jim Gartland, SJ, continues to serve as president of Cristo Rey Jesuit High School.

Mike Heidkamp now serves as academic dean at Josephinum Academy, an all-girls Catholic high school in Chicago, and as an adjunct professor of education at DePaul University.

Br. Dave Henderson, SJ, also part of the founding team, continues to serve as the school's director of facilities.

Germán Indacochea, a founding faculty member, continues to teach at Cristo Rey.

Preston Kendall spent three and a half years as vice president for work study and administration at the Cristo Rey Network, which now has four full-time employees and two part-time employees. In 2007 Preston transitioned out of his work at the Network into a new role as VP for the Corporate Internship Program at Cristo Rey Jesuit High School and Christ the King Jesuit College Preparatory School, the Cristo Rey-model school that will open on the West Side of Chicago in 2008. In this new role, Preston will work to achieve synergies between the two schools in staffing, transportation, sponsor relations, and, possibly, training.

Julie Minikel-Lacocque currently lives in Madison, Wisconsin, where she is teaching and completing her PhD in ESL and Bilingual Studies at the University of Wisconsin.

Mary Morrison left Cristo Rey at the end of the 2005–6 school year. At her final assembly, the students presented her with a bouquet of flowers and a standing ovation.

Fr. Ted Munz, SJ, continues to serve as president of Loyola Academy in Wilmette, Illinois.

Sr. Judith Murphy, OSB, Cristo Rey's founding principal, returned to education after a brief hiatus and is currently serving as principal of St. Martin de Porres High School, a Cristo Rey–model school in Waukegan, Illinois.

Rick Murray currently runs Equity Schools, an educational consulting company that provides services both to small start-ups and to large established institutions.

Fr. Sean O'Sullivan, SJ, continues his work as Cristo Rey's director of counseling.

Fr. Steve Planning, SJ, continues to serve as president of Arrupe Jesuit High School in Denver, Colorado. In the spring of 2007, Arrupe celebrated its first graduation. Brent Dexter, Stephan Graham, Jeff Susor, and Dan O'Brien attended the graduation. Dexter and Graham, who'd both taught at Cristo Rey, were part of Arrupe's founding faculty and continue to teach at the school. O'Brien, who'd worked in Cristo Rey's CIP office, was Arrupe's founding work program director and served the school in that capacity until he returned to Chicago in December of 2007 to become director of development at Christ the King.

Rosa Sánchez, hired in Cristo Rey's second year, continues to teach at the school.

Fr. Bradley Schaeffer, SJ, concluded his term as provincial in 1997. From 1997 to 2006, he served as president of the Jesuit Conference—

the administrative office of the Jesuits in the United States. In 2006, he began work as rector at the Jesuit community of the Weston Jesuit School of Theology.

Sr. Frances Thibodeau, a founding faculty member, continues to teach at Cristo Rey.

Jeff Thielman continues to serve as executive director of the Cassin Educational Initiative Foundation and as vice president for development and new initiatives at the Cristo Rey Network.

Jim Wall is currently teaching at St. Francis High School in Wheaton, IL, and working on a new play about education called *No Principals—Just Fish Sticks*. He was nominated for a Golden Apple Award in 2006.

The Students

Billy Holiday, who enrolled with his cousin Sam at De La Salle North Catholic High School in 2001, was suspended from school as a freshman for selling drugs. He says he thought he was "gone." Much to his surprise, the administrators at DLSNC wanted him to stay. They put him on strict probation for the remainder of his freshman year. Billy stayed away from drugs and stayed off probation for the rest of his time at De La Salle. He graduated in June 2005 and enrolled at the University of Nevada, Las Vegas, where he's currently studying business with a minor in real estate. He returned to De La Salle to speak at a luncheon for benefactors in 2005. In his speech, he said, "I thank the school for giving me a second chance, because I'm not sure where I would be if I weren't given that." He went on to say, "The school really opened up doors for me, so I feel like I have no choice but to walk through and be successful. By far I have not had the best life, nor have I done all of the right things. But I want to let every kid know who has gone or is going through what I had to overcome that there *is* hope."

He concluded his speech by saying that he didn't realize the value of his experience at De La Salle while he was there. "But I can tell you the seeds that were planted landed in fertile soil and have blossomed in so many ways." He then spoke about his relationship with God, and closed by saying, "De La Salle exposed me to the true spirit of Christ, not just through lectures or Bible lessons, but through providing me a place to see Christ's spirit in action every day. A place where a second chance was not just a second chance, but an opportunity to change my destiny."

Frank Rojas spent more than a year in the hospital in the wake of his shooting and then another year bedridden at his parents' home, where his mother nursed him back to health. "With the love and support of my family, especially my mom, I'm coming out on top," Frank says. Fr. Sean O'Sullivan accompanied Frank through much of his recovery. "I visited him in his room," O'Sullivan recalls, "and he would always talk about how great his family is, and how God had saved his life for some reason. He often asked me to pray with him, and to bless a picture of Our Lady of Guadalupe that was at the end of his bed. He said she was watching over him, making sure he was going to get better." Frank has made enormous improvement, and O'Sullivan says watching the progress—first mumbling words, then moving a hand, then a leg, and eventually walking with the help of an uncle and a walker—gave him a feeling of "indescribable satisfaction."

Frank was tutored by Chicago Public School staff when he moved back home and eventually enrolled at Curie Metro High School. He graduated in June 2006 and is currently working his way slowly through an intensive tutoring program designed to prepare him for classes at West Side Technical Institute, one of the City Colleges of Chicago. Frank plans to study counseling or social work so he can help young people stay out of gangs. He has returned to Cristo Rey to speak to parent groups about the dangers of gangs.

"Cristo Rey is a part of my heart," he says. "The school showed me there are people out there who want to help each other."

Leo Maldonado graduated from Lewis University in December 2003. Fr. Steve Planning flew to Illinois for the graduation. On August 17, 2004, Leo's girlfriend gave birth to their son, Audelio Javier Maldonado. Planning returned to Chicago to baptize the baby. Today Leo works as an assistant lending manager at a bank in Little Village. The bank has long been a sponsor of Cristo Rey's Corporate Internship Program. Leo serves both as a banker—helping individuals from the community finance the purchase of new homes—and as a mentor to the Cristo Rey students working at the bank, helping them prepare to follow in his footsteps. He's contemplating returning to school to get his MBA and frequently returns to Lewis to tutor Latino students.

"Cristo Rey definitely helped me," Leo says. "I tell the students at the bank, 'You might hate Cristo Rey now with all the work, but it'll help you.' It really helped me, especially Fr. Planning. For me, it wasn't so much the learning. It was the motivation, the teachers saying, 'You can do it.' The teachers were constantly telling us, 'You can do this.'"

Maritza Santibáñez-Luna majored in Hispanic studies and Portuguese and Brazilian studies at Brown University. During her four years there, she received additional private scholarships from the Hispanic Scholarship Fund, The Pilsen Neighbors Community Council/Fiesta del Sol Guadalupe A. Reyes Scholarship Program, and the Hispanic Alliance for Career Enhancement. During her junior year, she spent a semester in Brazil. On May 28, 2006, Maritza and fifteen hundred of her classmates graduated from Brown. Three of Maritza's classmates from Cristo Rey—Ramiro Gónzalez, Christian Lara, and Armando Piña—drove sixteen hours to Providence for the ceremony. Maritza's mom, brother, and sister were also there.

"I still can't believe it," Maritza says of her graduation. "It seems so surreal." Walking across the stage, she says, felt "incredible." "I was thinking, *I finally did it. I made it, and now I have a diploma from Brown to prove it.* I knew my grandmother was watching me from up above. My grandfather was proud, too, and my father, who passed away during the spring of my junior year, was with me as well."

After graduation, Maritza returned to Chicago, where she now works as an assistant account executive at Edelman in the multi-cultural practice. In spring 2007, Maritza's memoir essay, entitled "Do You Speak English?" was published in *Windows into My World: Latino Youth Write Their Lives*, a collection of essays on life in college for Hispanic students edited by Sarah Cortez and published by Arte Público Press.

Maritza admits to having mixed feelings about Cristo Rey. She says she wished the school would have challenged her more and feels she wasn't adequately prepared for college. To catch up with her class-mates at Brown, she says, "I did a lot of extra studying on my own." Her desire to learn and her willingness to teach herself undoubtedly make many of her former teachers proud. Five years after graduating from Cristo Rey, Maritza believes the Corporate Internship Program and the teachers who took an interest in her were the two most formative elements of her education. "CIP was very valuable for me. It took me out of the neighborhood and placed me at a job that, at fourteen, nobody else can get. It made me feel like a participant in my own education, because I was paying for my own education. It helped me to believe that one day I'd be able to work there on my own."

Joey Garcia continued to work as a security guard at local grocery stores during the two years after his graduation. He applied to DePaul University again. Three of his former teachers wrote enthusiastic letters on his behalf, but he didn't submit the letters before the deadline and decided to just "let the whole thing go." He also served as Cristo Rey's director of basketball operations while working at the grocery stores. During that time, he expressed a desire to go to college so he could get a degree in teaching and return to Cristo Rey to teach chemistry—a tribute to Stephan Graham, his chemistry teacher. Joey's future, though, may be in management. As director of basketball operations, he hired an assistant whom he paid three dollars out of the eight he was making each hour. He also convinced the school to allow students to complete their community-service requirements by helping at basketball games. "I'm a boss now," Joey said during his final season there, "I'm really just here to supervise." Either way, he and his staff always had the gym ready for games and always had someone working the official scorebook and scoreboard. The operation, though, ground to a halt one day in January each year, the anniversary of his mom's death, when Joey spent the afternoon at the cemetery instead of in the gym.

On April 4, 2005, Joey enlisted in the United States Army. He completed his basic training at Fort Sill, Oklahoma, and then completed the twenty-week Advanced Individual Training in C4I (Command, Control, Communications, Computers, and Intelligence) at Fort Bliss, Texas. In April 2006, he was sent to Iraq, where he worked primarily on a counter rocket, artillery, and mortar mission at a variety of bases as part of the 82nd Airborne Division. His tour in Iraq concluded in April, 2007. He's currently stationed at Ft. Bragg, North Carolina, where he is a specialist in the 108th Brigade.

In September of 2007, Joey proposed to France Nicole Jordan. They plan to be married before he returns to Iraq in April of 2008.

"Being at Cristo Rey has made it possible for us to live on and be happy for what we have done, to accomplish our goals and to be what we are meant to become," Joey says. "Cristo Rey has taught us the values we need to succeed in life no matter what we do after high school, whether it's going to college, working, or, in my case, joining the army."

Mayra Hernandez's first semester at Xavier University proved incredibly difficult. She missed her mom, her brothers and sisters, and their apartment, and her boyfriend. Every couple of weeks, she took a Greyhound bus back to Chicago for a long weekend. Mayra's mom, Maria, was struggling financially and was relying on her siblings for help. "I hated the way they'd treat her because she needed help," Mayra said. She felt awful about being away, ostensibly enjoying herself. She wanted to be home helping her mom get by.

In mid-November, she decided she wouldn't return for the second half of her first year at Xavier. She took all her exams and passed all her classes. Then she packed up her belongings and walked away from her scholarship. She came home and enrolled at Richard J. Daley College, one of the City Colleges of Chicago. To date, Mayra has completed approximately one year of college credits at Xavier and

Daley. She's currently working in the billing department at the Alivio Medical Center in Pilsen and is saving money so she can complete her associate's degree in general arts at Daley. She then hopes to enroll at Loyola University, where she'd like to study criminal justice or psychology.

"Cristo Rey had a great impact on my life," she says. "The surroundings at Cristo Rey were so different than my home or the schools I'd attended before. Just about every teacher who crossed my path tried to help me in some way, even with just a few words of advice. Cristo Rey has been my second home and continues to be today."

❈

Paul Purcell, Cristo Rey's board chair, says much of the board's energy is currently devoted to coming up with ways to better prepare Cristo Rey's students for the cultural challenges of college. "Preparing them for the college course work isn't enough," Purcell says. "If they aren't prepared to be college students, they won't stay in college."

Mayra isn't the only Cristo Rey student to leave college. In fact, while 98 percent of Cristo Rey's graduates are accepted to and enroll in college, a considerably smaller percentage finish college (both the school and the network are currently working to collect more precise data). "The students who are coming back have made it clear to us that we need to do more to prepare them for being students in a new environment, and we're listening to them and looking for ways to respond," says Pat Garrity, Cristo Rey's principal.

Cristo Rey, eleven years after its founding, remains focused on the needs of its students.

Acknowledgments

THIS BOOK WAS A labor of love for me, just as the development of Cristo Rey Jesuit High School and the Cristo Rey Network has been a labor of love for the hundreds of people around the country who have given their time, talent, and treasure to make it happen. It's a privilege to tell a story about which so many people care deeply, and I'm grateful to Cristo Rey Jesuit High School's leadership team for giving me an opportunity to do so. I'm also indebted to my wife, Tara, who encouraged me to write this book.

My attempts to tell this story would have failed miserably were it not for the generous contributions of so many people. I'm especially grateful to Leo Maldonado, Maritza Santibáñez-Luna, Joey Garcia, Mayra Hernandez, Frank Rojas, and Billy Holiday for their willingness to share so much of their lives and experiences with me.

Many of the folks who helped dream up Cristo Rey and helped turn those dreams into reality were incredibly generous in sharing their recollections and experiences with me. Rick Murray spent many hours explaining the genesis of the Corporate Internship Program and the finer points of the business plan that launched the school. Fr. John Foley, SJ, over the course of many interviews, offered a series of wonderful stories and a very honest look at the many highs and lows of the school's early years. The amount of work Preston Kendall did at Cristo Rey simply can't be overstated. Neither can his contributions to this book. He was, despite an incredibly busy schedule, available for countless interviews, for detailed discussions about tax law, and for trips into the depths of Cristo Rey's basement to dig for documents and pictures dating back to the school's earliest days. Jeff Thielman's razor sharp memory was invaluable. Mike Heidkamp and Jim Wall's generosity in offering their recollections of, and reflections on, the curricular development of the school was critical to understanding what was happening in Cristo Rey's classrooms.

I'm grateful to Fr. Brad Schaeffer, SJ, for recounting the Jesuits' move into Pilsen and to Frs. Jim Gartland, SJ and Ted Munz, SJ, for sharing their recollections and insights into the feasibility studies that laid the foundation for the school. Many past and present members of Cristo Rey's faculty, staff, and administration offered their reflections and recollections or helped me collect information about the development of the school and the students. They include: Carolyn Alessio, Peter Beale-DelVecchio, Dan Considine, Carlos De La Rosa, Brent Dexter, David Dixon, Jason Dillon, Deirdre Fisher, Matt Franke, Josh Hale, Br. Dave Henderson, Pat Garrity, Araceli Goméz, Octavio Gonzalez, Stephan Graham, Elizabeth Hauck, Germán Indocochea, Julie Minikel-Lacocque, Marjorie Maclean, Maricruz Maynez, Kate McCann, Mary Morrison, Judy Murphy, Chris Nanni, Tony Ortiz, Fr. Sean O'Sullivan, Fr. Steve Planning, Blanca Rabiela, Bridget Rush, C. C. Ryan, Rosa Sánchez, Mike Staff, Andy Stanner, Jeff Susor, and Sr. Frances Thibodeau. I'm also grateful to Cristo Rey graduates Verónica Cortez, Belinda Hernandez, Nick Morales Jr., and Gustavo Rodríguez for sharing their experiences with me and for helping me understand more of the students' experience at Cristo Rey. Board members Rosemary Croghan, Dave McNulty, Steve Baine, Jack Crowe, Peggy Mueller, and Fr. Ted Munz, SJ, provided great insights into the critical role the board played in developing and refining the Cristo Rey model of education.

Both Jesuits and lay staff members from the Chicago Province of the Society of Jesus were enormously helpful. Frs. John Costello, Dan Flaherty, Jim Stoeger, and Brian Paulson shared their insights into the school's development. Tim Freeman and Kay Smolinski, both of whom were involved in early feasibility study meetings, were also very helpful. Annie DiMattina of the province's communications office, shared many of the Cristo Rey pictures she's collected over the years.

Jason Ashley, Marty Hegg, and Matt Powell of De La Salle North Catholic pitched in to help me get up to speed on how the Cristo Rey model had been used in Portland.

B. J. Cassin and his assistant, Bobbi Dolan, have made many contributions both to the Cristo Rey Network of schools and to this book.

I'm grateful to Mike Heaton of O'Keefe, Lyons & Hynes, Tony McGuire of McGuire Engineers, Edward Shealy of Katten Muchin Rosenman, LLP, and Moria Waddy of Sidley Austin, LLP, for their insights into the lives of Cristo Rey students at work, and especially for their insight into the contributions students make each day at work.

Fr. Dan Flaherty read early drafts and offered invaluable feedback. Leo, Maritza, Joey, and Mayra also proofread much of the book and were enormously helpful with fact checking. So, too, were John Foley, Jim Gartland, Mike Heidkamp, Preston Kendall, Ed Schmidt, Jeff Thielman, and Jim Wall. I'm grateful, too, to Matthew Lynch and Catherine Cassidy of Chicago Jesuit Academy for reading through a complete, mostly unedited, early draft of the book.

I will be forever indebted to Jeremy Langford, who very generously guided me through much of this process, commenting extensively on early drafts and helping me prepare the book for submission.

Finally, I am grateful to the editorial team at Loyola Press for their many efforts at turning this manuscript into a story that will, we hope, both inform and inspire others to attempt to change what so often seems unchangeable. Matthew Diener, Joe Durepos, and Tom McGrath helped shape the project. Heidi Hill and Vinita Wright made myriad improvements to the manuscript and helped transform it into a cohesive story, while Carrie Freyer and Molly Hart identified and sought out different audiences. I said above that it's a privilege to get to write a story that so many people care so deeply about. It's a privilege, too, to work with a publishing company that cares just as deeply about the subject and the story.

Sponsoring Businesses and Organizations

CRISTO REY SCHOOLS WORK because their students work and because hundreds of businesses around the country have given their students an opportunity to work. The list below highlights the more than nine hundred companies and not-for-profit organizations that are sponsoring Cristo Rey students during the 2007–2008 school year.

Baltimore, MD
Cristo Rey Jesuit High School

Aegon Direct Marketing Services
Allegis Group
Baltimore Symphony Orchestra
Catholic Charities
DLA Piper Rudnik Gray Cary US
Gallagher, Evelius & Jones
Good Samaritan Hospital
Gordon Feinblatt
Greater Baltimore Medical Center
Immediate System Resources
Johns Hopkins Medicine
Laureate Education
Legg Mason
Loyola College in Maryland
M&T Bank
Maryland Science Center
Mercantile Bankshares Corporation
Mercy Medical Center
Monumental Life
MuniMae Municipal Mortgage & Equity
National Aquarium in Baltimore
RCM&D
Semmes, Bowen & Semmes
St. Agnes Hospital
St. Joseph Medical Center
University of Maryland
Whiteford, Taylor & Preston
Whiting–Turner Contracting Company
YMCA of Central Maryland

Birmingham, AL
Holy Family Cristo Rey High School

Alabama Public Television
Altec Industries
Arlington Properties
Barfield, Murphy, Shank & Smith
Birmingham Botanical Gardens

Birmingham Civil Rights Institute
Blue Cross Blue Shield of Alabama
Bodnar Investment Group
Brasfield & Gorrie General
   Contractors
Bruno Event Team
CABWC
Children's Health System —
   Children's Hospital
Coca-Cola Bottling Company United
Colonial Properties Trust
Compass Bank
Diocese of Birmingham in Alabama
Dr. Jacqueline Stewart
EWTN Global Catholic Network
First American Bank
First Commercial Bank
Gallet & Associates
Giattina Aycock Architecture Studio
Golden Flake Snack Foods
Hunter Systems
Innovative Depot
Junior Achievement of Greater
   Birmingham
Kirklin Clinic (University of
   Alabama Health Services)
L. Paul Kassouf & Co.
The Land Title Company of Alabama
Liberty National
McWane Science Center
Medical Center East (St. Vincent's
   East)
Miller Hamilton Snider & Odom
Monumental Contracting Services
Motion Industries
NCCJ
O'Neal Steel
Park-Rite
Pathways
PricewaterhouseCoopers
Protective Life
Regions Bank
Robins & Morton

Serra Honda of Birmingham
St. Rose Catholic School
St. Vincent's Hospital (Seton Health)
The Stewart Organization
Synovus Mortgage Corp.
UAB Department of Anthropology
UAB Department of Neurology
UAB School of Public Health
VIVA Health
Vulcan Materials Company
White Plume Technologies
YMCA of Birmingham
YWCA of Birmingham

Cambridge, MA
North Cambridge Catholic
High School

Abt Associates
American Red Cross of
   Massachusetts Bay
Arlex Oil Corp.
ATG
Beth Israel Deaconess Medical
   Center
Bingham
Boston Business Journal
Boston College
The Boston Foundation
Boston Medical Center
Braver
Brodeur
Cambridge College
Cambridge Health Alliance
Cambridge Savings Bank
Cambridge Trust Company
Catholic Charities of Boston
Center for Women and Enterprise
The Charles Draper Laboratory
CIMIT
Citizens Bank
Congregation of the Sisters of Saint
   Joseph

Crosby Benefits Systems
Cushman & Wakefield
Deloitte & Touche
Edwards Angell Palmer & Dodge
Elkus Manfredi Architects
Emmanuel College
Ernst & Young
Goulston & Storrs
Hanify & King
Harvard Business School
Harvard Pilgrim Health Care
Holland & Knight
Hollister
International Institute of Boston
Jimmy Tingle's Off Broadway Theater
Junior Achievement of New England
MassDevelopment
McDermott Will & Emery
Monitor Company Group
Mount Auburn Hospital
Museum of Fine Arts, Boston
Neighborhood Health Plan
New England Aquarium
New England Association of Schools
    & Colleges
Newton–Wellesley Hospital
Northeastern University
Nutter McClennen & Fish
O'Neill and Associates
Office of Secretary of the
    Commonwealth of MA
One Family
Partners HealthCare
Pine Street Inn
Pitney Bowes Management Services
PricewaterhouseCoopers
Regis College
S. R. Weiner and Associates
Sisters of St. Joseph
St. Catherine of Genoa School
State Street Bank
The TJX Companies
Trinity Property Management

Tufts Associated Health Plan
Tufts University
Turner Construction Company
Verizon
Xerox
Youville House

Chicago, IL
Cristo Rey Jesuit High School

Alivio Medical Center
American Cancer Society / HSBC
American Dental Association
Apex Insurance Managers
Arthur J. Gallagher & Co.
Barbara J. Pope
Barnes & Thornburg
Blue Cross Blue Shield of Illinois
Brinks Hofer Gilson & Lione
Cabrera Capital Markets
The Catholic Church Extension
    Society
Chicago Federation of Labor-WAC
Chicago Partners
The Chicago Province Jesuit
    Development Office
Chicago Underwriting Group
Citadel Investment Group
Clifford Law Offices
CME Group
CNA
Corboy & Demetrio
Corcoran Expositions
Cremer Kopon Shaughnessy & Spina
Daniel Murphy Scholarship
    Foundation
Deloitte & Touche
DLA Piper Rudnick Gray Cary
Drinker Biddle Gardner Carton
Electric Arts
Equity Lifestyle Properties
First Industrial Realty Trust
Foley & Lardner

Gary Lee Partners
General Growth Properties
Gofen & Glossberg
Goldberg Kohn
Golden Country Oriental Food
Grant Thornton
GTCR Golder Rauner
Hinsdale Bank & Trust Company
hinton + grusich
HSBC Bank USA
Huron Consulting Group
INROADS Chicago
Insurance Auto Auctions
International Truck & Engine
    Corporation
Jenner & Block
The John Buck Company
Jones Lang LaSalle
JPMorgan Chase
Katten Muchin Rosenman
Kirkland & Ellis
KPMG
LaSalle Bank
Leo Burnett USA
Lock, Lord, Bissell & Liddell
Loyola Press
Loyola University Health System
Madden, Jiganti, Moore & Sinars
Madison Dearborn Partners
Marsh USA
Mayer Brown
McCracken & Frank
McDermott, Will & Emery
McKinsey & Company
Mercer
Mercy Hospital and Medical Center
Mesirow Financial
Morningstar
Museum of Science and Industry
MWH Americas
National Museum of Mexican Art
Neal, Gerber, & Eisenberg
Northern Trust Company

Northwestern Memorial Hospital
NYSE Group
O'Keefe Lyons & Hynes
Office of Illinois Attorney General
    Lisa Madigan
Office of the Illinois Comptroller
    Dan Hynes
One Equity Partners
Poder Learning Center / St.
    Procopius Elementary
Recycled Paper Greetings
Reliable Asphalt Corp.
Robert W. Baird & Co.
RR Donnelley
RREEF
Schiff Hardin
Seyfarth Shaw
Sidley Austin Brown & Wood
Smurfit-Stone Container
    Corporation
TCF Bank
TLC Management Company
The University of Chicago
    Hospitals
US Soccer Federation
USG
Wayne Hummer Wealth
    Management
Wiedner & McAuliffe
Wildman, Harrold, Allen & Dixon
William Blair & Co.
Winston & Strawn
Wm. Wrigley Jr. Company
Women's Center, Northwestern
    University

Cleveland, OH
St. Martin De Porres High School

ACS Global Learning
Admiral Products
Baker Hostetler

Beverage Distributors Inc.
Big Brothers Big Sisters
Brown Gibbons Lang & Company
Calfee, Halter & Griswold
CGI
Cleveland Botanical Garden
Cleveland Clinic
Cleveland Foundation
Cleveland Indians
Cleveland Municipal Court
Congressman Dennis Kucinich
Cuyahoga County Deparment of
   Children and Family Services
Cuyahoga County Department of
   Justice Affairs
Cuyahoga County Engineer's Office
Cuyahoga County Prosecutor's
   Office
Cuyahoga County Treasurer's Office
Cuyahoga Physician Network
Cystic Fibrosis Foundation —
   Rainbow Chapter
The DiGeronimo Companies
Diversity Center of Northeast Ohio
Eaton Corporation
Fairview Hospital
The Fedeli Group
Fifth Third Bank
FireFighters Community Credit
   Union
Forest City Enterprises
Goodrich–Gannett Neighborhood
   Center
Greater Cleveland Regional Transit
   Authority (RTA)
Hahn & Pollock / Sheerer &
   Goodwin / Steven Wolkin Law
   Offices
Henkel Consumer Adhesives
HoseMaster
Hudec Dental Associates
Huntington National Bank
International Partners in Mission

John Carroll University
Junior Achievement of Greater
   Cleveland
Life Line Screening
Littler Mendelson
McDonald Hopkins
Medical Mutual of Ohio
The MetroHealth System
National City Bank
Ohio Savings Bank
Park View Federal Savings Bank
Parker Hannifin Corporation
PricewaterhouseCoopers
Real Living Title Agency
Realty One Real Living
Reminger & Reminger Co.
Renillo Court Reporting Records
Robert W. Baird & Co.
Scott Care
The Sherwin–Williams Company
Squire, Sanders & Dempsey
Third Federal Savings & Loan
Towards Employment
Tucker Ellis & West
Weltman, Weinberg & Reis Co.
West Side Catholic Center

Denver, CO
Arrupe Jesuit High School

AIMCO
Alliance for Choice in Education (ACE)
Anthem Blue Cross & Blue Shield
Apartment Realty Advisors (ARA)
Archdiocese of Denver
Archstone Smith
Aspect Energy
Ballard Spahr Andrews & Ingersoll
Brownstein Hyatt Farber Schreck
Campbell Bohn Killin Brittan & Ray
Catholic Health Initiatives
Centura Health
CH2M HILL

The Children's Hospital
Chipotle Mexican Grill
Citywide Banks
Clinica Tepeyac
Colorado Business Bank
Colorado Housing and Finance
    Authority
Davis Graham & Stubbs
Denver Health
Ehrhardt Keefe Steiner & Hottman
Encana Oil & Gas
Escuela de Guadalupe
Exempla Healthcare
Exempla Saint Joseph Hospital
Fairfield and Woods
Fleet Car Carriers
Fortner, Bayens, Levkulich and Co.
Frederick Ross Company
Gates Corporation
Gensler
GHP Horwath
Great-West Life and Annuity
Hogan & Hartson
Holland & Hart
Holme Roberts & Owen
HUB International
IMA of Colorado
Janus Capital Group
Jones & Keller
Judicial Arbiter Group
Kaiser Permanente
Kennedy Childs & Fogg
K-M Concessions, Inc.
LARASA (Latin American Research
    and Service Agency)
Leprino Foods Company
Lockton Companies of Colorado
McConnell Siderius Fleischner
    Houghtaling & Craigmile
Mercy Housing
Messner & Reeves
Mile High United Way

Minor & Brown
Montgomery Little Soran & Murray
MWH
Newmont Mining
OppenheimerFunds
Panorama Orthopedics & Spine
    Center
Pinnacol Assurance
Ready Foods
RedPeak Properties
Regis University
Resolute Natural Resources
    Company
Sage Hospitality
Saint Joseph Hospital Foundation
Seeds of Hope
Senior Care of Colorado
Sherman & Howard
Smith Barney
Snell & Wilmer
St. Anthony Central Hospital
St. Anthony North Hospital
U. S. Bank
UMB Bank
University of Colorado Hospital
University of Denver
Village Homes
Wells Fargo Brokerage Services
Wheeler Trigg Kennedy

Indianapolis, IN
Providence Cristo Rey High School

Advantage Health Solutions
AIT Laboratories
August Mack
Baker & Daniels
Barnes & Thornburg
Bingham McHale
BKD
CSO Architects

Deloitte & Touche
Dow AgroSciences
Duke Realty Corporation
Eli Lilly and Company
Ice Miller
Indiana Business College
Indianapolis Convention & Visitors
	Association
Kite Realty Group Trust
Marian College
Marian Inc.
Marriott Indianapolis Downtown
OneAmerica Financial Partners
Rje Interiors
Shiel Sexton Construction
St. Vincent Health
The Steak N Shake Company
Wells Capital Management

Kansas City, MO
Cristo Rey Kansas City High School

ABC'nD Enterprises
American Red Cross KCKS
Andrews & McMeel
Avila University
Bishop Sullivan Center
Cable–Dahmer Chevrolet
Carondelet Health Network
Catholic Community Services
Christian Foundation for Children
	and Aging
CompResults
Coterie Theatre
Country Club Bank
Diocese of Kansas City-St. Joseph
Dismas House
Donnelly College
DST Systems
Duchesne Clinic
El Centro, Inc.

The Family Conservancy
Freightquote.com
GEHA
Greater Kansas City Chamber of
	Commerce
Greater Kansas City Community
	Foundation
Guadalupe Center
Guadalupe Center / Plaza de Ninos
	Preschool
Habitat for Humanity / ReStore
Hispanic Chamber of Commerce
Hotel and Lodging Association of
	Kansas City
Hyatt Hotel & Resorts
Inergy Gas Services
JE Dunn Construction
Kansas City Free Health Clinic
Kansas City Life Insurance
Kansas City Public Library
Kansas City Southern Railway
Lankford + associates
Logic Inc.
Main Street Corridor Development
	Corporation
The Marriott Downtown Hotel
Maxus Properties
Media / Professional Insurance
MedTrak Services
Miller Law Firm
Missouri Repertory
National Catholic Reporter
	Publishing Company
Nazarene Headquarters
Neighborhood Housing Services
Phoenix Family Housing
Plaza Primary Care & Geriatrics
Polsinelli Shalton Flanigan Suelthaus
Providence Medical Center
Redemptorist Social Services Center
Retina Associates
Robert E. Miller Insurance Agency

Sanctuary of Hope
Security Bank of Kansas City
Seton Center Family & Health Services
Shook Hardy & Bacon
Smiles Change Lives
St. Aloysius Parish
St. Luke's Hospital of Kansas City
State Street Bank
Stinson, Morrison & Hecker
Straub Construction
The Studio Knitting and Needlepoint
UMKC School of Dentistry
United Way of Wyandotte County
University of Kansas Hospital
Valley View Bank
Walton Construction
West Central Missouri Area Health
    Education Center (AHEC)

Lawrence, MA
Notre Dame High School

AAA Merrimack Valley
Anika Therapeutics
Bank of New England
Caritas Holy Family Hospital
CGI Information Systems
Challenge Unlimited — Ironstone
    Farms
City of Lawrence Community
    Development Department
Commonwealth Motors
Copanion
Curriculum Associates
Dadgar Insurance Agency
DeLuca Family of Dealerships
Diagnostic Laboratory
The Eagle–Tribune
Flir Systems
Fred C. Church Insurance
The Gem Group
Greater Lawrence Community
    Action Council

Jabil Circuit
Kollsman
Kraft Foods
Lahey Clinic Medical Center
Lawrence Community Works
Lawrence Family Development
    Charter School
Lawrence Firefighters Federal Credit
    Union
Lawrence General Hospital
Lawrence Public Library
Lawrence Pumps
MassInnovation
Nevins Nursing and Rehabilitation
    Center
Northeast Rehab Health Network
Northern Essex Community College
Kevin O'Brien, MD — Chiropractic,
    Orthopedics, Neurology
Our Lady of Good Counsel School,
    Lawrence
Penacook Place
Pentucket Medical Associates
Putnam Investments
Raytheon
RiverBank
Salem Co-operative Bank
Savings Bank Life Insurance
Shaheen Bros.
Sovereign Bank
St. Mary School
St. Michael's Parish
St. Patrick School
Stoneham Bank
TD Banknorth
Team Coordinating Agency
Trexel, Inc.
United Way of Merrimack Valley
Verizon Wireless
Whittier Rehab Hospital
Wignall Animal Hospital
Zwicker & Associates

Los Angeles, CA
Verbum Dei High School

A Place Called Home
The Aerospace Corporation
AIDS Project Los Angeles
Allen Lund Company
Archer Norris
Baker, Keener & Nahra
Bank of the West
Bannan, Frank & Terzian
Belkin International
Bingham McCutchen
Bob Smith Toyota
Braille Institute of America
Buchalter Nemer
California Chicano News Media
    Association
California Hospital Medical Center
California National Bank
Campaign for College Opportunity
CAP-MPT
Catholic Healthcare West
CB Richard Ellis
Centinela Freeman Regional Medical
    Center
Century Housing
CHIRLA (Coalition for Humane
    Immigrant Rights of Los Angeles)
CLUE (Clergy and Laity United for
    Economic Justice)
Comerica Bank
Countrywide Home Loans
Cushman & Wakefield
Deloitte & Touche
Dewey Ballantine
DMJM H&N
Ernst & Young
Foley & Lardner
Friends of California African
    American Museum
Gilbert, Kelly, Crowley & Jennett
Girardi & Keese

HealthCare Partners
Heart of Los Angeles
Hennigan, Bennett & Dorman
Herbalife
Immaculate Conception School
Imperial Capital Bank
IndyMac Bank
Institute for Educational
    Advancement
Jefferies & Company
Jet Propulsion Laboratory
Keenan & Associates
Kirkland & Ellis
LA Harley–Davidson
LA's Best
Latham & Watkins
Lightfoot, Vandevelde, Sadowsky,
    Crouchley, Rutherford & Levine
Lord, Bissell & Brook
Los Angeles Times
Loyola Marymount University
Macerich Co.
Maguire Properties
MALDEF — Mexican American
    Legal and Educational Fund
Marsh Inc.
McDermott, Will & Emery
Mellon 1st Business Bank
Merle Norman Cosmetics
Merrill Lynch & Co.
Mildred Cursh Foundation
Monteleone & McCrory
Morris Polich & Purdy
Munger, Tolles & Olson
Nike
O'Melveny & Myers
Operating Engineers Fund
Palmer Investments
Payden & Rygel
Psomas
QueensCare Family Clinics
Robie & Matthai
Shea Properties

Sidley Austin Brown & Wood
South Central Los Angeles Ministry
    Project
Southern California Edison
St. Francis Center
St. John Chrysostom
St. Joseph Center
The Sullivan Group
Thomas Properties Group
Trench Shoring Company
Trust Company of the West
UBS
Union Bank of California
Union Rescue Mission
US Bank
Venice Family Clinic
Western Asset
Westfield Shopping Centers
Winston & Strawn

Minneapolis, MN
Cristo Rey Jesuit High School

AgMotion
Allina Hospitals & Clinics
American Engineering Testing
The Basilica of St. Mary's
Best Buy Co.
C. H. Robinson Worldwide
Capella University
Catholic Charities of St. Paul and
    Minneapolis
Children's Hospitals and Clinics of
    Minnesota
Deloitte & Touche
Dorsey and Whitney
Geek Squad
General Mills Shared Financial
    Services
Linquest & Vennum
Opus Corporations
Robins, Kaplan, Miller & Ciresi

Ryan Companies US
Salo IT Solutions
STS Consultants
SuperValu
Wells Fargo Brokerage Services
Wells Fargo Home Mortgage

New York, NY
Cristo Rey New York High School

Arquitectonica
BDO Seidman
Bear Stearns
BearingPoint
The Bond Market Foundation
Booz Allen Hamilton
BrainLink IT Crisis & Management
    Solutions
Brown Brothers Harriman
The Capital Group Companies
Capuchin Franciscans
Catholic Medical Mission Board
Christian Brothers Investment
    Services
Citigroup
City Parks Foundation
Classroom
Common Ground
Credit Suisse
Debevoise & Plimpton
Deloitte & Touche
Denihan Hospitality Group
Deutsche Bank
El Museo del Barrio
Ernst & Young
Eurotech Construction
Exec / Comm
Farrell's Limousine Service
Ford Marrin Esposito Witmeyer &
    Gleser
Goodwill Industries

Hargraves McConnell & Costigan
Hartford Financial Products
Horizon Asset Management
HSBC
Human Rights First
ING Financial Services
Jones Day
JPMorgan Chase
Keefe Bruyette & Woods
Kelley Drye & Warren
Kramer Levin Naftalis & Frankel
Law Offices of John C. Dearie
MarketAxess
Mayer Brown
Merrill Lynch & Co.
MetLife
Museum of the City of New York
National Corporate Research
National Council on Economic
    Education
New York City Housing
    Development Corp.
The New York City Department of
    Small Business Services
New York Historical Society
New York Life Insurance Company
New York State Capital Defender
    Office
New York State Supreme Court
O'Dwyer & Bernstien
Pfizer Animal Health
Pitney Bowes
Practising Law Institute
PricewaterhouseCoopers
Proskauer Rose
Putney Twombly Hall & Hirson
Rockefeller Group Development Corp.
Russell Reynolds Associates
Sandler O'Neill
Satterlee Stephens Burke & Burke
Shearman & Sterling
Sher Herman Bellone Tipograph

Sidley Austin
Simpson Thacher & Bartlett
Skadden Arps Slate Meagher & Flom
Sullivan & Cromwell
Terence Cardinal Cooke Health Care
    Center
Thacher Proffitt & Wood
U.S. Trust
Weil Gotshal & Manges
White & Case
William H. Sadlier
Xerox
YMCA

Newark, NJ
Christ The King Preparatory School

AarhusKarlshamn USA
Archdiocese of Newark
Bendit Weinstock
Broadway House Continuing Care
Catholic Health and Human Services
City National Bank
Durkin & Durkin
Essex Community College
FAPS Inc.
Gibbons
Horizon Blue Cross Blue Shield of NJ
HSBC Bank
Kirkpatrick & Lockhart, Preston,
    Gates, Ellis
La Casa de Don Pedro
Maher Terminals
New York Community Bancorp /
    Penn Federal Savings Bank
Newark Museum
The North Ward Center
PSE&G
Railroad Construction Company
Seton Hall University School of Law
The Star–Ledger

Omaha, NE
St. Peter Claver High School
Alegent Health System
American National Bank
Blue Cross Blue Shield of Nebraska
Boys & Girls Club
Catholic Mutual Group
CETAC Technologies
Chicano Awareness Center
Child Saving Institute
COX Communications
Creighton University
Durham Western Heritage Museum
ENOA (Eastern Nebraska Office on
    Aging)
First National Bank
Koley Jessen
Metropolitan Community College
Midwest Maintenance Co.
Midwest Neuroscience
Mutual of Omaha
The Nebraska Medical Center
Omaha Children's Museum
Omaha State Bank
US Bank
Woodmen of the World Life
    Insurance Society

Portland, OR
De Lasalle North Catholic
Albertina Kerr
American Red Cross
Archdiocese of Portland
Black Helterline
Black United Fund of Oregon
Children's Relief Nursery
Columbia Sportswear
First Call Heating & Cooling
Freightliner

Goodwill Industries
Guardian Management
Legacy Health System
Lifeworks Northwest
Loaves & Fishes Centers
McMenamins–Kennedy School
Meyer & Wyse
Meyer Memorial Trust
Miller Nash
Mkg Financial Group
Mottau & Co.
Multnomah County District
    Attorney's Office
National Multiple Sclerosis Society
NW Natural
OHSU (Oregon Health Sciences
    University)
OnPoint Community Credit
    Union
Oregon Catholic Press
Oregon Steel Mills
Oregon Zoo
PCC Structurals
Perkins Coie / Pitney Bowes
Police Activities League
Portland General Electric
Portland Radiology Group
Providence Health System
Reed College
Rose City Printing and Packaging
Schwabe, Williamson & Wyatt
Stoel Rives
Sysco Food Services
Tektronix
Tonkon Torp
Trailblazers
UBS Financial Services
University of Portland
Urban League of Portland
Xerox

Sacramento, CA
Cristo Rey High School, Sacramento

A. Teichert and Son
Adval Properties
All Hallows–St. Peter Parish
American Red Cross Sacramento
   Sierra Chapter
Anderson Pharmacy
Big Brothers, Big Sisters of Greater
   Sacramento
Big Hairy Dog Information Systems
Capitol Area Development
   Authority
Catholic Healthcare West
Cedar Valley Construction
Davison Iron Works
Diocese of Sacramento
Downey Brand Attorneys
Geremia Pools
Granite Consruction Company
Harbison–Mahony–Higgins Builders
HSBC
Knox, Lemmon & Anapolsky
Matheny, Sears, Linkert & Long
Mercy General Hospital
Mercy Hospital of Folsom
Mercy San Juan Medical Center
Methodist Hospital of Sacramento
National Corporate Research
Pacific Coast Companies
Pacific Coast Supply
PRIDE Industries
Raley's Supermarkets
River City Bank
Roebbelen Contracting
The Sleep Train
Sutter General Hospital
Sutter Health
Sutter Memorial Hospital

Tony's Fine Foods
UC Davis Medical Center
Vanir Construction Management
Vision Service Plan
Waste Connections

Tucson, AZ
San Miguel High School

Advanced Ceramics Manufacturing
Advanced Ceramics Research
Arizona Daily Star
Automated Presort Services
Bank of the West
Better Business Bureau
Caid Industries
Carondelet Health Network
Chestnut Construction
Chicanos Por La Causa
City of Tucson
Compass Bank
Diocese of Tucson
Donovan and Grob (Orthodontics)
Edmund Marquez Suzuki
El Rio Health Clinics
First Magnus Financial Corporation
Fluoresco Lighting & Signs
Goodwill Industries
Grenier Engineering
Hispanic Chamber of Commerce
   (Raytheon)
Holy Hope Cemetery
Hotel Arizona
HSL Properties
Intuit
La Frontera Center Inc.
Law Offices of Sipe & Landon
Metropolitan Domestic Water
   Improvement District
National Bank of Arizona
Pima Community College

Pima Community College — East
Campus
Radiology Ltd.
Restor-To-Nu
Romanoski Glass and Mirror
Company
San Miguel High School
SCF Arizona
Securaplane Technologies
Skin Spectrum
Southwest Gas
St. Elizabeth's Health Center
St. Mary's Managed Pharmacy
Programs
T. L. Roof & Associates Const. Co.
Texas Instruments
Tucson Citizen
Tucson Electric Power
Tucson Medical Center
Tucson Museum of Art
Tucson's Newspapers
Tucson Old Pueblo Credit Union
University Medical Center (UMC)
University of Arizona
University Physicians Healthcare

Washington, DC
On Bosco Cristo Rey High School

Akin Gump Strauss Hauer & Feld
American Health Lawyers
Association
Boland
Catholic Charities of DC
Chevy Chase Bank
C-SPAN
Fannie Mae
FBB Capital Partners
Georgetown University
Gleason Flynn Emig & Fogleman
Holy Cross Hospital

Howrey
Impact Office Products
Jones Day
Miller & Long Concrete
Construction
Montgomery County State 's
Attorney's Office
National Federation for Catholic
Youth Ministry
NIH–NOAA Recreation and Welfare
Association
Opus East
PAHO / WHO Federal Credit Union
Reznick Group
St. Thomas More Nursing and
Rehabilitation Center
Summit Marketing
Warren Communications News
Winston & Strawn
WorldSpace Satellite Radio

Waukegan, IL
St. Martin De Porres High School

Abbott
Academy of Our Lady
Acco Brands
Akzo Nobel
ALEC–Abbott Credit Union
Allstate Financial
Baxter Credit Union
Baxter International
Cancer Treatment Centers of
America
Cardinal Health
Catholic Charities
Condell Medical Center
First Insurance Funding Corp
First Midwest Bank
Fortune Brands
Gewalt Hamilton Associates

Glen Flora Country Club
Holy Family Church
Hospira
Joel Kennedy Construction Corp.
Lake County Clerk
Lake County Health Department
Lake County Recorder of Deeds
Lake County Sheriff
Lake County State's Attorneys
Lake Forest Bank
Lake Forest Grad School
Learning Resources
Libertyville Bank & Trust Co.
LTD Commodities
MacLean–Fogg Company

NorStates Bank
PACTIV
Rosalind Franklin University
Stericycle
STS Consultants
Technical Concepts
United Way of Lake County
Verizon Wireless
Village of Gurnee
Vista Health
Walgreens
Waukegan Public Library
YMCA of Lake County
YWCA

By purchasing this book, you have already helped support the Cristo Rey dream; a portion of both the publisher's and author's proceeds from the sale of this book will go to Cristo Rey Jesuit High School and the Cristo Rey Network of Schools.

If you're inspired by this story and the work of these schools, you may wish to make a personal contribution to Cristo Rey, the Cristo Rey Network, or the Cristo Rey model school in your area.

To make a contribution to Cristo Rey Jesuit High School in Chicago, please visit **www.cristorey.net** or send a check to:

> Cristo Rey Jesuit High School
> 1852 W. 22nd Pl.
> Chicago IL 60608

To make a contribution to the Cristo Rey Network (a not-for-profit organization that provides resources to all the schools in the Cristo Rey Network), please visit **www.cristoreynetwork.org** or send a check to:

> Cristo Rey Network of Schools
> 2244 S. Wolcott Street
> Chicago IL 60608

You can also use the Cristo Rey Network's online giving page to direct a gift to any of the 19 schools in the Cristo Rey Network. If you prefer to send a check, contact information is available for each school by accessing the school directory at **www.cristoreynetwork.org**.

Thank you for supporting this ongoing work that turns dreams into reality.